◆

THREATS AND PROMISES

◆ ◆ ◆

Threats and Promises

The Pursuit of International Influence

James W. Davis, Jr.

The Johns Hopkins University Press
Baltimore and London

2000 THE JOHNS HOPKINS UNIVERSITY PRESS
All rights reserved. Published 2000
Printed in the United States of America on acid-free paper
2 4 6 8 9 7 5 3 1

The Johns Hopkins University Press
2715 North Charles Street
Baltimore, Maryland 21218-4363
www.press.jhu.edu

Library of Congress Cataloging-in-Publication Data
will be found at the end of this book.
A catalog record for this book is available
from the British Library.

ISBN 0-8018-6296-5

◆

In memory of my father,

JAMES W. DAVIS

◆

CONTENTS

♦

ACKNOWLEDGMENTS

Without the support of a number of friends, colleagues, and institutions, as well as my family, I would have been unable to complete this project. It is only fitting that I take a moment to acknowledge my debts and appreciation. During the course of my research I was fortunate to have received financial support from the United States Arms Control and Disarmament Agency's Hubert H. Humphrey Fellowship and from the President's Fellowship of Columbia University. Columbia University's Institute of War and Peace Studies provided office space, access to computers, copiers, and, perhaps most importantly, coffee, for which I am extremely thankful. Manuscript revisions were in large part made possible by a postdoctoral fellowship in the John M. Olin Institute for Strategic Studies at Harvard University and completed with the help of a number of student research assistants at the Geschwister-Scholl-Institute of the Ludwig-Maximilians-Universität in Munich. At various stages, my research and writing benefited from critical and constructive comments from Andrew Cortell, Barbara Farnham, Geoffrey Herrera, Paul Huth, Charles Kupchan, Jeffrey Legro, Martin Malin, James McAllister, Rose McDermott, Kathleen McNamara, Jonathan Mercer, Laura Miller, and Marc Trachtenberg. For assistance with translating Russian documents and sources I thank Alexander Motyl and Sergei Tikonov. Gregor Nowotny produced the maps in chapter 6. Special thanks go to an anonymous reviewer for the Johns Hopkins University Press who read multiple drafts of the manuscript, provided pointed critiques, and forced me to reconceptualize a large portion of the analysis. The manuscript is much improved as a result. My greatest intellectual debts are to my teachers. First and foremost to my dissertation advisor, Robert Jervis, who has influenced the way I think about international politics in ways I continue to discover. It is a joy and a privilege to work with him. Jack Snyder was a faithful critic and friend who helped me find my way out of numerous dead ends, real and imaginary. David Baldwin's work on positive sanctions provides much of the basis for this analysis, and his critiques of earlier drafts helped sharpen the conceptual apparatus presented in chapter two. Friedrich Kratochwil read the entire manuscript and helped me make appropriate links to broader international relations debates. Richard Ned Lebow's support went beyond collegiality. He not only provided valuable critiques of the manuscript, he also shepherded a younger scholar trying to market his first book. Finally, I would like to thank my family and friends, especially Dorsie Hecht, who always manages to keep me sane.

◆

THREATS AND PROMISES

· *I* ·

Threats and Promises

Folk wisdom maintains that honey offers a more effective bait than vinegar and thereby suggests an answer to one of the pervasive questions of social life: *How can I influence someone else's behavior? How can I get someone else to do what I want her to do?* Parents often face the choice: the switch or sweets, punishments or rewards? Politicians do too. Party bosses, presidents, and prime ministers confront the issue on a daily basis. In an effort to secure a congressman's vote on a crucial bill a president might ask: Should I threaten to withdraw support for the weapons program located in the congressman's district, or promise an increased budget for weapons acquisition? To gain greater access to the Japanese market a prime minister might wonder: Should I threaten to increase tariffs on Japanese products, or promise to lower them? Which will prove more effective, threats or promises?

If folk wisdom suggests that rewards are often more appropriate tools of influence than punishments, the proposition has largely been rejected by contemporary students of international politics. For example, in his defense of mainstream Realist analysis, John Mearsheimer argues that international anarchy compels states to acquire the means for punishing others. But Mearsheimer fails to consider whether states might sometimes find necessary the capability to reward.[1] This is regrettable, for whereas direct evidence supporting the proposition that threats are effective tools of international influence is sparse and methodologically often problematic, there is considerable evidence demonstrating the effectiveness of rewards and promises, even in the anarchic environment of international politics. Promises have been successfully used in strategies designed to defuse crises and avert war, often proving more effective than threats. And if promises can be used to influence decision makers who are highly motivated to initiate aggression, they are likely to prove even more effective tools of influence in less acute situations.

This book is about influence. More specifically, this book demonstrates that *both* threats and promises are effective tools of inter-state influence when statesmen bargain in the shadow of war. In contrast to the volumes of scholarly analysis devoted to the use of threats, there exists little theoretical or empirical research on the use of promises in international relations.[2] To fill this gap in the literature the role of promises in strategies of inter-state influence is a central focus of this study. My aim is to identify the conditions under which threats are appropriate tools of conflict management and when, by contrast, promises are more likely to influence a decision maker's calculations over war and peace.

THE LEGACY OF THE COLD WAR

The twentieth century's great superpower rivalry between the United States and the Soviet Union had in many respects an adverse impact on our understanding of international politics. The Cold War narrowed the focus of American scholarship in the field, led to a stylized understanding of the security challenges faced by states in anarchy, and consequently simplified questions of strategy in both theory and practice.

The failures of appeasement in the 1930s and the breakdown of allied cooperation in the 1940s produced widespread rejection of negotiation and conciliation as routes to conflict management in the wake of the Second World War. Thus, in searching for an answer to one of the central questions of international politics—how one leader can influence another's decisions over war and peace—analysts and policy makers enjoyed access to only a limited range of alternatives. However, in a world where the United States confronted only one significant security challenge, the disadvantages of a reduction in the range of strategic means appeared to be tolerable insofar as they were offset by a reduction in the complexity of the international system.

For American decision makers and students of international politics, one question came to dominate all others during the Cold War: Given an expansionist Soviet Union, how can the United States protect its global interests and yet avoid war? In his "long telegram" of 1946, George Kennan offered an answer in the strategy of containment. But whereas Kennan originally articulated a *political* strategy of containment that contemplated using a mix of threats to deter expansion and rewards for moderation in Soviet behavior, in practice (with the important exception of detente) the strategy of containment was little more than a *military* strategy of deterrence.[3]

Moreover, during the course of the Cold War the development of ever more sophisticated nuclear weapons and the means for their delivery, coupled with the emergence of strategic parity, produced a situation wherein the military strategy of deterrence came to be driven largely by the logic of weapons systems, further obscuring its political origins and goals.

The primacy of deterrence as both a conceptual framework and national strategy during the Cold War is reflected in the massive body of academic literature focused on the use of threats to achieve security goals.[4] Deterrence is arguably the most developed theory in the study of international statecraft.

Although the Cold War provided a strong impetus to identify the fundamentals of international relations, most of the resulting theories offer highly stylized depictions of the security challenges facing states in anarchy. Because the Cold War conflict was bilateral, or could at least be reduced to two competing blocs, models of strategic relations between two actors appeared to capture the essentials of the international system.[5] Deterrence theory was likewise characterized by models where two players bargained over outcomes which were the product of interdependent decision making.[6]

Of course, abstracting from the complexities of social life is necessary for the furtherance of knowledge. However, abstraction is defensible only to the degree to which those items left out of a model are irrelevant to explaining the issues or phenomena that concern the analyst.

The fundamental issue for deterrence theorists was how one could manipulate the utility calculus of an adversary in pursuit of maintaining the status quo. In theory one can manipulate a decision maker's utility calculus by increasing the benefits as well as costs associated with certain outcomes. In practice, however, deterrence theorists concentrated their analysis on "the use of threats to induce an opponent to behave in desirable ways."[7]

With the peaceful resolution of the superpower rivalry, many credit deterrence with having prevented a third world war. But as I show in chapter 3, to the extent to which deterrence theory can be said to offer an explanation for the lack of war between the United States and the Soviet Union, it cannot be said to do so merely in terms of the successful use of threats. However, the shortcomings of deterrence theory are broader and deeper than a critique of the explanation it offers for the absence of war between the superpowers.

The Cold War context within which deterrence theorizing progressed influenced the basic assumptions driving the enterprise with important implications for its generalizability. For if the Cold War was more unique than representative of international politics, analyses grounded in assumptions derived from the character of the Cold War may offer lessons of rather limited applicability. The assumption that most deterrence encounters can be understood chiefly as struggles between two actors is historically inaccurate as this book will demonstrate. The assumption that all aggressors resemble Hitler's Germany or Stalin's Soviet Union, and that deterrence is therefore a universally applicable response, is likewise problematic.

During the Cold War bipolarity and the nuclear stalemate created a measure of stability in the international system such that many were comfortable overlooking the limitations and contradictions of deterrence theory's stylized account of security competition. Despite its narrow focus, the abstract deductive model of deterrence provided enough guidance to decision makers charged with promoting and defending states' interests.

As early as 1974 influential scholars were lamenting the fact that deterrence theory was developing independently of a broader theory of internation influence that recognized the utility of both positive and negative sanctions.[8] With the end of the Cold War continued reliance on an overly stylized account of international politics is even more problematic. The radical changes that both accompanied and followed the end of the Cold War call into question the applicability of the model of politics offered by standard deterrence theory. Among the developments giving rise to skepticism are (1) the collapse of the Soviet Union and subsequent movement from bipolarity to multipolarity in the international system, (2) the acceleration of the proliferation of weapons of mass destruction, and (3) increased border violations not by military troops but mass migrations of refugees fleeing the anarchy of failed states or the effects of civil war.

The end of the Cold War would appear to present an opportunity to rediscover the range of tools available for the conduct of statecraft. Many argue that with the end of the Cold War nonmilitary means of influence will predominate in relations among states, particularly among the advanced industrial democracies.[9] Others argue that promises should be incorporated into American policies aimed at fostering transitions to democracy in former authoritarian states.[10]

A BROADER THEORY OF INFLUENCE

If security goals can be promoted through the use of promises as well as threats, the critical task is to establish the conditions under which one or the other is the more appropriate tool of influence.[11] This is especially important because the effects of misapplied threats are not always benign. Thus, as Robert Jervis suggests, "we are particularly interested in when threats protect the state and when, by contrast, they set off a spiral of counterthreats that leaves both sides worse off than they would have been had the state adopted an alternative policy."[12]

Threats sometimes provoke the very actions they aim to deter. When the costs associated with the continuation of the status quo are seen as high, decision makers may see no option but to adopt aggressive foreign policies. When decision makers adopt aggressive foreign policies because of perceived strategic or political vulnerability, deterrent threats tend to backfire because they reinforce fears of loss, and the belief that the state is surrounded by a hostile environment.[13]

Statesmen who are motivated to challenge the status quo by fear of losses and a sense of strategic vulnerability are best influenced through the use of assurances and promised rewards. To state the argument in terms of cost-benefit calculus: When the continuation of the status quo portends losses and is perceived as costly for a given state A, logically another state B can decrease the incentives for A to attack by adding to the value of the status quo, promising rewards for peaceful relations.[14]

Not all aggression is motivated by fears of loss. The history of international politics is replete with examples of statesmen who sought territorial aggrandizement because they viewed the costs and risks of doing so to be low relative to the prospective gains of success; that is, they were motivated by a sense of strategic opportunity. Rewarding aggression of this type is likely to encourage the aggressive state to increase its demands, because it reinforces the estimation that the state's environment offers opportunity for gain. When aggression is motivated by perceived opportunity to make gains at reasonable cost and risk, threats, not promises, are the appropriate means of influence.

This twin dichotomy of motives for aggression and influence techniques suggests a simple 2 × 2 matrix to capture the essential argument of this book (see figure 1). When a challenger is motivated by perceived opportunity and is met with credible threats, restraint is the likely outcome. This is the class of events captured by standard deterrence theory. Restraint is also likely to obtain when challengers motivated by vulnerability are met with promises. However, when opportunity-driven aggressors are met with promises, increased demands for revision in the status quo are the predicted

Aggressor's Motivation

		Opportunity	Vulnerability
Tool of	Threat	Restraint (Deterrence)	Spirals
Influence	Promise	Increased demands	Restraint

Figure 1. Matrix

outcome. And when aggression is motivated by a sense of vulnerability, threats are predicted to produce counterthreats and deepening spirals of crisis, if not war.

THREATS, PROMISES, AND THE GERMAN QUESTION

Germany presents an interesting focus for a study of threats and promises for a number of reasons. First, from the mid–nineteenth century to the present, the status quo among the great powers has been intimately connected with the German question, and conflict with or over Germany has been a recurrent theme in the modern history of great power relations. Thus, the sheer number of crises involving Germany from 1848 to the outbreak of the First World War solves a problem frequently facing students of international politics: the paucity of cases with which to construct tests for theoretical propositions. Because many of these crises involved the same issues, states, and decision makers but had different outcomes, focused comparisons are facilitated in a way not generally available to the social scientist.[15]

Second, as subsequent chapters demonstrate, understanding the impact of threats and promises on decision making requires more than establishing a correlation between a putative threat (or promise) and a particular outcome. Whereas we can do little more than point to apparent correlations for more recent crises, the volumes of documentary material available on the motives, expectations, and calculations of the German leadership for the period under investigation allows the making of clear causal connections between the use of threats and promises on the one hand and German behavior on the other.

Finally, analysis of the German question from the standpoint of strategic interaction provides new answers to long-standing questions relating to nineteenth- and twentieth-century German diplomatic history. For years historians have debated the wellsprings of imperial Germany's foreign policy, with two schools vying for hegemony: those who stress the primacy of Germany's position in the international system (*der Primat der Aussenpolitik*), and those who stress the pernicious effects of the internal makeup of the Prussian-led German Reich (*der Primat der Innenpolitik*).

Scholars in the first tradition highlight the fact that Germany's geographic location in the heart of Europe, surrounded by powerful states, created an essential vulnerability unique among the great powers. In the nineteenth and early twentieth centuries the German leadership had to contend with the possibility of invasions from France, Russia, and even Austria-Hungary. Consequently, the impulse to fight preventive wars was an inescapable result of Germany's position in the European state system. Late unification and industrialization only enhanced German weakness relative to the other great powers, who were busy dividing much of the rest of the world among themselves. Thus, Germany was caught in an intense security dilemma. German political and economic development directly threatened the continental balance of power and thus the interests of the other powers. But without an assertive policy, Germany was condemned to mediocrity.[16]

This position has been challenged by a second school of historians who argue that the institutional structure of the Bismarckian Reich and the domestic political consequences of late industrialization combined to produce aggressive, expansionist foreign policies in Germany. Compared with the other Western European states, Germany followed a "special path" or *Sonderweg* into the twentieth century. Whereas early textile-led industrialization produced a diffusion of economic power and tended to promote the development of a liberal middle class, convergence of agricultural and commercial interests, and support for free trade, late industrialization in Germany was characterized by rapid development of heavy industry, concentration of economic power in the hands of a few industrialists and finance capitalists, and the failure to create a middle class supportive of economic liberalism.[17] At first the new economic elite competed for political influence with the traditional Prussian agrarian ruling class, the East Elbian Junkers. But by the late nineteenth century, the concentrated interests of the Junkers and the industrialists were forged into a coalition of iron and rye, producing industrial and agricultural protectionism, pressures for imperial expansion, and the construction of a high seas battle fleet, while retarding political development of an anachronistic absolute monarchy.[18] The most provocative representative of this school has been Fritz Fischer, who fueled the debate by advancing the thesis that the First World War resulted from a political bargain struck among German elites intent on promoting their economic interests while preserving their social position and the prestige of the imperial regime.[19]

Despite the insights provided by these two historical schools, claims that German foreign policy can be adequately explained by an analysis of Germany's position in the international system or by the particularities of Germany's domestic institutions are not persuasive, for from 1871 to 1914 both of these structural features remained essentially constant. Consequently we would not expect German foreign policy to have displayed much variation across the period.

However, German foreign policy did vary. Germany was not uniformly aggressive or expansionist after the founding of the Reich. Bismarck did not act on incentives for preventive war with France in 1875 or 1887.[20] And the imperial impulse waxed and waned in a fashion not directly attributable to the dynamics of domestic coalition building. Both structural explanations suffer from the inability to account for variations in German foreign policy without ad hoc appeals to other causal factors. Neither approach leaves much room for individual choice.

German foreign policy between 1848 and 1914 was in large part a function of the policies and strategies adopted by the other powers. For the student of international politics this is not surprising. Yet to stress this point challenges many traditional historical interpretations, a number of which have been accepted by political scientists, too often indiscriminate consumers of the historian's product.

WHY DOES IT MATTER?

The role of promises in international politics is of more than academic interest. At the center of debates over how best to avert renewed Russian imperialism lies conflict over the use of threats versus promises.[21] Promises of economic assistance proved crucial to securing Ukrainian ratification of the Strategic Arms Reduction (START) accords and adherence to the Nuclear Nonproliferation Treaty (NPT).[22] Ongoing efforts to foster an Arab-Israeli peace in the Middle East and to bring peace to the warring factions in successor states to the former Yugoslavia frequently come down to questions of carrots versus sticks. Promises of energy assistance and official diplomatic relations defused a crisis over North Korea's nuclear program, although a stable resolution of the problem remains elusive.[23] As a contribution to both international relations theory and our understanding of the practice of statecraft, this study should be of interest to the academic student of international politics as well as those charged with the formulation of states' foreign policy.

The book is structured as follows. The next chapter develops a definition of promises that allows one to distinguish them from threats and assurances. Chapter 3 moves toward the formulation of a more complete theory of influence, one that provides guidance on the question of when threats, promises, or assurances are the most appropriate tool of influence. Chapters 4 through 7 evaluate a series of historical cases through the theoretical prism developed in chapter 3. Finally, the conclusion seeks to identify the broader theoretic and policy implications of the study.

◆ 2 ◆

Tools of Influence

> The typical student of politics either fails to distinguish
> positive from negative sanctions or ignores positive sanctions.
> The need for thinking about promises in politics is at least as
> great as the need for thinking about threats—perhaps greater.
> David Baldwin, *Thinking about Threats*

Before we can analyze the power of promises in international politics we need to answer a basic question: What are they? The difficulty of conceptualizing threats and promises has most often led analysts to assume that threats and promises are merely flip sides of the same coin. All threats are said to imply promises, and all promises assumed to imply threats. But the relationship of promises to threats and the distinctions between the two are far less trivial and obvious.[1]

DEFINITIONS

At a basic level threats imply punishments, and promises imply rewards. The proffered punishment or reward is generally contingent on the behavior of the party at which the threat or promise is directed. Threats and promises are used in an effort to influence the behavior of others. They are tools of social influence.

Influence attempts in social life are characterized by at least three components: (1) a source, (2) a signal, and (3) a target. Threats and promises are signals sent by a source to a target in an effort to influence the target's behavior.[2] They take the general form of "if-then" statements. "If you renounce terrorism then we will agree to negotiations on autonomy." "If you invade Western Europe, then we will bomb Moscow."

Although the existence of such an if-then statement constitutes an objective criterion for identifying cases of attempted influence, the characterization of a particular signal as a threat or promise is not exclusively dependent on its taking a particular linguistic or logical structure. For example, a message from a servant to a king may take the same form as that of the king to his servant, but the former is less likely to affect the king's behavior or perceptions.[3] Threats and promises imply a relationship between a source and target and must be analyzed in terms of power defined in relational terms.[4] Thus, the identification of threats and promises requires an evaluation of the broader context of interdependence within which an influence attempt takes place.[5]

Moreover, in determining whether a signal is a threat or promise, an analysis of the target's expectations is critical. Common usage dictates our associating threats with contingent punishments and promises with contingent rewards. But although a source may intend a particular if-then statement as a threat—believing the contingent outcome to be something the target would want to avoid—the target, in view of previous beliefs and expectations about the future, might actually welcome the contingency. Whether the target regards a contingent outcome as positive (and thus a reward) or negative (thus a punishment) is a function of the target's prior expectations.[6]

In his discussion of promises Thomas Schelling follows a similar line of analysis, arguing that promises usually have the following characteristics:

1. What is promised must appear to the second party, the one to whom the promise is made, as being in his interest. (Incurring an obligation to punish in the event of his misbehavior we would call a threat.)

2. What is promised should be something that one would not ordinarily be expected to do or bring about, absent the promise: promising to be home at dinnertime is vacuous if I always go home on time for dinner and there is no reason to suppose that today is different.

3. What is promised should be something that the second party perceives to be within the promisor's control. My promising the sun will be eclipsed at noon should not affect your expectations that event will happen nor get me any credit for having brought it about.[7]

Distinguishing promises from threats requires two steps. First, one must establish whether the contingent outcome is perceived by the target as positive or negative. Second, one must establish whether or not the outcome was expected or represents an improvement or deprivation relative to some baseline of expectation. In order to distinguish rewards from punishments and thus promises from threats, one must first establish the target's baseline of expectations at the moment the sender's influence attempt begins.[8] *Promises are contingent improvements in a target's value position relative to its baseline of expectations. Threats are contingent deprivations relative to the same baseline.*

Distinguishing threats from promises as they relate to the target's baseline of expectations has the advantage of allowing for the isolation of a third conditional commitment technique, namely *assurances*.[9] It is sometimes argued that whether one speaks of the threat to punish or the promise not to punish, one nonetheless describes the same conditional influence attempt. However, Baldwin's arguments to the contrary are most compelling:

> The fallacy in this line of reasoning lies in the assumption that withholding a reward is *always* a punishment and withholding a punishment is *always* a reward. If rewards and punishment (and, correspondingly, promises and threats) are defined in terms of B's expectations at the moment A begins the influence attempt, it is clear that a conditional commitment not to reward if B fails to comply is not *necessarily* a threat. "If you do not do X, I shall not reward you" is a threat to punish if—and only if—B had a prior expectation of receiving the reward. "No bonus for you tomorrow unless you work hard today" means one thing on the day before Christmas bonuses are traditionally handed out and quite another on the day after such bonuses have been distributed.[10]

Isolating assurances as a category distinct from both threats and promises allows for more precise scholarly analysis and may provide statesmen with a broader range of potential influence techniques. Whereas it is conceptually possible to threaten a target without simultaneously implying that a reward will accompany compliance, all threats imply a corresponding assurance that in the event of compliance, the threatened punishment will be withheld. Assurances serve to buttress the target's base expectations, reducing uncertainty about the future. For a threat to prove effective at deterring undesired action on the part of the target, both the threatened punishment and the corresponding assurance must appear credible and within the control of the sender.

One might hypothesize that the character of an influence attempt in which a threat was coupled with a promised reward (as distinct from an assurance) in the event of compliance would differ from the previous example. Statesmen probably regard rewards as normatively inappropriate in some instances, yet appropriate and altogether necessary for successful implementation of a threat in others.

For example, it is hard to imagine that any American president would have coupled a reward to the compellent threats issued to the Iraqi leader

Saddam Hussein after he had occupied Kuwait. The president's position was clear: One cannot reward aggression.

American statecraft appears to be guided by the general proposition that you offer rewards to friends, and even then only when based on merit. Adversaries lack merit and are to be avoided or punished. Influencing an adversary is thus seen as a matter of threats. However, even if rewards are ruled out of the question, the neglect of assurances may render bargaining strategies ineffective. For example, the fact that certain highly placed administration officials as well as prominent members of the U.S. Senate questioned whether it was a sufficient American objective to force Iraqi withdrawal to the pre-invasion borders, in effect restoring the status quo ante, probably weakened the effect of American threats by calling into question the ability of President Bush to make good on his assurances that American aims were limited.

In the case of the Cuban missile crisis the mix was different. Compellent threats were coupled with promises and proved successful at persuading Soviet Premier Khrushchev to remove offensive weapons from the island. The threat of U.S. escalation beyond the naval quarantine that was carried by Robert Kennedy to Soviet Ambassador Anatoly Dobrynin on 27 October 1962 included a promise to remove U.S. Jupiter missiles deployed in Turkey and a contingent promise not to invade Cuba. From the perspective of explaining Soviet behavior, it is not important that the president had intended to remove what most officials believed to be militarily insignificant missiles from Turkey in any event. What is important is that the missiles presented an ongoing irritant to the Soviets, one that Khrushchev had raised as an issue at the 1961 Vienna summit. The Soviet baseline of expectation included the continued presence of these American missiles in Turkey aimed at the Soviet Union; their removal represented an enhancement relative to that baseline. Had the Soviets had access to the earlier American deliberations, perhaps through espionage or public debate over the proposed withdrawal, their baseline might have shifted such that what in the end was seen as a promise would only have been viewed as a cynical American ploy.

Scholarship as well as diplomatic practice has often neglected the importance of promises and assurances. Both are potentially powerful components of a strategy of influence. To be effective, threats and promises must serve as both signals and commitments. The perceived ability of the sender to carry out a commitment is an important factor in the success or failure of any influence attempt.[11]

TYPES OF PROMISES

Promises are contingent improvements in the target's value position relative to a baseline of expectation. However, promises are not all of one type. Distinguishing among different types of promises highlights important characteristics that may affect their utility as tools of international influence. By focusing on the nature of the proffered reward, two typologies of promises can be constructed. A third is suggested by analysis of the behavior the source seeks to promote on the part of the target.

The Difference between Private and Shared Rewards

Economists often distinguish between private and public goods. Private goods are characterized by rivalry of consumption; that is, the consumption of the good by one actor limits or forecloses its being enjoyed by another; the total quantity of a good consumed being equal to the sum of the quantities consumed by individuals.

By contrast, public goods are characterized by non-rival consumption. For example, one pedestrian's walk past a city streetlamp does not ordinarily preclude another from enjoying the benefit of its light. Public goods are also nonexcludable. Provided to one they are available to all; again, the light of a city streetlamp provides a nice example. And because an individual can generally expect to enjoy the benefits of a public good without paying for them, public goods are underprovided for in perfect markets.

As most international bargaining situations involve either two actors, or very small groups of actors, neither scenario approximating a perfect market, the difficulty of providing public goods is greatly reduced. Because we are in general speaking of dyadic or small group relations, I will substitute the term "shared" for "public," although the benefits of shared rewards may in some cases be enjoyed by other parties.

The rewards associated with promises can thus be categorized as either *private* or *shared*. After first outlining the characteristics that differentiate each reward type, I will introduce the behavioral consequences thereby suggested.

Private Rewards

Private rewards represent transfers of value between or among actors. They are often, but not always, material or tangible. Parties to a dispute can often reach an agreement by trading items each values differently, the resulting exchange producing gains for both. In international relations examples of private rewards include cash payments, territorial cessions, the granting or transferral of resource rights, as well as transfers of arms and food.

If international relations theory has neglected their potential, statesmen have recognized the utility of private rewards in inter-state bargaining. In 1890 London ceded the North Sea island of Heligoland to Germany as part of a policy aimed at deterring what were seen as imperial aspirations on the part of Kaiser Wilhelm II in Africa. United Nations Security Council Resolution 242 represented an attempt to induce Arab recognition of Israel and deter another Arab-Israeli war by exchanging "land for peace." In yet another Middle East conflict, Washington allowed Syria to consolidate its control over most of Lebanon in 1991, in exchange for Syrian participation in the war against Iraq.

Private rewards are usually quantifiable in terms of some metric that allows for their specification and limitation. They are often part of a state's reserves and available for immediate use. But this is not always the case. Sometimes private rewards can take the form of actions undertaken by the source that remove some preexisting condition that the target state finds disagreeable. These rewards may be quantifiable in the way that the U.S. missiles in Turkey were: That is, one could count the number of weapons the United States removed from Turkey as a result of the agreement ending the Cuban Missile Crisis. However, it is difficult to quantify the level of improvement the reward provided the Soviet Union. Indeed, the benefit was ongoing and qualitative as long as no new missiles were introduced to replace them.

Shared Rewards

Whereas private rewards take the form of transfers between or among states, shared rewards are usually achieved through coordinated behavior based on the mutual exchange of promises. The resulting common value is enjoyed by both parties simultaneously. Shared rewards are often nonquantifiable. They generally provide qualitative enhancements to actors' value positions and frequently represent obligations on the part of state actors that will be ongoing and unlimited. Actors' expectations for the future are subjective and based on assigning some probability to a particular outcome. Promises of shared rewards may serve to increase the probability of a given outcome, decreasing uncertainty in the relationship. Such promises often include the recognition or establishment of behavioral norms. For example, in an effort to stabilize and limit the offensive arms race and deter a new race in defensive arms, the United States and the Soviet Union promised in May 1972 to limit the deployment of antiballistic missile systems (ABMs) to two cites and "not to develop, test, or deploy ABM systems or components which are sea-based, air-based, space-based, or mobile land-based."[12]

Hypotheses

Promises can offer private or share rewards. Undoubtedly, in many cases promises offer rewards of both types. However, for purposes of generating hypotheses, it is useful to focus on the pure types. Some hypotheses are logically deducible from differences between the two reward types. Others are based on the findings of behavioral psychologists who study people's responses to promises and rewards.[13]

The Role of Costs Among others, Baldwin notes that threats tend to cost when they fail, promises when they succeed. However, when promises are disaggregated into types, one sees that the relationship is more complex.

Because private rewards require the source to transfer value to the target upon compliance, they are indeed costly when believed and successful. If the target complies with the source's demands, the proffered reward must be forthcoming. Thus, the costs are generally tangible, immediate, but usually limited. Rational employment of these promises requires that the costs associated with provision of the reward be offset by the gain of cooperative relations; that is, the fulfillment of the obligation to reward must be cheaper for the source than continued conflict or escalation.

The situation is somewhat different for promises of shared rewards. The costs of these are often not tangible (they may be political) or represent instrumental costs associated with carrying out an obligation (such as the cost of removing the missiles from Turkey). The costs associated with on-going relationships based on obligation may be incremental and unlimited rather than immediate and limited; however, these too should be offset by the gains of continued cooperation. When the promised reward is based on a state's *refraining* from action, the reward might actually result in some net tangible savings to the source (such as the savings associated with a foregone ABM race). Unlike promises of private reward, these promises tend to bring costs to the source when they are *not* believed and allow for continued conflict.

Whether a state will base a bargaining strategy on the promise of private or shared rewards may thus depend on the nature of the costs involved and the state's sensitivity to such costs. When immediate costs loom large for the state, promises that allow for the creation of ongoing shared benefit should be preferable to promises that require transfer of wealth. However, in crises where the stakes are very high, where large-scale war appears quite likely, the immediate costs associated with promises of private reward should appear relatively small.

Credibility   There is more to the general unease with which statesmen view the use of promises in international politics than the asymmetry associated with their costs as compared to threats. Indeed, it is possible to establish the conditions under which the use of costly promises is more rational than the use of threats. Yet one of the distinguishing features of international anarchy is the inability of statesmen to appeal to higher authority for the enforcement of obligations. There is nothing to prevent the target from continuing with a challenge once it has reaped the benefits of a reward offered in an effort to dissuade it. Thus, promises may cost when they succeed, but also when they fail. Hitler was not appeased after he was given the Sudetenland, nor was Stalin after granted the territories of eastern Poland.

For their part target states know all to well that promises are as Lenin remarked, "like pie crusts—made to be broken." It is often difficult to convince an adversary that one will follow through with a promised reward in the event of compliance.

Because they generally require the source to carry out its obligation immediately, it is probably easier in a relationship of distrust to establish the credibility of promises that are based on private rewards than those that promise shared rewards.[14] One can often provide a portion of the reward as an index of one's intentions and commitment to peaceful relations.[15] This is the basis of Charles Osgood's GRIT (graduated and reciprocated initiatives in tension reduction) strategy.[16] A state pursuing GRIT devises a series of small initiatives it can take unilaterally without endangering its own security in an effort to induce cooperation from an adversary. In general, the decomposition of a large issue into a number of smaller issues allows the source more opportunities for the establishment of credibility with the target.

Rewards that are enjoyed incrementally should offer less incentive for defection on the part of the target. However, because private rewards are generally limited rather than ongoing, once the last increment has been received, the target has the opportunity to return to the posture that gave rise to the promise in the first place. Insofar as the benefits associated with shared rewards are often ongoing, the incentives for defection should be reduced. The credibility of such promises will be easier to achieve when the benefits to the target are linked to benefits the source itself will receive because the incentives for the source to default on the promise are thereby reduced.[17]

Motivations behind the Target's Challenge When statesmen contemplate aggression owing to a sense of vulnerability, promises offer a potent tool of influence. Feelings of vulnerability can result from immediate needs or fears arising from statesmen's uncertainty regarding the future. Japan's immediate need for resources in the 1930s may have contributed to its aggressive designs in East Asia. One factor leading to the outbreak of the First World War was the fear an uncertain future inspired in the European leadership. The German leadership, in particular, believed its future position—both domestically and internationally—to be in jeopardy. They perceived themselves to be facing relative economic decline and increasing strategic vulnerability.[18]

Challenges to the international status quo based on immediate need are probably best met with promises of private rewards. Challenges resulting from vulnerability associated with an uncertain future call for promises of shared rewards.

The Soviet leadership's uncertainty regarding the reliability of their own ABM technology, especially against U.S. MIRV (multiple independently targeted reentry vehicles) deployments, and how they would fair in a defensive arms race probably contributed to their willingness to sign SALT I.[19] Similarly, the introduction of "stability" into the offensive arms race provided the major justification for American acceptance of SALT I and II.[20] Promises intended to deter aggression arising from a sense of uncertainty regarding the future probably need not appear 100 percent credible to the target in order to succeed. Rather, a promise that enhances the target's expectations for a stable future—raising the probability that the expected outcome will come about from something that was already greater than zero, to something still less than one—will probably suffice.[21]

Potential for Transforming Relations among Adversaries   Schelling points out the lamentable fact that it is usually easier to destroy than to create.[22] As a corollary to Schelling's point, Boulding notes that there is a limit to total destruction whereas there is no upper limit to the amount of good man can create over time.[23] Threat-based strategies may in some cases succeed in preventing challenges to the status quo, but they do so by suppressing behavior and constraining choice. Threats do little to change underlying motives.[24]

The most successful bargaining strategies would appear to be those that not only induce the other side to change its behavior but also change its preferences and expectations regarding the value of the status quo and cooperative relations. By showing how a new good can be created through joint action and thus changing underlying actor preferences, promises can transform relations among adversaries in a way that threats cannot. Moreover, psychologists find that cooperation in pursuit of shared gains increases affective and behavioral commitment on the part of individuals.[25]

Most increases in a state's stake in the status quo probably come from increased wealth. Both private and shared rewards can contribute toward increasing another state's wealth; however, they do so in different ways.

Private rewards, insofar as they provide transfers of value as compensation for an aggrieved position, may at best be zero-sum transactions. The limited increases they provide a target state's endowment may serve to appease a challenge for the moment, but they may do little to increase the target's long-run stake in peaceful relations.

By contrast, shared rewards often allow for positive-sum exchange that is ongoing and unlimited. For example, granting of most-favored nation trading status to a state offers increased benefits from trade that are limited only by the state's ability to produce products for export to the new market. To the extent that promises of shared rewards promote the norm of reciprocity between actors, they hold greater prospect for transforming relations from conflictual to cooperative over a range of issues.[26]

Promises and rewards foster cooperative relations in another way. When a state is the target of a deterrent threat, a common strategy on the part of the target is to act as though it did not hear or understand the threat. If the threat is not heard or is misunderstood, the source will find its strategy thwarted and carrying out the punishment more difficult.[27]

With promises, however, the target's strategic incentives are different. It is likely to make every effort to show it has heard the source and is behaving accordingly in order to reap the reward. Threats promote deceptive behavior on the part of targets, distrust on the part of the source. In contrast, promises can promote open and honest action on the part of targets and may promote greater trust in the overall relationship.

The Difference between Concessions and Compensation

Promises are contingent improvements in a target's value position relative to a baseline of expectation. One can distinguish among different types of promises as they relate to and improve the baseline. Specifically, do the promised rewards conceed disputed issue/s, or are they intended to improve the target's value position on another dimension? The rewards associated with promises can represent either *concessions* or *compensation.* Diplomatic history is replete with examples where statesmen promised concessions and/or compensation in an effort to influence the behavior of another state.

Concessions

Concessions are rewards that address the target's specific needs or grievances. The traditional concept of appeasement, "the policy of settling international quarrels by admitting and satisfying grievances through rational negotiation and compromise, thereby avoiding resort to armed conflict," focused on this type of reward.[28] The most successful concessions would correspond to the revisionist state's minimum essential needs.[29]

In 1961, responding to American plans to introduce tactical nuclear weapons into Germany and amid calls by many Germans for German control over these weapons, Soviet Premier Khrushchev pressed for the recognition of Germany's divided status through the negotiation of a peace treaty by the World War II belligerents. The resolution of the crisis was characterized by the United States' acquiescing to construction of the Berlin Wall, stopping the flood of refugees from the East, and promising to enter into negotiations over outstanding issues relating to Berlin and a divided Germany.[30] In this way Kennedy found concessions sufficient to deter further Soviet action against Berlin. Thirty years later Saddam Hussein successfully dissuaded Iran from joining the allies during the Gulf War, by conceding Iranian positions across a range of unresolved issues arising from the stalemated Iran-Iraq War.

Compensation

Compensation is more like the game theorist's notion of "side payments." Promises of compensation may correspond to the notion of a trade, or "social exchange."[31] The defender of the status quo offers compensation for the aggrieved position of the revisionist state rather than compromise the issue motivating the challenge.

For example, in 1904 France deflected British opposition to its plans for Morocco, essentially compensating Britain by relinquishing French claims in Egypt. Austria successfully restrained Turkey in the Bosnian annexation crisis of 1908–9 through financial compensation. And in 1939 the Germans successfully averted a Soviet alliance with Britain and France by promising "non-aggression" as well as territorial compensation in Eastern Europe.

Hypotheses

States interested in preserving the status quo can promise a revisionist state (1) compensation for its aggrieved position in exchange for the maintenance of the status quo, (2) negotiation of the issues motivating the challenge and concessions on some issues, or (3) a combination of concessions and compensation.

States probably fear that if they concede certain issues to an adversary they will gain a reputation for lacking resolve. But the state can try to limit the inferences drawn from the concessions by isolating its behavior from other issues and claiming that special circumstances explain its actions. Decision makers will thus consider a strategy that incorporates concessions to the extent to which they can plausibly demonstrate that such circumstances are not likely to recur.[32]

Although inferring a state's future behavior from its willingness to grant concessions in the past is not straightforward, it is even more difficult to make an inference based on a state's willingness to offer compensation. The fact that the state will sacrifice much to maintain the status quo tells one little. Because the state did not give in on the specific issue motivating a challenge, the state could gain a reputation for being resolute. But in choosing to offer the challenger compensation elsewhere, one might infer that the state is unwilling to risk a war over the issue. Recognizing that the process whereby states gain reputations is complex and poorly understood, decision makers will probably be more likely to incorporate compensation into deterrent strategies when the potential for influencing third parties is low.[33]

The targets of deterrent encounters also fear for their reputation. Schelling argues that reputations are one of the few things worth fighting for.[34] When compliance with the terms of another's threats confronts a decision maker with loss of face both abroad and at home, escalation may appear preferable to retreat.[35] Deterrence strategies that incorporate promises of compensation, however, may present the aggrieved party with an opportunity to retreat and yet save face and maintain equality of status vis-à-vis the source.[36] Compensation that holds symbolic value may introduce an aspect of symmetry to the deterrent encounter, which psychologists have found enhances the degree of credibility the promise engenders on the part of the target. If the compensation appears wholly unrelated to the behavior demanded, or if it appears unrealistically large, it will most likely be regarded as incredible.[37] And for both psychological and domestic political reasons, compensation that allows the target to frame compliant behavior as a cost incurred to achieve some benefit will elicit less hostility and resistance than will deterrent threats.[38] Thus, President Kennedy's promise to remove U.S. missiles in Turkey in exchange for the removal of Soviet missiles in Cuba may have been critical to the success of his policy as it both introduced symmetry into the encounter and allowed Khrushchev to frame his retreat as a cost incurred in pursuit of the larger security gain represented in the diminished threat from U.S. missiles.

The Difference between Deterrence and Compellence

In his classic work on coercive diplomacy Thomas Schelling delineates important differences "between a threat intended to make an adversary do something and a threat intended to keep him from starting something. The distinction is in the timing and in the initiative, in who has to make the first move, in whose initiative is put to the test."[39] With an exclusive focus on threats, Schelling argues that it should be easier to deter than to compel.

If deterrent threats enjoy a number of inherent advantages over compellent threats, the relationship appears quite different when analysis moves to promises. Once again, timing and initiative provide the basis for evaluating the relative efficiency and efficacy of deterrent and compellent promises. Whereas deterrence enjoys an advantage over compellence when threats are employed, compellence is probably easier to achieve through promises than is deterrence.[40]

To deter through threats, one generally sets the stage and leaves to the adversary the initiative, the choice, the "last clear chance" in Schelling's words, to avert crisis.[41] The goal of deterrence tends to be of indefinite duration. One hopes that the occasion to implement a threat never comes. Deterrence often enjoys the benefit of clarity and specificity. "Do nothing!" is easily understood.

By contrast, compellence requires the adversary to act, to change behavior, and immediately raises a host of questions. "In addition to the question of 'when,' compellence usually involves questions of where, what, and how much."[42]

If the target is required to act, so too must the source of the compellent threat: "The compellent threat has to be put into motion to be credible, and *then* the victim must yield."[43] This issue of timing and initiative can create problems at home for the statesman issuing compellent threats. If the compellent action requires sustained application of the punishment until the other acts, the action must prove acceptable to the initiator over whatever amount of time is needed to bring about compliance. In an era of "real time" news coverage, unpleasantries associated with compellent actions can give rise to international as well as domestic opposition. Because the punishments associated with deterrent threats are brought to bear only if the threat fails, debates over the legality or morality of a particular form of punishment are generally less focused and intense.

Consider, for example, the difference in the debates generated by two types of coercive bombing actions. The Nixon administration's efforts to compel the North Vietnamese to the negotiating table by the so-called Christmas Bombings of December 1972 brought protestors to the streets and widespread outrage. One news magazine wrote: "Civilized man will be horrified at the renewed spectacle of the world's mightiest air force mercilessly pounding a small Asian nation." The response of the public to a strategy of deterrence based on the threat of strategic nuclear bombing of Soviet targets was, if not one of disinterest, quite muted by comparison.[44]

The fact that threats imply assurances means that deterrent threats may fail not because the threat is incredible, but because the target does not believe the corresponding assurance will be honored. The relationship between threats and assurances is even more problematic when the goal is compellence. Schelling writes of the tendency to emphasize the threat:

[It] is natural when deterrence is our business, because the prohibited misbehavior is often approximately defined in the threatened response; but when we must start something that then has to be stopped, as in compellent actions, it is both harder and more important to know our aims and to communicate. It is particularly hard because the mere initiation of an energetic coercive campaign, designed for compellence, disturbs the situation, leads to surprises, and provides opportunity and temptation to reexamine our aims and change them in mid course. Deterrence, if wholly successful can often afford to concentrate on the initiating events—what happens *next* if he misbehaves. Compellence, to be successful, involves an action that must be brought to a successful closure.[45]

If compellent threats are to succeed, one must convincingly communicate that the corresponding punishment can and will be stopped in the event of compliance; otherwise there is no incentive for cooperation on the part of the target. The object of any threat is to give the adversary a choice. Similarly, one must convincingly demonstrate that one's own aims are limited and that compliance on the part of the adversary will not lead to further demands.

The objective of most strategies of deterrence is the maintenance of the status quo into the indefinite future. By definition, the punishments associated with successful deterrent threats are never imposed. Aside from the costs associated with establishing the credibility of such threats, deterrent threats are cheap when successful.

Successful deterrent promises are often costly. This is especially true when the promised rewards represent transfers of value. And what proved sufficient for deterring an adversary today may not be enough tomorrow. If the defender of the status quo does not appear resolute, the challenger may be persuaded that he can push further than originally contemplated. Since Munich appeasement has come to be associated exclusively with defeat.[46] When incorporated into deterrent strategies, promises risk bringing costs to the source when they are successful as well as when they are not.

A somewhat related issue arises in the issue of counterfactual analysis. How does one know successful deterrence when one sees it? How can one be certain a challenge would have been forthcoming in the absence of the deterrent?[47] Statesmen may hesitate to issue deterrent promises when uncertain of a potential challenge. They may well provide a reward that is not necessary for the maintenance of the status quo.

Whereas the use of promises in deterrent strategies always carries some risk that the source will be taken advantage of, or receive a "sucker's" payoff, the situation is rather different if one considers the potential of *compellent* promises. With compellence the promised reward can be withheld until the proper behavior is evidenced in the adversary. In this way compellent promises may cost when they succeed but not when they fail.

Successful compellence when based on promised rewards may be more efficient than compellence based on threats. Whereas compellence by threats requires the source to initiate action, the requirements of compellence based on promised rewards are more like those of threat-based deterrence. The source sets the stage, structures the incentives, then waits for the other side to move.

Of course, depending on the nature of the desired change, there is the potential for the adversary to resume the original behavior. However, the same can be said for compellence based on threats and punishments. The best strategies for deterrence and compellence are probably those that combine both threats and promises. For example, once a compellent promise has achieved the desired action on the part of the adversary, deterrent threats might be employed to support the new status quo.[48]

Compellence based on rewards has another advantage over that based on threats. In contrast with deterrence, successful compellence brings action on the part of the adversary that "is more conspicuously compliant, more recognizable as submission under duress, than when an act is merely withheld in the face of a deterrent threat. Compliance is likely to be less casual, less capable of being rationalized as something that one was going to do anyhow."[49] Often one need not only convince a single leader to comply, but also important domestic groups. When the target of compellence based on promises complies, the associated rewards should provide some basis on which to justify compliance to domestic as well as international audiences.[50] The relationship appears to be less unidirectional and embedded in a context in which the parties are interdependent.[51] The most successful compellent promises would target rewards to those elements within the opposing society that are most committed to defiance in an effort to influence their calculations.[52]

For compellent promises to successfully influence an adversary they must appear credible. Sometimes one can enhance the credibility of a performance obligation by using third parties as guarantors. Such was the case in the release of American hostages from Iran. Previously frozen Iranian assets were transferred from U.S. banks to accounts in Algeria, the Algerians agreeing to release those funds upon release of the American diplomats.[53] If the source of a promise is unable to guarantee performance via third parties, it must structure the promise such that it would be costly to renege on provision of the associated rewards should target compliance occur.[54] The most obvious factor inhibiting lying in international politics is the state's reputation, but the reputational effects of broken promises or unfulfilled threats have not been subjected to much serious analysis.[55]

· 3 ·

A Theory of Influence

Threats, promises, and assurances are analytically distinct concepts, and each offers the statesman a potential tool of influence. A general theory of influence in international politics must incorporate all three and ideally identify when, how, and in what combination each can be effectively employed. In this regard deterrence—which examines the use of threats for coercive ends—and "reassurance"—which looks at the effects of promises and assurances—are incomplete at best. Nonetheless, identifying the short-comings of existing scholarship is a necessary first step toward the construction of a broader theory of influence.

THE POVERTY OF DETERRENCE THEORY

Deterrence theory represents the most developed attempt to answer one of the central questions of international politics: how one leader can influence another's decisions over war and peace. Many consider it to be "the most influential school of thought in the American study of international relations."[1]

A Crisis of Identity

The prevailing rationalist-deductivist theory of deterrence suffers from a twofold identity crisis. Does deterrence theory make normative or explanatory claims? If the latter, what does the theory purport to explain?

The tension between normative assertions and explanatory claims is already apparent in Schelling, but it is most pronounced in later efforts to construct a rational deterrence theory. With foundations in abstract models, many borrowed from game theory, rational deterrence theory as developed in the 1970s and 1980s attempts to superimpose the structure of strategic games on the structure of the international system, or it posits that abstract games capture the essential dynamics of strategic interaction between states that are assumed to be rational unitary actors. The strongest claim for such models is that they provide determinate solutions or dominant strategies and thus can both inform and explain the choices of rational actors.[2]

However, because many abstract games (like most real-world conflicts) do not have determinate solutions, what deterrence theory prescribes for one actor is often dependent on the opponent's actions and beliefs. Thus, in a game of Chicken, "if you think the other side is going to defect, you have to cooperate, because although being exploited (CD) is bad, it is not as bad as total breakdown (DD). As the familiar logic of deterrence shows, the actor must then try to convince the adversary that he is going to stand firm (defect) and that the only way the other can avoid disaster is to back down and cooperate."[3]

Strategic models of the deterrence problem, like Chicken, have the advantage of making explicit the fact that crisis outcomes are the product of interdependent choice and are thus superior to many models of decision making that fail to recognize the interactive nature of international crises or do so only implicitly. But because what one side should do is dependent on what the other will do, it is usually difficult to deduce positive propositions from any given international conflict: There are simply too few *objective* bases upon which to do so. Because structure appears indeterminate in all but the most extreme cases of international conflict, the strongest normative claims of deterrence theory cannot be sustained.

Many deterrence theorists shy away from prescribing strategy and instead claim only to explain outcomes.[4] But here too a crisis of identity emerges. Is the theory cast at the level of foreign policy or the international system? Does deterrence theory claim to explain strategic choices, crisis outcomes, or both? Perhaps the proponents of rational deterrence theory find comfort in the ambiguity, for when one asks the question and begins to explore the explanatory claims, one quickly discovers numerous inconsistencies and inadequacies.

Most claims to explanation of national behavior—or the choices of decision makers—rest on an assumption of rational actors engaged in subjective expected utility (SEU) maximization. But if crisis outcomes are the result of interdependent choice, this presents a problem. To the degree that SEU gives rise to determinate predictions over individual choice, it often does so at the expense of insights that could have been generated through strategic analysis. Thus, where Bruce Bueno de Mesquita argues that it is rational for a state to go to war when the expected gains outweigh the expected costs, a game theoretic analysis would suggest that in such situations the adversary has strong incentives to make concessions to avoid war, something a rational actor should anticipate.[5]

The claim that knowledge of outcomes in strategic situations provides unambiguous data over individual choice is also problematic.[6] The fallacy of this line of argument is most apparent when one considers the now common assertion that the absence of war between the United States and the Soviet Union was the result of successful deterrence. First, the absence of superpower war can be explained independently of deterrence theory.[7] Second, the absence of war may indicate absence of prior intent to attack rather than the successful use of deterrent threats.[8]

Moving from knowledge of outcomes to an explanation of individual choice is further complicated if international crises are not independent of one another. If deterrence theorists are correct, and the state's reputation, commitments, and other's expectations are interdependent, then outcomes in a particular case will not be amenable to explanation by means of straightforward decomposition. A challenger's decision to stand firm may have less to do with the immediate issues at stake or the defender's resolve or capabilities, and more to do with redressing the effects of retreats in previous crises or influencing third parties, be they domestic or foreign.[9]

Furthermore, the claim that an explanation of outcomes presupposes an explanation of individual choice rests on assumptions over decision making processes that are rooted in logical deductions rather than empirical evidence. When logical truths appear to be empirically violated, proponents of rational deterrence theory often retreat to arguments that approach tautology or dismiss the inferential value of the data. Thus, Christopher Achen and Duncan Snidal assert that *if initiators are deterrable* they will back down when threats to retaliate are costly and credible, implying that deterrence applies to actors who are deterrable![10] And when confronted with comparative case study data inconsistent with the expectations of rational deterrence theory, the same analysts argue that such studies "inherently [provide] too little logical constraint to generate dependable theory and too little inferential constraint to permit trustworthy theory testing."[11]

Given the inconsistencies and problems arising from the failure of theorists to agree on core issues (such as what is to be explained), the result of some thirty years of scholarship has been not so much a "theory of deterrence," as a number of theories, each based on different, often contradictory, assumptions, understandings, and claims to validity. But the shortcomings of deterrence theory are not limited to issues associated with the crisis of identity.

It's Never Just about Threats

Neither logic nor the empirical record will sustain the argument that successful deterrence is solely a matter of threats. As Schelling makes clear, "any coercive threat requires corresponding *assurances*; the object of a threat is to give somebody a choice." Logically, successful deterrence requires credible threats *and* assurances. "'One more step and I shoot,' can be a deterrent threat only if accompanied by the implicit assurance, 'And if you stop I won't.'"[12] Thus, a credible threat may fail to deter because the corresponding assurance of peace is in doubt.

Although in the first instance a matter of logic, the interdependence of deterrent threats and assurances has important practical implications. Many of the means by which a state can enhance the credibility of its threats—brinkmanship, for example—will tend to undermine the credibility of the corresponding assurance that compliance will be met with restraint. Unfortunately most scholars have followed Schelling's lead and restricted their analyses to the use and effects of threats. There is no scholarly treatment of the role of assurances in coercive diplomacy.

Guided by an underdeveloped analytic framework that mistakenly isolates threats as explanators, most empirically oriented research has been biased and narrow. Failures of deterrence are generally assumed to have resulted from either incredible threats or ambiguous commitments. Rarely examined is the question of whether decision makers believed that compliance with a deterrence threat would be met with restraint on the other side. What evidence there is suggests the difficulty of deterring decision makers who, perceiving their state to be facing long-term relative decline in a hostile environment, have concluded that war is inevitable.[13]

Assurances are probably even more important for successful compellence. Schelling noted the connection but failed to examine it in any detail: "Because in the West we deal mainly with deterrence, not compellence, and deterrent threats tend to convey their assurances implicitly, we often forget that *both* sides of the choice, the threatened penalty and the proffered avoidance or reward, need to be credible. . . . When we do engage in compellence, as in the Cuban crisis or in punitive attacks on North Vietnam that are intended to make the North Vietnamese government act affirmatively, the assurances are a critical point of the definition of the compellent threat."[14]

Such may have been the case in the fall of 1997 when Iraqi leader Saddam Hussein refused to grant American members of the United Nations weapons inspection team continued access to suspected arms production facilities and storage depots. Some analysts concluded that Hussein was motivated by the conviction that the United States was no longer content with Iraqi disarmament and that compliance with United Nations resolutions aimed at the destruction of weapons of mass destruction would not bring an end to the economic sanctions that were imposed after the Iraqi invasion of Kuwait in 1990 and extended in an effort to compel Iraq's compliance.[15]

When Are Threats Appropriate?

In both its normative/prescriptive and explanatory variants, deterrence theory is underspecified. Despite the preoccupation with threats, or perhaps owing to it, the theory tells us nothing with respect to *when* threats are appropriate tools of influence. One suspects that many theorists view deterrence as an end in itself, thus conflating deterrence with foreign policy, or at least security policy.[16]

As a result, many tend to assume that threats are *always* appropriate tools of influence. But as Alexander George and Richard Smoke argue, "whether deterrent threats are necessary and useful in a particular historical situation cannot be judged either in theory or in practice on the basis of a prescriptive theory that narrowly confines itself to indicating how to make threats."[17] What is needed is a theory of foreign policy or inter-state influence in which deterrent threats would represent but one of a number of potential tools of statecraft.[18]

REASSURANCE

George and Smoke are not alone in criticizing the failure of scholars to identify deterrence theory's scope conditions. Based on systematic analysis of cases of deterrence failure, Janice Gross Stein has concluded that threats are often "provocative, ineffective, or irrelevant" as tools of statecraft.[19] Together with Richard Ned Lebow, Stein has worked to broaden scholarly analysis and redress the limitations of deterrence—both as theory and strategy—by seeking to identify the conditions under which threats are most appropriate. The results of these studies not only suggest factors that may contribute to deterrence failure but also demonstrate that "reassurance" can be an effective approach to conflict management.[20]

A basic axiom of deterrence theory is that variation in outcomes is explainable by variations in actors' opportunities. Decisions are assumed to be driven by externally given incentives that in principle are amenable to influence by way of either threatened punishments or promised rewards. Most deterrence theorists make a second assumption, that aggression is primarily the result of states' efforts to exploit opportunities for gain. Thus, deterrence aims to manipulate the cost-benefit calculus of a potential aggressor by means of threats that increase the costs and/or risks associated with aggression.[21]

But all aggression is not similarly motivated. Empirical studies have demonstrated that deterrence failures are often characterized by challengers who are motivated by strategic vulnerability or domestic weakness rather than opportunity for gain. Threats appear to have little impact on the calculations of these decision makers, or worse—they may enhance the incentives to initiate a challenge.[22] Moreover, decision makers motivated by insecurity and fear of loss tend to display relatively high tolerance for risk and brinkmanship.[23]

Although threat-based strategies of deterrence appear counterproductive when employed against a risk-acceptant, loss-minimizing decision maker, strategies captured under the rubric of "reassurance" have proven successful at forestalling their resort to violence. Recognizing that aggressors are sometimes motivated by insecurity, "strategies of reassurance attempt directly to reduce the incentives to the threat or use of force and indirectly to make the use of force less likely through reduction of uncertainty and the establishment of norms that can regulate the management of conflict."[24] Theorists have identified at least five general strategies of reassurance, each of which contemplates a mix of promises and assurances.[25]

Whereas rationalist deductivist theories of deterrence either make universal claims or are silent with respect to the conditions under which they apply, empirically grounded analyses such as those of Lebow and Stein have provided clues as to when threats are appropriate tools of influence. Threats appear to be most effective at preventing resort to force when directed at aggressors motivated by opportunity for gain, but dangerous when employed against an actor motivated by fear of loss. Strategies based on promises and assurances appear to be most successful when the state is confronting an adversary driven by security concerns and not intent on exploiting opportunity for relative advantage. By drawing our attention to the variety of motives giving rise to aggression, as well as the utility of reassurance as a means of conflict management, Lebow and Stein have succeeded in pointing the way toward a broader theory of international influence. However, their work suffers from at least two important limitations.

First, their insights result from empirical analysis of deterrence failures. Before we can judge the validity of inductively derived propositions regarding the conditions under which deterrence and reassurance will prove effective, we must engage in a systematic comparison of cases selected on the independent variable, as Lebow and Stein themselves acknowledge.[26] Second, although they offer an interesting collection of inductively derived insights, Lebow and Stein fail to unify their propositions regarding deterrence and reassurance within a single theoretic framework. A broader theory of influence would link the two realms with one logic, subsuming cases of deterrence and reassurance under the same deductive framework.

PROSPECT THEORY AND INTERNATIONAL INFLUENCE

A broader theory of influence should provide analytic leverage over cases of deterrence as well as reassurance. It should establish conditions under which threats are appropriate tools of inter-state influence, and when, by contrast, promises are more likely to prove effective in strategies of conflict management. A theory of influence based on assumptions borrowed from behavioral decision theory, in particular prospect theory, provides such leverage.

An Introduction to Prospect Theory

Prospect theory offers a psychologically based alternative to rational models of choice under risk and uncertainty.[27] Whereas expected utility theory assumes that a person's utility for a particular good is a function of the net amount of that good possessed and that choice is driven by a desire to maximize net expected utility, prospect theory holds that people are more sensitive to *changes* in their endowment and that choice is driven by an overwhelming psychological desire to avoid loss.

Informed by a series of laboratory studies, Daniel Kahneman and Amos Tversky conclude that people evaluate the utility of prospective outcomes not only against each other, but more importantly against a reference point that is regarded as neutral. The framing of prospective outcomes in terms of a reference point establishes a psychological domain of gains (all outcomes above the reference point) and losses (those outcomes that fall beneath the reference point) with important behavioral implications.[28]

The reframing of an identical outcome in terms of a loss rather than a gain has been demonstrated to produce a reversal in preferences and corresponding choice. For example, when given a choice between (1) a sure gain of $100 and (2) a 50 percent chance of a $200 gain and a 50 percent chance to gain nothing, an overwhelming percentage of people will chose the sure bet. However, when confronted with a choice between (1) a sure loss of $100 and (2) a 50 percent chance of losing $200 and a 50 percent chance of losing nothing, most people will take the gamble. In terms of subjective expected utility, the two choice situations are essentially the same. The reversal of preferences thus represents a deviation from rational choice.[29]

In general, losses loom larger in our calculations than do gains: "The common reluctance to accept a fair bet on the toss of a coin suggests that the displeasure of losing a sum of money exceeds the pleasure of winning the same amount."[30] Mounting evidence suggests that the attribute, which Tversky and Kahneman have termed *loss aversion,* is widely shared. Because of loss aversion, differences between two outcomes in the domain of losses produce greater psychological impact than corresponding differences between two outcomes in the domain of gains. Thus, we would expect the difference in subjective value between a loss of $100 and a loss of $200 to be greater than the subjective difference between a gain of $200 and a gain of $100.

Because of the psychological asymmetry between losses and gains, the value individuals place on an object generally increases when it becomes part of their endowment. This *endowment effect* leads people to demand much more for an item they own than they themselves would be willing to pay to acquire it.[31] If inconsistent with the tenets of rational theories of choice, the phenomenon has gained expression in common folk wisdom: "A bird in the hand is worth two in the bush."

Moreover, people tend to accommodate to gains easier than to losses. The endowment effect appears to be almost instantaneous, whereas accommodation to losses can take years. And contrary to the expectations of rational choice, decisions often fail to reflect calculations of incremental costs. Rather, the influence of past states has been shown to lead actors to focus on sunk costs and strive to recoup past losses.[32]

The framing of choice in terms of gains and losses also affects individuals' tolerance for risk as illustrated in the aforementioned example of preference reversal. Once outcomes are framed around a reference point, most people are risk averse with respect to gains, yet risk seeking with respect to loss. Because people appear to value that which they have more than that which they covet, most people will take greater risks to avoid a loss than they will to secure a comparable gain.[33]

Furthermore, behavioral decision research has demonstrated that contrary to the norms of expected utility, people exhibit nonlinear responses to probabilities. They overvalue outcomes that are certain as compared to those that are merely probable: Highly probable yet uncertain outcomes are treated as if they are were certain, and outcomes of extremely low probability tend to be discarded in the editing of options. Together with loss aversion, this *certainty effect* leads to the expectation that people will chose a sure (or almost sure) bet rather than take a chance on a larger gain that is merely probable, even if the latter offers higher expected utility. Relatedly, they will bet on a larger probable loss rather than accept a certain (or nearly certain) loss, even when the certain loss represents an outcome of higher expected utility (consider again the case of preference reversal above).

Tversky and Kahneman thus hypothesize that most people's utility or value functions follow an S shape: concave for gains, convex for losses, with the slope steeper in the domain of losses than in the domain of gains (see figure 2).[34]

Prospect Theory and International Politics

A growing literature finds plausible links between prospect theory and foreign policy decision making.[35] Coupled with auxiliary assumptions (e.g., that political decisions display similar dynamics to those demonstrated in laboratory experiments), prospect theory gives rise to a number of interesting hypotheses. For example, Jack Levy has suggested that prospect theory would lead us to expect the following:

1. Decision makers will take greater risks to maintain their positions domestically and internationally than they will to enhance those positions.

2. Decision makers will find accommodation to political losses difficult and will often run high risks to recover them.

3. It is easier to deter an actor from beginning an action than to compel him to stop an action already underway.

4. It is easier to deter an actor from making gains than from attempting to recover losses.

5. Cooperation over the distribution of gains will be easier than over distribution of losses.

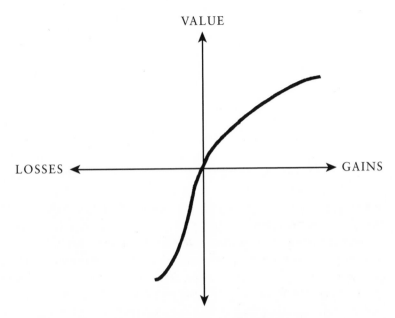

Figure 2. Hypothesized Value Function

6. It will be easier to achieve agreement on preventing the degradation of public goods than in securing contributions for their provision.[36]

Janice Stein finds in loss aversion a possible explanation for escalation in limited wars: "If [the state's] leadership fears certain and immediate losses from continuation of the status quo, then the larger risks of escalation which are probable rather than certain may be preferable."[37]

Prospect theory also offers a compelling set of assumptions on which to base a general theory of influence. This is true for at least three reasons. First, in international politics decision making is almost always conducted under conditions of uncertainty, the domain prospect theory purports to explain. Second, classifying outcomes in terms of gains and of losses vis-à-vis a reference point corresponds to the definition of threats and promises—as contingent deprivations or improvements relative to a baseline of expectation—offered in chapter 2. Finally, when applied to cases of crisis bargaining, prospect theory and the assumption of loss aversion reconcile the findings of both deterrence and reassurance theorists to a single (psycho-) logic. The argument requires elaboration.

The Implications for Statecraft

If political leaders frame choices around a reference point and respond differently to prospective gains and losses vis-à-vis the reference point, then prospect theory provides answers to fundamental questions of statecraft. For if prospect theory is valid outside of the laboratory,[38] we should expect threats to be most effective when the target is evaluating options in the domain of gains. By contrast, promises will be powerful tools of influence when directed at leaders confronting loss. And to the degree to which they reduce uncertainty and increase the probability that the reference outcome will obtain, assurances can reduce fears and anxieties that have often led to assertive or aggressive foreign policies.

If statesmen value what they have more than what they covet, few will be willing to incur heavy costs or run high risks to secure gains. The decision maker evaluating options in the domain of gains will be highly sensitive to threats that increase the costs or risks associated with a policy of aggrandizement. Deterrence is the appropriate strategy when the adversary is motivated by perceived opportunity for gain.

If prospect theory is correct, threats that increase the prospective costs associated with a given course of action may be highly effective at deterring a decision maker operating in the domain of gain but ceteris paribus will be less effective when decision makers are in the domain of loss. Threats that manipulate risk or "leave something to chance"[39] will also prove less effective in the domain of loss than the domain of gains, because actors are relatively more risk acceptant when contemplating loss. And because the certainty effect biases assessment of utility, the *uncertain* prospect of a defender response—even when the balance of interests and capabilities suggest that a response would bring heavy losses—is unlikely to deter a state motivated by what it considers to be a *certain* (or near certain) loss. Moreover, in the wake of a challenge motivated by loss aversion, the issuance of immediate deterrent threats, *particularly when credible*, may lead the state to take ever larger gambits.[40]

Because the endowment effect is instantaneous, whereas renormalization[41] occurs much more slowly, shifts of assets between actors in a sequential interaction can quickly result in a situation where *both* sides are evaluating options in the domain of loss. For example, imagine that at T-1 France loses Alsace and Lorraine to Germany. At T-2 France escalates the crisis in an effort to recover the recent loss. Germany, in turn, having renormalized to the new status quo, would be expected to run high risks in an effort to avoid the "loss" of the former French territories. The psychological processes associated with loss aversion thus provide a possible explanation for outcomes associated with the "spiral model" and the failure of deterrent threats.[42]

Where threats are inappropriate, promises hold potential for successful inter-state influence. Prospect theory leads to the expectation that bold gains-seeking behavior will be relatively rare in international politics; aggressive foreign policies will most often reflect an underlying desire to minimize loss. When confronting loss, decision makers should be highly receptive to promised rewards. Because it postulates that people's utility functions are generally steeper in the domain of losses than in the domain of gains, prospect theory leads us to expect that promised rewards can be relatively modest and yet achieve significant return in terms of increased target utility.[43] The most effective promises should be those that offer the reduction or elimination of the target's losses rather than those that augment another attribute, because the corresponding increase in utility takes place on a steeper limb of the value function.[44]

If threats are appropriate tools of influence when the target is evaluating options in the domain of gains, and promises are more effective at influencing an actor considering loss, when should assurances be incorporated into strategies of conflict management? Schelling's insight—that assurances are constitutive of threats and thus both deterrence and compellence—was raised in the context of the general critique of rational deterrence theory offered above. However, the potential for influence by means of assurances is broader.

One of the pernicious effects of international anarchy—the absence of legitimate authority above sovereign states—is the security dilemma: The actions one state undertakes to enhance its own security generally menace the security of others, often leading them to respond in kind. These countermeasures may not only negate any measure of security the first state achieved, but provoke it to undertake ever more energetic actions. When the security dilemma is particularly virulent, fear and uncertainty regarding others' motives give rise to incentives for preventive or preemptive war, something Schelling called "the reciprocal fear of surprise attack." History offers numerous cases where the security dilemma and associated incentives for preemption produced war scares and diplomatic crises.[45]

Because statesmen frequently underestimate the degree to which their actions appear menacing to others, they often fail to recognize fear as a possible motive for behavior.[46] Consequently, they overlook the need to integrate assurances into the state's foreign and security policies. Yet the timely provision of assurances can help resolve disputes, defuse war scares, and more importantly prevent diplomatic crises in the first place.

For a status quo power the goal of foreign policy should be to facilitate other states' accommodation to the prevailing distribution of values in the international system and then to reinforce the expectation that the status quo will persist. If successful, challenges should be rare because incentives for gains seeking as well as loss avoidance will be limited.

Assurances offer a means of reinforcing the expectation that the status quo will persist.[47] For example, it is now acknowledged that President Kennedy's promise not to invade Cuba was crucial to the resolution of the 1963 missile crisis.[48] Somewhat less widely appreciated was the importance the Brezhnev Politburo attached in 1970 to securing President Nixon's assurance that he would continue to respect the Kennedy commitment.[49] Where Kennedy's promise contributed to the resolution of a superpower dispute, Nixon's assurance may have helped to prevent one.[50] If the most risk-acceptant actors are those who conclude that inaction portends loss, the most effective assurances will be those that reduce uncertainty and thus mitigate security fears that can impel even satisfied states to evaluate outcomes in the domain of loss.

To this point the discussion has focussed on rather ideal-typical situations. Based on insights taken from prospect theory, I have proposed a model of foreign policy decision making that assumes decisions are framed around a neutral reference point that separates prospective outcomes into a domain of gains and a domain of losses. Because people react differently to prospective gains than to losses, successful influence requires knowledge of the domain within which actors consider options. If confronted with an aggressive adversary who is evaluating outcomes in the domain of loss, the state should base its influence strategy on promises that reduce the adversary's prospective loss. Aggression motivated by opportunity for gain should be deterred through use of threats. Assurances can help reduce uncertainties, stabilize expectations, and thereby promote continued peaceful relations amongst status quo powers.

Though analytically distinct, both gains-seeking and loss-avoiding motives may arise in a particular empirical case. Thus, although the German government hoped to gain some advantage by supporting Austrian demands against Serbia in July 1914, it is also true that an assertive policy was regarded as the only means of avoiding relative decline.[51] Similarly, whereas

Khrushchev's primary motives for introducing missiles into Cuba were not offensive (he sought to deter an American invasion of Cuba and redress Soviet strategic inferiority), the Soviet leader probably thought that a successful deployment of Soviet missiles to Cuba would facilitate a more assertive policy on other issues, such as the status of Berlin.[52]

Because of multiple and complex linkages in international politics,[53] foreign policies are often formulated in response to numerous pressures, disputed issues are rarely analyzed in isolation, and outcomes in one area tend to have implications across a range of others. Owing to this multidimensionality, motives for behavior will often be characterized by admixtures of need and opportunity, and foreign policies will frequently reflect offensive as well as defensive goals.

If interconnections are common and motives for aggressive or assertive foreign policies frequently mixed, at least two implications follow. First, a particular tool of influence may produce a range of effects resulting from the different ways in which it impacts on the multiplicity of values at stake or motives giving rise to the target's behavior. A threat to certain values might simultaneously represent an improvement vis-à-vis others. Thus, although American threats led Turkish Premier Inönü to abandon plans for an invasion of Cyprus in 1964, they simultaneously strengthened his hand in the domestic power struggle with the Turkish generals.[54] The reverse can also occur. Although the promise of U.S. assistance in exchange for peace with Israel helped stabilize a deteriorating Egyptian economy and thereby brought certain political benefits to President Anwar Sadat (especially in the business community), it also provoked the Islamist opposition and further aggravated Egypt's relations with other Arab states.[55]

Second, if mixed motives are pervasive, quests for dominant strategies will often prove futile. When devising strategy, statesmen must consider the range of pressures giving rise to the target's behavior and try to gauge the underlying mix of need and opportunity as well as interrelations between the issues at stake and other important values. Successful influence will then require skillful mixes of threats, promises, and assurances—both to address the mixed motives giving rise to a challenge and to manage undesired "side effects" produced by one or the other tool of influence as a result of interconnections.

Such mixed strategies are inherently demanding and often appear incoherent or self-contradictory because of the trade-offs they require. The difficulty of increasing the credibility of threats without simultaneously undermining the credibility of corresponding assurances has already been noted.

But a strategy that seeks to combine threats and promises may be even more exacting, in terms of both influencing the target and generating requisite domestic and allied diplomatic support.

A first challenge results from the difficulty of communication through diplomatic signals. Even simple signals are often misinterpreted in international relations;[56] nuanced strategies that combine threats and promises are likely to allow for an even wider range of conflicting interpretations on the part of the target. Because people tend to assimilate ambiguous information to preexisting belief structures, targets are likely to focus on those signals that most readily lend themselves to reinforcing established opinion at the expense of those that do not. Thus, in the run-up to the Spanish-American War, the new Liberal government in Madrid failed to appreciate the seriousness of a threat issued by President McKinley in a speech before Congress. Convinced they could reach a negotiated settlement with the Cuban rebels, Spanish decision makers celebrated the president's avowed skepticism regarding the desirability of Cuban independence.[57]

In democracies the pursuit of mixed strategies is also confounded by the need to generate domestic support for the state's foreign policy. Simple and direct policies are generally easier to explain and justify than are mixed strategies that result from attempts to influence behavior on multiple dimensions or target multiple actors.[58]

Although demanding, the successful execution of mixed strategies is not impossible: Mixed need not imply complex or unintelligible. Adopted as a response to the deployment of intermediate-range nuclear forces (INFs) in the western portion of the Soviet Union, NATO's "dual-track" decision of December 1979 consisted of a threat to deploy U.S. INFs in Western Europe and an offer to engage in arms control negotiations to obviate the need for such deployments. The mixed strategy represented both an attempt to influence the course of Soviet deployments (and eventually reverse them), as well as to calm western publics' unease with the prospect of a new arms race. Certainly INF deployment was regarded unfavorably by a majority of western publics and provoked vocal protests from the peace and nuclear freeze movements. However, the dual-track policy succeeded in securing sufficient domestic support to allow deployment of cruise and Pershing II missiles in 1983.[59] Moreover, the strategy was eventually effective in promoting a treaty banning INFs.

The father of modern Realism, Hans Morgenthau, was right: motives matter. Decision makers will invite war if they incorrectly assess the motives animating others' foreign policies: "A nation that mistakes a policy of imperialism for a policy of the status quo will be unprepared to meet the threat to its own existence which the other nation's policy entails." However, "[a] nation that mistakes a policy of the status quo for a policy of imperialism will evoke through its disproportionate reaction the very danger of war which it is trying to avoid." The art of diplomacy lies in correctly assessing the mix of motives giving rise to the other's behavior and devising a strategy that places the proper emphasis on one or the other tool of influence: "A diplomacy that puts most of its eggs in the basket of compromise when the military might of the nation should be predominately displayed, or stresses military might when the political situation calls for persuasion and compromise, will likewise fail."[60]

FROM THEORY TO PRACTICE: THE QUESTION OF DIAGNOSTICS

If the search for dominant strategies deduced from original principles or assumptions is usually futile, then the need for diagnostics is clear. In considering whether to adopt a strategy based on threats, promises, assurances, or a mixture of these, statesmen need to diagnose both the motives giving rise to the target's behavior as well as the range of effects any one tool of influence is likely to produce.

Insights from prospect theory lead to the expectation that choice will be highly reference dependent; that is, once outcomes have been framed around a reference point, we expect decision makers to be risk averse with respect to outcomes above the reference point, yet risk seeking with respect to outcomes falling beneath it in the choices they make.

Thus far, however, behavioral decision research has not produced a theory of framing. Evidence suggests that actors often frame prospective outcomes around their own subjective definition of the status quo. But the propensity to frame outcomes around social norms, focal points, or aspirations is not insignificant. Researchers have only begun to examine the question of how decision makers choose among multiple relevant reference points.[61]

Yet most political decision makers can imagine multiple reference points for any set of outcomes, and the proper referent is often the subject of intense political debate. For example, in a given year Israeli leaders might measure a proposed American aid package against the previous year's level of assistance; against the current year's requested level; as a function of the total amount of assistance the United States sends abroad in the current year; or perhaps as it relates to the amount of aid given to Egypt. The

Israeli government's choice of frame is likely to condition American influence and the effectiveness of U.S. diplomacy. Thus, a worthwhile goal of American political and intelligence analysis would be to establish precisely how the Israeli government was framing the issue.

The lack of a theory of framing is regrettable. Nonetheless, if the theory holds, effective influence will hinge on the state's ability to establish the target's frame and thus develop and appreciate the motives animating its behavior.

EVALUATING THE THEORY

For the scholar the testing of hypotheses deduced from prospect theory is less problematic. Through the post hoc reconstruction of an actor's definition of a given situation with particular attention paid to the construction of the decisional frame, prospect theory's hypotheses regarding the behavior of choice under conditions of risk, uncertainty, or both should be susceptible to empirical refutation.

Because this book looks at decisions concerning war and peace, and because motives for behavior are regarded as key explanators, the analysis is cast at the level of decision making.[62] However, the idiosyncrasies of individual decision makers are discussed only insofar as they provide background to the cases and are not accorded causal primacy. The goal is to identify generalizable patterns of decision making in an effort to establish when threats or promises are better tools of influence. When helpful, the general argument is refined and the explanation of individual cases enriched by insights from cognitive and social psychology.

Chapters 4 through 7 present a series of case studies taken from German diplomatic history. Across the range of cases German motives for contemplating challenges to the status quo vary, as do the methods used by the other powers to influence German decision making. The cases thus show variation in both independent variables: motive for aggression and influence technique. Sometimes deterrence succeeded, and German decision makers backed away from contemplated aggression. In many cases deterrence failed, Germany attacked, and war broke out.

The analysis focuses on the motives and expectations of the principal decision makers in each crisis, most often the Prussian king (later the German kaiser), the chancellor, and the foreign minister when this position was held by someone other than the chancellor. The coding of motives is based on a reading of the work of historians as well as data from diplomatic documents, diaries, letters, and memoirs. The next chapter presents cases where Prussian leaders were motivated to expand their territory by the perception that the strategic environment provided opportunity to do so at little cost and manageable risk. Chapters 5 and 6 examine cases where German leaders were strongly motivated by fears of loss and the perceived need to defend the status quo.

After establishing the motives for German behavior, analysis turns to the methods adopted by the other powers in their effort to influence German policy. In a third step, the processes by which threats, promises, and assurances were identified and incorporated into German policy deliberations are examined with the goal of establishing the effects of such signals on German behavior. Did threats deter opportunists? Did threats produce spirals when German leaders were acting out of fear of loss? When were promises effective tools of conflict management, and when did they only encourage further aggression?

In addition to intensive analysis of individual cases, cross-case comparison provides a means of testing whether an individual actor's responses to threats and promises varied according to the context within which a given influence attempt took place. This is accomplished by demonstrating variation in outcomes (dependent variable) for similar cases where German motives (first independent variable) are held constant, but where the influence technique employed by those seeking to deter Germany (second independent variable) varies, and cases where outcomes varied when influence technique is held constant but motives for aggression vary.

· 4 ·

Confronting Prussian Ambition:
Influence in the Domain of Gains

> Great crises are the weather which Prussia's growth de-
> mands—as long as we use them fearlessly, perhaps even
> unscrupulously. If we wish to continue to grow, we must not
> be afraid to stand alone with our 400,000 men, especially as
> long as the other states are fighting each other.
> > Otto von Bismarck to Manteuffel, 15 February 1854

How can states influence the policies of revisionist powers bent on exploiting opportunity for gain? This was the essence of the German question
from 1848 to 1871 as the Prussian leadership set out to transform one of
the weakest into one of the strongest of the great powers. Although the
dictates of international competition and the spread of nationalism as a
political ideology were probably sufficient conditions for the emergence of
a unified German state in the nineteenth century, there was nothing inevitable about a Prussian-dominated Germany extending from Schleswig in
the north to Bavaria in the south, from the border of Poland in the east to
the provinces of Alsace and Lorraine in the west. Rather, Prussian expansion at the expense of Denmark, Austria, France, and numerous independent German states reflected to a large extent the failure of the European
powers to successfully defend the status quo in Germany as defined by the
Vienna settlements of 1815.

In 1848 and again in 1863 Prussia provoked an international crisis by
trying to detach the duchies of Schleswig and Holstein from Denmark. With
Austrian assistance Prussia succeeded in 1863 but turned on its erstwhile
ally the following year, defeating Austria at Königgrätz (Sadowa) and thereby
securing Prussian hegemony in Germany north of the Main River.

The cases are both theoretically and methodologically interesting. In each, Prussian challenges are largely gains driven. Each crisis provoked efforts on the part of the European great powers to influence Prussian decisions over war and peace. Yet because the responses of the European great powers vary across the cases, we would expect to see variation in outcomes.

To the extent that Prussian challenges to the status quo in Germany can be characterized as having been gains seeking and opportunity driven, the argument developed in chapter 3 would lead us to expect that Prussian decision makers would be relatively risk averse and highly sensitive to threats. Gains seeking and weak in relation to the great powers, Prussia should have been an easy target for a strategy of deterrence.

The cases are analyzed in parallel fashion. First, I establish the motives giving rise to the Prussian challenge. Was Prussian aggression motivated by a desire to make gains or avoid loss? I then turn to the reconstruction of the decisional frame. What was the reference point against which prospective outcomes were judged as gains or losses, and what was the baseline against which Prussian decision makers evaluated the actions of other states? In a third step I present the responses of the European great powers to Prussian efforts at expansion. Last, I turn to an examination of outcomes. How did Prussian decision makers react to the influence attempts of other European states?

THE FIRST SCHLESWIG-HOLSTEIN CRISIS

The settlement of 1815 at the Congress of Vienna proved decisive for the future course of Prussian expansion and German unification. To secure the establishment of the new Polish state, Russian Tsar Alexander I persuaded King Friedrich Wilhelm III to relinquish his Polish holdings. The Prussian monarch was compensated in the west with two-fifths of the Kingdom of Saxony, Swedish Pomerania, and the Kingdom of Westphalia. These new territories effectively shifted Prussia's center of gravity westward with profound strategic implications, as the focus of Prussian exertions shifted from extending influence in the east to consolidating and expanding in the west, a development that continued to the outbreak of the First World War.

However, the Vienna settlement also established the German Confederation under a federal constitution, an arrangement for Germany that promised to keep Prussia weak in relation to the other great powers. Thus, the emergence of a unified German state in the center of Europe would have a dramatic effect on the balance of power and would certainly affect the interests of France, England, and Russia. If Prussian expansion and some form of German unification were to come about, the consensus regarding the appropriate constitution of Europe that emerged among the great powers during the Concert would either have to be renegotiated, or collapse.

The factors leading to the demise of the Concert of Europe are many, but two interrelated events are crucial to the course of Prussian expansion and German unification: first, the spread of nationalist-republican revolutions throughout Europe in 1848, and, second, the particular result of the revolution in France: the election of Louis Napoleon as president of the French Republic on 10 December of the same year.

In February 1848 King Louis Philippe was dethroned, and the Second Republic was proclaimed in France with a call to revive nationalism across Europe. The revolutionary spark landed on dry tinder in Germany, where radicals and liberals had been mobilizing public opinion in favor of national unity for months. By March hundreds of barricades were manned across Germany, and bloody street battles broke out between army troops and revolutionaries in Berlin.[1]

The revolutions of 1848 revealed the inherent weakness of the German Confederation. Intended by Metternich as a bulwark against liberalism and nationalism, and a means for securing Austrian predominance in Germany, it was clearly a failure, with Metternich himself forced to flee the Austrian revolution to London in disguise. Under pressure from the revolutionaries, the Diet in Frankfurt dissolved itself and a revolutionary parliament assembled in the Paulskirche (St. Paul's Church) as the "German Constituent National Assembly."

The revolution's early successes receded relatively rapidly, and debates in the Paulskirche led nowhere. Nonetheless, two political movements emerged from the revolution, each promoting a unified German state. The *grossdeutsch* (great Germany) movement maintained that the German portion of Austria was an essential part of any future German state. For the *kleindeutsch* (little Germany) movement, the inevitability of a Prussian-led Germany that excluded Austria was already accepted.[2]

Apparently shocked by bloodshed in the streets of Berlin and the high level of support at the barricades, the Prussian monarch attempted to divert the focus of attention away from discontent at home and toward the cause of national unity. On horseback, and draped with the black, red, and gold imperial tricolor, King Friedrich Wilhelm IV, accompanied by generals and ministers, road the streets of Berlin giving speeches and reading his royal proclamation: "To my people and the German nation. . . . We can only be rescued from our dangers by the most intimate union of German princes and peoples under one leadership; I take over that leadership. . . . I have today taken the old German colors and placed my people under the venerable banner of the German Empire. Prussia is henceforth merged with Germany!"[3] If the specter of further revolution at home inspired the king to adopt nationalist rhetoric for domestic consumption, an unexpected opportunity for external expansion presented itself in Schleswig-Holstein.

The question surrounding the duchies of Schleswig and Holstein had a long and complicated history.[4] By 1848, however, a succession dispute combined with the rise of nationalist animosities to make the future of the two rather obscure duchies an issue of major import to the great powers of Europe.

The duchies had been associated with each other since the Middle Ages when the noble estates of each agreed to elect the Danish king, Christian of Oldenburg, duke. Considering themselves "forever united," the nobles first secured a charter in 1460 in which Christian was made to affirm that he was ruler by election rather than hereditary right, and that only his male heirs would be eligible for election as duke. He was further made to guarantee that the close association between the duchies would never be impaired.

Although united under personal union with the Danish crown, Schleswig and Holstein enjoyed different status with regard to Germany. Holstein, by virtue of its earlier membership in the Holy Roman Empire and exclusively German-speaking population, was a member of the Confederation. The Danish monarch, by virtue of his position as Duke of Holstein, was a member of the federal Diet at Frankfurt. Schleswig, by contrast, was German in its southern part, predominately Danish in the north. It had never been a part of the Holy Roman Empire, was not a member of the German Confederation, and thus was subject only to the authority of the Danish king.

With the rise of liberalism and nationalism across Europe, the 1840s brought animosity to the relations between Germans and Danes in Schleswig. Supported by the Danish nationalists in Schleswig, the so-called Eider-Danes, the new king of Denmark, Christian VIII, began to move toward the formal incorporation of Schleswig into Denmark.[5] In opposition to the Eider-Danes stood the German nationalists who comprised the national, or Schleswig-Holstein, party. Their aim was the establishment of a unified German state to include the duchies of Holstein, Schleswig, and Lauenburg.

Compounding the fierce clash of Danish and German nationalism in the duchies was the impending extinction of the direct male line in the royal house of Denmark. The Crown Prince, later King Friedrich VII, had no children nor prospects for any. The Danish throne would pass to the nearest heir of the last king according to the *lex regia* of 1665, which meant through the female line to his youngest sister. Because the Salic law applied in the duchies, a fact guaranteed in the charter of 1460, the duchies would pass to the nearest male line, which happened to be that of the Dukes of Augustenburg.[6] Hence, the kingdom and the duchies would be divided.

In response to pressure from the Eider-Danes and other quarters within Denmark, the king issued an "Open Letter" in 1846, declaring the succession in Schleswig to be that of Denmark. The king conceded that it applied only to a portion of Holstein. The estates of Holstein promptly appealed the matter to the federal Diet.[7] The situation became further radicalized as revolution spread throughout Europe. In March 1848, with the Eider-Danes holding the upper hand in Copenhagen, a new constitution was established for Denmark and Schleswig. The estates rebelled and established a provisional government for "Schleswig-Holstein" and appealed to the Diet for protection. Groups from across Germany rose to support their cause. Provincial diets, universities, mass meetings, conservatives as well as liberals called for the federal Diet to defend the "German" nationality in Schleswig-Holstein.

In reality the only member of the Confederation with the requisite military strength and proximity to the duchies was Prussia, and Friedrich Wilhelm was poised to take advantage of the opportunity to appease nationalist fervor at home and make gains abroad.[8] Thirty thousand Prussian troops crossed into the duchies on 10 April and by month's end were beginning an invasion of Jutland, part of Denmark itself. The question of the duchies' future at this point became a matter for the great powers, as Denmark appealed to Britain, France, and Russia for support under terms of a 1720 treaty. For a variety of reasons, each was interested in the preservation of the status quo in the duchies.

The British Foreign Secretary, Lord Palmerston, considered the Schleswig-Holstein affair to be a powder keg that could ignite a major European conflict. Although supportive of the general thrust of German unification, Palmerston saw the maintenance of the status quo in the duchies as essential because it kept control over the Baltic and the Danish straights out of the hands of a major power and thus contributed to the preservation of British maritime supremacy.[9] As long as Prussia was denied access to the ports of Schleswig, its efforts to build a strong naval capability would be thwarted. A Prussian navy was seen not only as a potential military but also as a commercial threat. A Prussian victory in the duchies might hurt British commerce on the continent through an expanded Zollverein with increased duties on British goods and bring about new competition in maritime trade.[10]

France, embroiled in revolutionary turmoil itself, was in no position to encourage Prussian aggrandizement in Germany. In Paris Bastide had taken over the foreign ministry from Lamartine and wrote to his representative at Frankfurt: "German unity would make of this people of more than twenty-five million a power very much more redoubtable to its neighbors . . . therefore I do not think we have any reason to desire this unity, still less, promote it."[11]

Russia was perhaps the most interested of the powers in the outcome of the crisis. Tsar Nicholas I feared that Denmark would join forces with the Scandinavian Union if defeated, a prospect that could complicate Russian designs for the Baltic. Nesselrode suggested dividing the duchies along nationalist lines.[12] Nicholas also feared that triumph of German nationalism in Schleswig-Holstein would encourage further nationalist agitation in Poland.

Under strong diplomatic pressure from England and France, and facing the prospect of war with Russia, Friedrich Wilhelm IV abandoned his invasion and concluded the Armistice of Malmö in July 1848. The armistice called for joint Danish-German administration of the duchies pending the conclusion of a peace treaty. Fighting broke out again in March 1849 when the Danes renounced its terms. Again the tsar threatened intervention against Prussia. The British threatened to stand aside if Prussia was attacked, and again Friedrich Wilhelm relented.[13]

Prussia began to withdraw its forces from Schleswig in 1849 and accepted the London Protocol in July 1850. The king of Denmark then asked the federal Diet to help him reestablish his authority in Holstein. At the request of the Diet, Austrian and Prussian troops occupied Holstein.

Prussia and Austria seized the opportunity to extract concessions out of the Danish monarch. Before they would agree to restore his authority in Holstein, they secured a promise from the king that there would be no de jure or de facto incorporation of Schleswig into Denmark or any efforts to weaken the traditional links between Schleswig and Holstein. Further, the Danish monarch promised to consult Prussia and Austria before undertaking any constitutional reforms in the duchies. On 8 May 1852, with the king of Denmark agreeing to these conditions, the Schleswig-Holstein question appeared to be settled as the five powers together with Sweden-Norway and Denmark signed the London Treaty.[14]

Decisional Frame

What motivated Friedrich Wilhelm to invade the duchies and how did Prussian decision makers frame their choices in the dispute with Denmark over Schleswig and Holstein? Among the king's advisors were reactionaries who rejected anything coming from the Paulskirche as well as supporters of German nationalism. Both groups competed for influence in a foreign policy decision making apparatus that was generally chaotic.[15] However, the opportunity presented by the crisis over Schleswig-Holstein served to unify elements from both camps, as they came to see that the goals of conservative restoration and Prussian-led German nationalism could be accomplished together through an aggressive policy in the duchies.

Prussian motives in the First Schleswig-Holstein Crisis were mixed. The invasion of the duchies was aimed both at correcting domestic weakness by coopting the nationalist cause and at securing territorial gains. The generalized chaos of the revolution presented a unique opportunity to extend Prussian hegemony at the expense of the weaker states and suggested a need to do so.[16]

In the run-up to the war with Denmark, Prussian decision makers framed outcomes to the crisis in terms of the political status quo among the European great powers. Although they sought to make territorial gains, they were unwilling to risk a wider conflict in order to do so. Believing that Prussian troops could drive Danish forces from Schleswig in less than a fortnight, they aimed for a quick victory by which they could present the powers with a fait accompli.

An intimate of the king, Joseph Maria von Radowitz recorded the course of the government's deliberations in his diary: "The present political-military crisis cannot drag on. It must come to a rapid conclusion." He further noted his own opposition to an eventual invasion of Jutland, arguing that a widening of the war to Denmark proper would lead to a rupture in relations with Russia with "unforeseeable consequences." If the duchies could be secured with a rapid drive through Schleswig he supported the effort, but Prussian gains in Schleswig and Holstein were not worth the cost of a wider conflict.[17] It was a position that unified Radowitz and his political rival, the influential General von Gerlach.[18]

Apparently influenced by military estimates, Foreign Minister von Arnim argued that Danish forces could be driven out of the duchies in eight days, at which time Denmark would be forced to sue for peace.[19] The king agreed to support an invasion of the duchies if the affair could be localized and brought to a rapid conclusion. However, he did not regard territorial gain to be worth a wider political dispute with Britain and Russia.[20]

The political status quo among the great powers was the reference point against which the Prussian leadership evaluated prospective outcomes. Control over the duchies without consequent deterioration in Prussia's relations with the other great powers would pose a gain, whereas a wider conflict with Russia or Britain would constitute a loss. The theory of influence developed in the previous chapter would lead us to expect that insofar as they were seeking gains in the duchies of Schleswig and Holstein, the Prussian leadership would be highly sensitive to threats that increased the costs and risks associated with an invasion. The Prussian leadership should have been deterrable.

Baseline of Expectation

Before turning to an analysis of the tsar's interventions and their effects on Prussian decision making, it is necessary to establish the prevailing expectations among the Prussian leadership with regard to the position other powers would adopt. What was the expected response of the European powers to an invasion of Schleswig and Holstein?

The Prussian leadership believed that Russia and England would not oppose an invasion of the duchies and that revolutionary upheaval in France precluded any independent French intervention. In the run-up to the crisis both British and Russian diplomacy had supported the general thrust of German unification. Palmerston had drafted a memorandum on the subject in the fall of 1847: "There can be no doubt that it is greatly for the interest of England to cultivate a close political connection and alliance with Germany, as it is also the manifest interest of Germany to ally itself politically with England. The great interests of the two are the same. England and Germany therefore have mutually a direct interest in assisting each other to become rich, united, and strong."[21] With both the Prussian monarch and the Frankfurt Parliament espousing the cause of German unity in March 1848, Palmerston instructed his minister in Frankfurt to support it: "We wish you to support . . . any plan which has for its object to consolidate Germany and give it more unity and political vigor."[22]

As the crisis developed, the Prussian foreign ministry came to believe that Britain could serve as a neutral intermediary between the warring parties. Von Arnim advised the king that "as a mediator, England would not approach the question in an enemy fashion."[23] The king was persuaded. To his sister, the wife of Tsar Nicholas, he wrote: "The horrible, lawless experience of the King of Denmark leads me, without love I confess, to drag him into the field. Wrangel commands the united federal troops, 25,000 against 15,000 Danes, and I hope that the status quo before the Danish invasion can be quickly reestablished. In order to negotiate, which the federation and England are prepared to do, the object of negotiation must be free."[24]

As long as the war was quick and limited to Schleswig and Holstein, the Prussian monarch was convinced he would enjoy the diplomatic support of Russia. Indeed, the tsar had consistently favored the reorganization of Germany under Prussian leadership. He regarded Prussia to be a more reliable partner than Austria on the Polish question and believed that a Prussian-led Germany would serve as a strong counterweight to France and the forces of republicanism. Meyendorff, the Russian minister at Berlin, reported to Nesselrode of his activities: "I do not cease to promote with all my efforts and counsels, anything which may prevent Germany from breaking up. . . . If a chance remains of saving Germany, it is from [Berlin] that the impulse must come. God grant that the effort may be successful! The feebler and more divided Germany becomes, the more open she will be to republican influences, the closer the danger approaches our frontiers. May the Germans, enlightened about their true interests, understand that Russia can wish only to see Germany powerful and united."[25] In correspondence with both his sister and the tsar, Friedrich Wilhelm betrayed his expectation of Russian support. Arguing that the Danish king was counting on Russian and Swedish assistance and was "thirsting for war," he asked the tsar to "*strongly admonish* Denmark." If the Danish stand was not softened, "unforeseeable difficulties" could result.[26]

Response of the Great Powers

Expecting a brief war during which the great powers would remain militarily neutral, and hoping to receive diplomatic support from the tsar, the Prussian monarch was surprised and disappointed with the actual policies adopted by the British, French, and Russians. For although Britain and Russia promoted the expansion of Prussian influence in Germany, neither Palmerston nor Nicholas I were prepared to countenance the defeat of the

Danish monarchy at the hands of the Prussian army.[27] Russian diplomacy did not offer tacit support of Prussian designs; rather, it aimed at a negotiated division of the duchies on nationalistic lines. On at least two occasions threats of Russian military intervention, supported diplomatically by Britain and France, forced Prussia to reverse course and proved crucial to the outcome of the crisis.

The first of these came in April 1848. With Prussian troops advancing toward Denmark, Nesselrode instructed Meyendorff to deliver a sharp message to the Prussian government: "The invasion, intended for Jutland, seriously injures the interests of all the powers bordering on the Baltic, and stretches to the breaking point the political equilibrium throughout the North which was established in treaties."[28] Meyendorff's message was reinforced by a letter from the king's sister, the tsarina: "It is your troops who have grabbed the weak Denmark with their superior force. This war can expand widely if you pursue it. Stop! There is still time! Think about the other difficulties Germany has to battle in order to bring about inner security, the dangers which threaten from the West. Do not force upon the Tsar the necessity to come to the assistance, with strong measures, of another state who's downfall Russia cannot regard with indifference and will not tolerate. It cannot come to pass that Denmark is absorbed by Germany; of this you can be certain."[29] The tsar ordered the mobilization of Russia's armed forces, sent a squadron of the Navy to Danish waters, and, supported by Sweden-Norway, threatened to declare war on Prussia unless Prussian forces were withdrawn.[30]

The second intervention came in May 1849 when the war resumed upon the Danish renunciation of the Armistice of Malmö. In a personal letter to Friedrich Wilhelm IV, Tsar Nicholas I used strong language demanding an end to the Danish war and a break with the nationalist movement represented in Frankfurt.[31] If the war continued, Russia would be forced to reach an understanding with France. The tsar urged the king to take the lead in the anti-revolutionary campaign in Germany. If Prussia put an end to war with Denmark, the tsar would lend support against the revolution. If it did not, "the troops intended to protect Prussia would cross its borders, the Russian fleet would land troops in Schleswig, and German ports would be blockaded." King Friedrich Wilhelm is said to have cried upon reading the letter.[32]

The tsar's communications confronted Friedrich Wilhelm with the wider conflict his strategy sought to preclude. They also shattered his expectation of at least tacit support for Prussian designs in the duchies. Representing contingent deprivations to the baseline of expectation, the Russian interventions can be clearly coded as threats. Moreover, in accordance with the expectations of the argument presented in chapter 3, they successfully led the king to shift course. After the warnings of April and May 1848 the king adopted the position that von Arnim went into Schleswig-Holstein foolishly and capriciously.[33] When faced with credible threats, he backed down.

However, the structure of the influence attempts is worth noting. In both cases the tsar's threats were accompanied by corresponding *assurances*; if the king was cooperative, the *status quo ante bellum* would obtain. In his correspondence with the Prussian monarch, the tsar was careful to assert his continuing personal regard for the king and his desire to maintain cordial relations with him despite their differences over Schleswig-Holstein.[34]

As argued in chapter 2, compellent threats are most likely to succeed when accompanied by promised rewards for compliance. Once Prussia had invaded Denmark, the tsar's goal was as much compellence as deterrence. By threatening intervention on the side of Denmark, the tsar hoped to force Prussia to the bargaining table. Addressing the domestic motives for Prussian aggression and providing some basis on which to justify compliance with Russian demands, the promise of support for the Prussian campaign against republicanism and radicalism probably enhanced the effectiveness of the tsar's strategy.

THE SECOND SCHLESWIG-HOLSTEIN CRISIS

"The Schleswig-Holstein question," Bismarck once remarked, "was a nut on which we might well have broken our teeth. Denmark didn't worry me; I could count on her making blunders and it was only a question of creating a favorable situation. Austria had to be brought to see that she would dissipate all sympathy in Germany if she didn't go with us; Russia had to be reminded of the services we rendered when Austria wanted to mobilize Germany against her; England had to be isolated so that she would confine herself to threats, as she always does when no one will pull the chestnuts out of the fire for her. The individual actions themselves were trifles; to see that they dove-tailed was the difficulty."[35] Although many of Bismarck's later writings and statements must be regarded with the skepticism one accords any policy maker's analysis of his or her own actions, this particular remark captures the essence of his overall strategy for securing Prussian control over the duchies. In order to accomplish the objective of annexation Bismarck needed to keep the great powers at odds with one another, thereby precluding any concerted action against Prussian expansion.

In this section I will examine what I call the Second Schleswig-Holstein Crisis. Remarkably similar in structure to the first crisis, the second attempt at expanding Prussian influence in the duchies is different in that Bismarck succeeded where Friedrich Wilhelm and Radowitz failed. Although he showed remarkable skill in his handling of the international aspects of the crisis, Bismarck's skill is not a sufficient explanation for his success. Rather, the inability of the great powers to intervene in support of the status quo, and their failure to utilize a strategy that incorporated credible threats of force, led Bismarck to believe he could manage the risks involved in his policy of Prussian aggrandizement. The evidence strongly supports the hypothesis that Bismarck was deterrable. At a critical juncture during the crisis, the threat of French entry on the side of Denmark prompted a German retreat. When the French threat receded, however, Bismarck resumed an aggressive policy. Thus, the outcome of the Second Schleswig-Holstein Crisis should be understood not as a failure of deterrence but as a failure on the part of the great powers to adopt a strategy of deterrence.

The containment of Prussia—both during the first crisis over Schleswig and Holstein as well as the dispute between Prussia and Austria over Hesse-Kassel in 1850—rested on the active engagement of Russia in inner-German affairs.[36] Were the Russian support removed from the European architecture supporting the status quo, the structure was bound to collapse. The Crimean War provided the shock that destroyed the consensus supporting the European status quo.

Russia's defeat in the Crimea—by Turkey and the western powers supported by Austria—provided Prussia with new found opportunities for gain. Russian power, so often critical to deterring Prussian expansion in Germany, was greatly diminished. Further, it was no longer well disposed toward concerted action with Britain and France, or entente with the Habsburg monarchy.

Although it had supported France in the Crimea, Austria itself fell victim to Napoleon a few years later. Napoleon's plans for a Kingdom of Northern Italy made up of Piedmont and Austrian possessions in Italy led to a Franco-Austrian war in 1859. In the compromise settlement at Villafranca, Franz Joseph ceded Lombardy to France, retaining Venetia. The Austrian defeat was indicative of an untenable position. Without its Russian ally, the task of defending against France in Italy and Prussia in Germany, all the while maintaining a lid on nationalist turmoil within the empire, was too much for its underdeveloped economy to manage.

Napoleon's Italian machinations earned him the mistrust of both Russia and England. Liberal England, however, was unwilling to support an absolutist regime in Russia, even to prevent further French gain. Unable to work together, and recognizing Austria's weakness, Palmerston and Alexander II each began to see a strengthened Prussia as a necessary counterweight to a revived France.

Thus, by the 1860s the environment was most advantageous for renewed Prussian efforts at expansion in Germany. The emergence of Otto von Bismarck as Prussian minister-president and foreign minister in September 1862 provided a leader willing to take advantage of this newfound opportunity.

The issue that precipitated yet another crisis over the "forever united" was a fresh attempt to incorporate Schleswig into Denmark. In March 1863 Friedrich VII issued a decree (the "March Patent") that proposed a new constitutional arrangement for the duchies, giving Copenhagen a much larger role in the legislative affairs of Schleswig and weakening the historic ties between the estates of Schleswig and Holstein.[37] The move was immediately viewed by the ducal estates as well as German nationalists as a violation of the promises of 1851. On 13 November the Danish parliament adopted the new constitution. However, they were unable to secure the necessary royal signature from Friedrich VII.

As had been the case in 1848–51, the constitutional question in the duchies was further complicated by the succession question when on 15 November Friedrich VII died. In accordance with the Treaty of London (1852), Prince Christian of Glücksburg assumed the titles King of Denmark and Duke of Schleswig-Holstein. On 18 November he signed the new constitution. Upon hearing of Friedrich's death, however, Prince Friedrich of Augustenburg proclaimed himself "Friedrich VIII, Duke of Schleswig-Holstein." Under the protection of the Duke of Coburg, he assembled a government at Gotha. The federal Diet as well as the German nationalist movement immediately adopted his cause.[38]

Under the constitution of the German Confederation, the Diet at Frankfurt was responsible for resolving succession disputes in member states. Although there was strong support in the Diet for the invasion of the duchies, the majority of members wanted action on the basis of the Augustenburg candidacy. Bismarck, however, insisted that any action proceed on the basis of the Treaty of London. Only on this basis could he minimize the international repercussions, keep Austria on board, and most importantly, hold open the option of annexation. Recognition of the Augustenburg pretender would preclude this possibility.

Thus, together with Austria, Bismarck engineered the passage of an order for federal execution in Holstein on 4 December.[39] On 24 December troops entered Holstein and Lauenburg. On 16 January 1864 the Austrian and Prussian ambassadors at Copenhagen issued an ultimatum to the Danish government demanding the withdrawal of the November constitution within forty-eight hours. The Danes refused, whereupon Austrian and Prussian forces began marching toward Schleswig.

If the consensus among the great powers for the maintenance of the status quo and the willingness of Russia to intervene in support of it were crucial to determining the outcome of the First Schleswig-Holstein Crisis, the powers' inability to agree on a course of action and unwillingness to intervene against Prussia were equally crucial to the outcome of the second. The aftereffects of the Crimean War have already been discussed. But concerted action against Berlin was further hindered in the winter of 1863–64 by the conviction—shared in foreign ministries across Europe—that Napoleon, not Bismarck, presented the real threat to peace.

In a speech from the throne on 15 November 1863, Napoleon sent shock waves across Europe: "The compacts of 1815 have ceased to be in force." The French emperor invited twenty crown heads of Europe to Paris for a general congress to revise the legal basis on which the stability of the European states system had rested for a half century.[40] Although the proposal came to naught, its emergence at the height of the crisis over constitutional reform in the duchies signaled further opportunity for Bismarck. With a Bonaparte preaching a revisionist message from the French throne, the powers of Europe were less inclined to view Bismarck as a major threat to the stability of Europe than they might have been had Napoleon III been content to support the status quo.

Bismarck was himself on relatively cordial terms with the French emperor. Napoleon favored the reconstitution of Europe along national lines. Guided in part by this principle and in part by the belief that Prussia might one day serve as an ally against Austria (with respect to Venetia), Napoleon supported Prussian expansion. Far from issuing a threat against the invasion of Schleswig-Holstein, Napoleon encouraged it. To the Prussian ambassador at Paris, Drouyn recommended annexing Schleswig-Holstein as well as some of the other neighboring states. He promised French support for this objective in exchange for compensation along the Rhine.[41]

The power most committed to the London Treaty was, not surprisingly,

England. But British policy throughout the crisis was exceedingly erratic. In July 1863 Palmerston adopted a decidedly pro-Danish line. In a speech before the House of Commons he declared: "I am satisfied with all reasonable men in Europe, including those in France and Russia, in desiring that the independence, the integrity and the rights of Denmark may be maintained. We are convinced—I am convinced at least—that if any violent attempt were made to overthrow those rights and interfere with that independence, those who made the attempt, would find in the result, that it would not be Denmark alone with which they would have to contend."[42] But Palmerston's position lacked strong domestic support.

The queen and much of her cabinet were unwilling to go to war over the Treaty of London, especially a war England would fight without allies.[43] A clear awareness of British isolation and military weakness informed their caution. Relations with America were uncertain owing to the U.S. Civil War; the Indian mutiny (1857–58) and the Crimean War had identified serious shortcomings in British military capabilities.[44] On the continent Britain lacked supporters. It further alienated Russia over the Polish question, the former still smarting from defeat in the Crimea. It had turned down French proposals for a general European congress, opposed French policy in Italy, and abandoned France in both the Mexican and Polish adventures.[45] Without allies and lacking domestic consensus, the erratic course of British policy under Palmerston and Russell is perhaps not surprising.

Although in the early days of the crisis Russell attempted mediation, he quickly abandoned the effort and supported prompt implementation of the federal execution as a way to restore order. This position, in turn, was dropped with fears that, once in the duchies, the German troops would be hesitant to leave. At the height of the crisis, in January 1864, Palmerston and Russell attempted to return to a hard line, sending a squadron of the fleet into Copenhagen harbor. However, the cabinet vetoed their decision and recalled the British ships. The cabinet's firm position was that without similar action by France, Russia, and Sweden-Norway, Britain would not intervene in the dispute militarily.

British weakness and isolation was not lost on Bismarck or his Austrian counterpart, Rechberg. Thus, in response to a threat from Palmerston that a German invasion of Schleswig would bring about French and Swedish intervention, Rechberg told the British ambassador that his own information did not lead him to suppose that Denmark would receive assistance from Sweden-Norway or France.[46] Recognizing the inability of Palmerston to back up his threats with intervention on the side of Denmark, Bismarck could safely reject every British proposal for compromise.[47]

Although Russian intervention was crucial to the outcome of the first crisis over Schleswig-Holstein, Alexander II's fear of France incapacitated him in the second. When the Danish ambassador sought Russian intervention against Prussia and Austria, the tsar "asked [the Danish ambassador] to look around him and then to state frankly whether he could advise the Russian government of to-day to act as the government of 1849 had acted."[48] The tsar was engaged in Turkestan and Afghanistan, feared further French agitation for an autonomous Poland, and was concerned that democratic tendencies in Denmark might have repercussions in Russia.[49] Russian weakness required Alexander II to maintain good relations with Bismarck.

Thus, at the height of the Schleswig-Holstein crisis, the strategic environment was such that Bismarck could pursue a policy of expansion in Germany without risking the intervention of the major powers.

Decisional Frame

Only two months into his premiership Bismarck wrote to King Friedrich Wilhelm IV: "The Danish question can only be settled in a way favorable to us through war; the occasion for war is to be found at whatever moment our situation in relation to the other Great Powers is most favorable for waging war."[50] Bismarck was also quite clear on what he regarded a favorable outcome in the Schleswig-Holstein affair.

At a New Year's Eve party in 1863 he told his family: "The 'forever united' must someday be Prussian. That is the goal toward which I am steering."[51] Annexation would represent a gain over the status quo, and it was the status quo—understood chiefly in terms of Prussia's political position in Germany—against which Bismarck evaluated the possible outcomes of the Schleswig-Holstein crisis.

Although annexation was his ultimate goal, Bismarck identified three possible solutions to the crisis: (1) annexation of the duchies to Prussia, (2) the continued personal union of the duchies to the Danish crown under the Danish king as duke, and (3) the independence of Schleswig and Holstein under the house of Augustenburg and their inclusion in the German Confederation.[52] In the event his ultimate goal of annexation proved unattainable, Bismarck preferred the second outcome to the third.

For Bismarck an independent Schleswig-Holstein under the Duke of

Augustenburg would represent a deterioration of Prussia's position in Germany. The creation of a new "middle state" would provide only another ally for the smaller German states—or indeed Austria—which could vote against Prussia in the federal Diet. He regarded the continuation of the status quo as a preferable outcome.[53]

Bismarck understood, however, that the outcome of the crisis was not his alone to determine. He would have to move cautiously, always ready to retreat should his movements provoke hostility among the great powers of Europe.[54] As a first step he would secure an alliance with Austria and adopt a policy of outward moderation. The preferences of the nationalist movement notwithstanding, Bismarck announced that Prussia would itself honor the conditions of the Treaty of London provided that Denmark abided by the promises of 1851.[55] But this conditional acceptance of the treaty was designed to provide a pretext for escalation. If Denmark did not withdraw the November constitution before its scheduled effective date (1 January 1864), and consult with Prussia and Austria regarding constitutional reform in Schleswig and Holstein, Prussia would no longer feel obliged to honor the terms of the treaty.

Baseline of Expectation

From Austria, Bismarck expected support—at least with respect to federal execution in the duchies if not with respect to his ultimate goal of annexation. He admitted as much to his Austrian counterparts: "Every action is for us based on the necessary assumption that Austria is in full agreement with us."[56] The hard reality was, however, that Austria had no choice but to support Prussia. It had alienated Russia with its policy in the Crimean War, and France with its refusal to participate in Napoleon's proposed congress. Within Germany it risked losing its traditional role as leader should it now fail to support the cause of Germans in the duchies. Bismarck could count on Austrian support.

From the other eastern monarchy Bismarck expected acquiescence to his policy of action against Denmark. Although the tsar supported the accession of his relative, King Christian, to the Danish throne, and for a time promoted the notion of British mediation, he was not prepared to fight Prussia over the status of the duchies. Bismarck was well aware of the limits on Russian support for the Danish position. On 23 January the Russian ambassador Oubril told Bismarck that Gorchakov favored the "peaceful occupation of Schleswig as a pledge for the fulfillment of Danish obligations." Bismarck "received this communication with satisfaction."[57] Gorcha-kov's main interest in the crisis was to ensure continued relations between England and Prussia and Austria. He did not want to endanger the tacit coalition against French expansion.[58] At the news of the Austro-Prussian ultimatum of 16 January the tsar declared that while he opposed the invasion of Schleswig, "Russia would never join any *démarche* which might wound Austria and Prussia. After all, it was better that Schleswig be occupied by them than by the minor states."[59] The tsar assured the Prussian ambassador that Russia would "never march against Prussia" over Schleswig-Holstein.[60]

Napoleon III gave every indication that he supported the expansion of Prussia's holdings in Germany although there is some indication that Bismarck was mistrustful of the French emperor's ultimate position.[61] With regard to the immediate issue, however, the French were quite clear in their unwillingness to come to the assistance of Denmark in the event of a war with the dual powers.

In accordance with diplomatic practice, envoys were sent from foreign governments in late December to congratulate King Christian on his accession to the throne. The British, Russian, and French envoys all pressed Denmark to make concessions to Prussia and Austria. To his fellow envoys, the French representative let it be known that he was ordered "to tell the Danish government explicitly that if Denmark became involved in a war with Germany, France would not come to her assistance; to advise in general terms moderation and concessions to Germany."[62] With the French urging concessions in Copenhagen and promising support for Prussian expansion to the Prussian ambassador at Paris, Bismarck was remarking at the "favorable posture" adopted by Napoleon as late as 21 December 1863.[63] Confident that France would not intervene in the crisis, Bismarck could ignore British threats.[64]

During the tense period from November 1863 to January 1864, British Prime Minister Palmerston and his foreign secretary, Russell, endeavored to secure cabinet approval for an active policy in support of Christian and the Danish cause. Palmerston was convinced that war could be deterred if Prussia and Austria thought that Britain was credible in its declarations supporting the Danish position.[65] Should they expand their action beyond the federal execution in Holstein, Palmerston and Russell favored supporting the Danish side. In December Palmerston wrote Russell: "Schleswig is not part of Germany, and its invasion by German troops would be an act of war against Denmark, which would in my clear opinion entitle Denmark to our active military and naval support. But you and I could not announce such a determination without the concurrence of the Cabinet and the consent of the Queen."[66]

The queen, however, succeeded in turning the rest of the cabinet against the pro-Danish policy of Palmerston and Russell, limiting their ability to pursue a determined and consistent course of action. Efforts to secure the support of Russia and France against Austrian and Prussian policy in the duchies were likewise unsuccessful.[67] If Bismarck had any fears of British military intervention in support of Denmark, they were certainly dispelled when news reached Berlin of the prime minister's remarks before parliament in early February 1864. In an effort to cover his diplomatic isolation and the ineffectiveness of British efforts to deter an invasion of Schleswig, Palmerston boasted of assurances from the Prussian and Austrian governments that "the invasion of Schleswig, however lamentable it may be and however much to be deplored, is not undertaken for the purpose of dismembering the Danish monarchy; and that they are committed to evacuate Schleswig whenever the conditions which they attach to the entrance shall have been complied with."[68] The prime minister in effect granted Prussia and Austria the right to establish the conditions for their own withdrawal. Bismarck would ensure that these were never met.

With Austria on board, France apparently supportive, Russia not averse, and Britain unable to act alone, Bismarck concluded that he could pursue an aggressive policy in Schleswig-Holstein without risking the intervention of the great powers.

Response of the Great Powers

Framing prospective outcomes vis-à-vis Prussia's position in Germany, the theory developed in chapter 3 would lead to the expectation that Bismarck would be risk averse with regard to gains and risk acceptant with respect to losses vis-à-vis the political status quo in Germany. In terms of the possible outcomes to the crisis identified by Bismarck, the theory would predict that he would be quite cautious with respect to Prussian annexation of the duchies (annexation regarded as a gain), but willing to engage in riskier policies in an effort to forestall the emergence of an independent Schleswig-Holstein under the Duke of Augustenburg (an outcome Bismarck regarded as constituting a loss).

While not afraid of war with Denmark and expecting no intervention on its behalf, Bismarck was indeed quite cautious in the campaign for Schleswig-

Holstein, lest he provoke a change of policy among the great powers.[69] Pflanze sees in Bismarck's conduct of the war a "step-by-step progression: first the confederate execution in Holstein, then Austro-Prussian occupation of Schleswig, finally the invasion of Jutland. Either excessive delay or precipitate haste could have brought disaster."[70] Bismarck himself regarded his strategy as cautious: "I never advance a foot until certain that the ground to be trod is firm and safe."[71]

At one point the tide did begin to turn against Bismarck. An analysis of the situation lends further support to the proposition that having been motivated to invade the Danish holdings by the perception that he could do so without great power intervention, a credible threat of such intervention would have deterred Bismarck from invading Schleswig-Holstein.

Upon the outbreak of hostilities the Danish government appealed to the signatories of the London Treaty for the defense of Schleswig. Britain, France, Russia, and Sweden-Norway all refused. The combined Austrian and Prussian forces made quick progress. During the night of 5–6 February, the Danish forces evacuated the *Dannevirke*, a series of fortifications constructed south of the town of Schleswig, and took up positions on the Düppel peninsula, the neighboring island of Alsen, and in Jutland. On 18 February Prussian forces pursued a party of retreating Danes over the border of Jutland and occupied the town of Kolding in Denmark.[72]

Reports of the invasion of Jutland "created a profound sensation in London and Paris."[73] Palmerston contacted the First Lord of the Admiralty and urged him to begin preparations to send a British squadron to Copenhagen. But it was from Paris that Bismarck's position was most seriously challenged. On 20 February Drouyn de Lhuys telegraphed Berlin and Vienna in an effort to ascertain the objectives of the escalation. The Prussian ambassador at Paris, von der Goltz, telegraphed Bismarck that "France was preparing to adopt an unfavorable attitude towards Prussia."[74] The French foreign minister allowed that the attitude in Paris was changing and the imperial government would need to reconsider its passive position in the Schleswig-Holstein affair. The invasion of Jutland gave rise to concern regarding Prussia and Austria's ultimate aims. As Goltz reported: "First we had seized Holstein on the pretext of Federal Execution, then although this security should have been enough for Schleswig too, we had occupied that duchy as a 'material guarantee'; we had declared, though in not very clear terms, that we only wanted to enforce the stipulations of 1851–52; now we have advanced into Jutland and are going to 'exterminate' the Danes; for what else can we intend."[75]

Bismarck had based his decision to invade the duchies on French assurances of support. The uncertainty presented in the reports from France led Bismarck to reconsider his position. In a discussion with the French ambassador he admitted that "Austria still refuses her consent to the entry of the allied troops into Jutland. Russia, frightened of a Scandinavian union, urges an armistice, a conference, and the integrity of the Danish Monarchy. England threatens us and, if Prussia has now to face the opposition of France as well, she will have to call a halt, for she cannot alienate the four Great Powers at once."[76] There is evidence to suggest that Bismarck's admission was genuine. In St. Petersburg Gorchakov commented on the "salutary impression produced in Berlin and Vienna" by the new French attitude. On 27 February the Prussian ambassador at London notified Russell of Berlin's acceptance of an invitation to a conference attended by the signatories to the London Treaty—with the addition of a delegate from the German Confederation—to discuss an end to the war.[77]

But Napoleon soon returned to a policy of detachment.[78] Consequently, Prussia and Austria decided to extend the war to the whole of Jutland on 5 March. By the opening of the London Conference, the last Danish fortifications in Schleswig were in German hands as was the whole of southern Jutland.

Unable to act in concert against the German powers on the battlefield, the great powers were likewise unable to support a common position at the peace talks. No longer under threat of French intervention, the Prussians were in any case not interested in a negotiated end to the war. Bismarck was intent on dictating peace to Copenhagen.

When a temporary armistice negotiated at the beginning of the conference expired at the end of June, the war resumed. With Austrian and Prussian troops making ever larger gains on Danish territory, the Danes accepted a new armistice on 20 July. A peace conference opened in Vienna on 25 July. On 30 October 1864 the King of Denmark ceded to the King of Prussia and the Emperor of Austria the duchies of Schleswig, Holstein, and Lauenburg and agreed to "recognize the dispositions they made" for these territories.

Summary

In 1864 Bismarck succeeded where Friedrich Wilhelm had failed in 1848. He wrested the duchies from the Danish monarchy and expanded Prussian influence in North Germany. Examining the two cases side by side highlights the contrasting policies adopted by the great powers. In response to the first attempt at Prussian expansion, concerted diplomatic activity on the part of Britain, France, and Russia as well as threats of intervention from the tsar persuaded King Friedrich Wilhelm to back down. Rather than confronting a hostile coalition willing to go to war in support of the status quo, Bismarck met assurances of neutrality and even support from the two powers most capable of deterring him, Russia and France. The evidence suggests that Bismarck was indeed deterrable. The apparent change in French policy after the invasion of Jutland led Bismarck to consider a retreat. But the ultimate inability of the great powers to assert themselves in opposition to the expansionist aims of the Prussian minister allowed for the isolation of Denmark and its eventual defeat.

THE AUSTRO-PRUSSIAN WAR

The successful completion of the Danish campaign did not signal the resolution of the duchies' relationship to Germany or Prussia and Austria or of the larger questions of Confederation reform and German unification. Rather, the defeat of Denmark brought about renewed competition between Austria and Prussia, with negotiations over the disposition of the duchies serving as a surrogate for the underlying conflict over primacy in Germany. As Prussia and Austria viewed the status quo in Germany quite differently, it is not surprising that they could not come to terms over the fate of Schleswig-Holstein, which each saw as essential to its own overall plan for a reconstituted Germany.

The Austrians supported the establishment of an independent Schleswig-Holstein under the House of Augustenburg, both as a means of limiting Prussian hegemony in North Germany and of securing the continued goodwill of the small and middle German powers. In Berlin Bismarck had convinced the king of the desirability of annexation, the minister's own long-time goal.

Throughout 1864 and 1865 the two sides were unable to reach agreement, and the friction between them grew. In late August 1864 Emperor Franz Joseph and King Wilhelm accompanied by their foreign ministers Rechberg and Bismarck, discussed the duchies' fate at Schönbrunn. The most they could agree to was continued collaboration in German affairs. At Bad Gastein in August 1865 the two sides agreed to the "provisional division" of the duchies: Holstein would be administered by Austria, Schleswig by Prussia, and Lauenburg sold to Prussia outright. But the Gastein

Convention proved to be a strategic error for Austria. With Prussia in control of Schleswig and certain military routes in Holstein, the provisional division of the "forever united" was unlikely to be reversed under terms other than those found agreeable to Bismarck.

In June 1866 the Austrians appealed to the federal Diet to resolve the succession question and final status of the duchies. Bismarck charged the Austrians with violating the terms of the Gastein Convention and bilateral agreements made in January 1864[79] and ordered General von Manteuffel to enter Holstein and reestablish Prussian co-sovereignty. Austria severed diplomatic relations with Prussia on 12 June, and two days later Bismarck withdrew Prussia from the German Confederation.

Armed conflict broke out on 16 June with the Prussian invasion of Saxony, Hanover, and Electoral Hesse. The decisive battle of the Austro-Prussian War took place on 3 July at Königgrätz, where a Prussian force of 280,000 routed 245,000 Austrians supported by 25,000 Saxons.

If there was any doubt as to Bismarck's expansionist motives, they were dispelled at the peace conference in Prague. Under the Treaty of Prague, signed on 23 August 1866, the Prussians were granted Schleswig-Holstein, Hanover, Electoral Hesse, Hesse-Homburg, Nassau, and the free city of Frankfurt.[80] Austria accepted the dissolution of the German Confederation and recognized the creation of a new association of states north of the Main River. The treaty provided for a new association of those states south of the Main that was to hold an independent international existence yet maintain national connections with the North German Confederation.

Decisional Frame

Over the course of the year proceeding the outbreak of war with Austria, the Prussian leadership almost unanimously supported an aggressive, expansionist policy for Prussia vis-à-vis the duchies and against Austria in Germany. The motivation for risking war was the perceived opportunity to contain its risks and make sizeable gains. Central to this perception was the expected neutrality of the other European powers, most particularly France.

As had been the case in the Danish War, Bismarck framed prospective outcomes in terms of Prussia's political position vis-à-vis Austria in the larger question of hegemony in Germany. The salient reference for Bismarck was the political status quo in Germany.

The clearest indication of Bismarck's motives for risking war with Austria over Schleswig-Holstein as well as his appraisal of possible outcomes are found in the minutes of the Prussian Crown Council of 29 May 1865. King Wilhelm convened the council to devise a Prussian strategy in the Schleswig-Holstein question, and Bismarck saw three possible courses of action.

The first amounted to the creation of a satellite state in Schleswig-Holstein. Repeating his long-standing opposition to such an outcome, Bismarck argued that the new state would eventually come under military pressures from irredentist elements in Denmark and might well ally itself with Austria or the smaller German states (the so-called third Germany) against Prussia in the federal Diet. A continuation of the status quo was preferable to the creation of even a satellite in Schleswig-Holstein.[81]

As an alternative, Prussia could buy off the pretenders to the ducal throne and hope that Austria would thereby drop its demands in favor of Augustenburg and accept Prussian annexation. However, Austria had made territorial compensation in Silesia a precondition for agreement to Prussian annexation of the duchies, and King Wilhelm was unwilling to cede any portion of Prussian territory.[82]

Bismarck's preferred course was the third: a formal demand for outright annexation. Although the probable result of such a demand was war with Austria, Bismarck found the moment opportune: "Such a war, given the political situation of Austria in Italy, and given that the neutrality of Russia and France could be expected, would place the Austrian Cabinet in a serious predicament. By contrast, the present moment offers Prussia favorable conditions for a collision with Austria which, given the traditional anti-Prussian policies of the Vienna Cabinet, cannot be avoided."[83] And Bismarck was not alone in his analysis of the strategic situation in Europe.

Helmuth von Moltke, Chief of the Prussian General Staff, shared Bismarck's analysis, although he saw only two courses of action: "either to indemnify the part owner or to make war on him (or make him declare war on you). The first would involve a cession of Prussian territory, and this has hitherto been absolutely rejected by the King; the other course, therefore, is not impossible, and its consequences are incalculable, as the whole of Europe must of necessity take sides, however unwilling some of the states might be, since France is engaged in Algiers, Mexico, and per chance North America, Russia has enough to do at home, and England is as powerless as she is presuming."[84] In the crown council von Moltke agreed with Bismarck that annexation was the best course of action and argued that "Prussia should not shrink from the prospect of war with Austria."[85] With the exception of only a single minister and the Crown Prince, the entire cabinet as well as the top military leadership endorsed the decision to risk war.

As the council concluded, Bismarck suggested that the result of war with Austria would be not only the annexation of Schleswig-Holstein but also "the establishment of a constitutional relationship between the middle and small states and Prussia."[86] For Bismarck the coming war was seen not only as a means for settling the narrow question of the duchies but also as an opportunity to overturn the system of Austrian and Prussian dualism in Germany and the establishment of Prussian primacy.

On 28 February 1866 the Prussian crown council moved closer to the collision that Bismarck had predicted the previous May. King Wilhelm opened the session with a bellicose statement in favor of annexation but admitting that the stakes were much higher. War with Austria would secure not only the addition of Schleswig-Holstein to the Prussian state but also Prussia's right to "decisive political preponderance in North Germany."[87] The decisive battle was only a matter of time, and Bismarck again asserted that conditions in Europe were at the moment most favorable for Prussia: "The present moment is favorable for Prussia because of the disposition of Italy, whose military forces threaten Austria but cannot be held together for long, because of the existence of friendly relations with Napoleon, and because of the superiority of our armaments."[88]

General von Moltke argued that Italian participation was indispensable to any war with Austria. In his military opinion a two-front war was necessary to secure a favorable balance of forces on the Bohemian front, as Austria would be forced to station a sizeable contingent of its troops in the south to protect against the Italians. The council agreed to solicit an offensive alliance with Italy and an understanding with France and to continue an aggressive policy with respect to Schleswig-Holstein and confederate reform, "without regard to the danger of a break and war with Austria."[89]

Having framed prospective outcomes in the crisis over Schleswig-Holstein around the political status quo in Germany, we would expect Prussian decision makers to be sensitive to costs and relatively risk averse with respect to gains vis-à-vis the status quo. We would expect the Prussian leadership to back away from expansionist goals if confronted with the threat of great power intervention. Prussia was an ideal candidate for a strategy of deterrence.

Baseline of Expectation

By the time armed conflict broke out in June 1866, Bismarck had every reason to expect that the war would be limited, with Prussia and Italy on the one side, and Austria on the other. He had spent the previous year preparing the other powers for the eventuality of an Austro-Prussian conflict and had succeeded in securing assurances of neutrality from most. The neutrality of the great powers had the practical effect of promoting Prussian designs in Germany, a fact noted at the time by the Austrian foreign minister.[90]

British neutrality was largely ensured through the inability of the prime minister and the queen to agree on a single policy for Germany. In a memorandum dated 30 March 1866, the queen proposed joint Anglo-French intervention against Prussia in the dispute over Schleswig-Holstein, but Russell would not support it. England had spoken out against the Austro-Prussian war on Denmark. Russell could not, therefore, accept that having "spoken in defense of right," England should now side with Austria "in the division of the spoil."[91] In fact, however, the prime minister supported Prussian expansion in North Germany.[92] Consequently, from the British ambassador at Berlin the most Bismarck heard were "friendly and confidential" suggestions for a negotiated settlement.[93] When Bismarck rejected a British offer for mediation in March 1865, Clarendon and the Prussian ambassador, Bernstorff, agreed that "the question is at an end" and relations between Prussia and England "remain as before."[94]

Throughout the spring of 1866 the tsar attempted to slow the pace of events by appealing to conservative solidarity in a series of letters to his fellow monarchs Wilhelm I and Franz Joseph. Gorchakov too urged compromise and direct Austro-Prussian negotiations on the matter of confederate reform, but the foreign minister denied rumors that Russia was considering intervention. Only a direct threat to its national interest would induce it to abandon the policy of neutrality.[95]

Russia was not in a position to contemplate military action in support of any but its most vital interests. In the wake of the Crimean War a revolt in Poland provided evidence of serious shortcomings in Russia's ability to maintain order at home.[96] Thus, the imperial cabinet adopted the position that "the Russian government must concentrate on internal development— all matters of foreign policy must be subordinated to this imperative need."[97] Although many in St. Petersburg sympathized with the Austrian position, the unwillingness of Austria to support Russia in the Danubian principalities and to entertain the Oldenburg candidacy in Schleswig-Holstein (favored by the tsar owing to dynastic linkages), and the importance of cordial relations with Prussia to tranquility in Poland, dictated a policy of detached neutrality.

The probable neutrality of Russia and England was appreciated in Prussian decision-making circles. In January 1866 Bismarck wrote to his ambassador at Florence: "The reports concerning an Anglo-French agreement are as groundless as the rumors about such a movement on the part of Russia."[98] In March King Wilhelm I received a letter from his nephew, Tsar Alexander II, in which the tsar indicated that he understood and shared the sentiments of his uncle regarding the tensions between him and the Austrian court. The tsar further expressed his confidence in the king's prudence and wisdom.[99] The difference between the tone of this letter and that sent by Tsar Nicholas to King Friedrich Wilhelm IV during the first crisis over Schleswig-Holstein cannot be overlooked. Whereas Tsar Nicholas spoke of Russian troop movements on the Prussian frontier, Alexander II spoke of his uncle's loyal heart and noble character.

Thus, as Taylor recognized, "both Russia and Great Britain had virtually eliminated themselves from the European balance; this gave the years between 1865 and 1866 a character unique in recent history. The struggle for mastery in Germany was fought out on a stage limited to western Europe; and Napoleon had to speak for Europe without any assistance from the other non-German powers."[100]

Napoleon relished the role of continental arbiter and was pleased to see Austria and Prussia at odds. The prospect of an Austro-Prussian war suited well his long-standing plans for a restructured Europe. By promoting a Prussian alliance with Italy, he hoped to further Italian unification in a way consistent with French interests. An Austro-Prussian war also held prospects for French territorial expansion and, in the event of an Austrian defeat, the expansion of French influence in southern Germany. As a by-product of such a war, the despised Treaty of Vienna would be cast aside.

Bismarck recognized that French neutrality was crucial to his plans for Prussian expansion in Germany. After the signing of the Gastein convention in August 1865, he hurried to Biarritz in an effort to reassure Napoleon that its contents were not directed against France. Despite the Austro-Prussian agreement, Bismarck admitted that war was likely. The Prussian minister-president hinted at rewards for French neutrality, suggesting that in exchange for Prussian gains in Germany, he would not object to French expansion "wherever French is spoken in the world."[101] Bismarck was not disappointed. Napoleon responded to the Prussian ambassador at Paris: "I beg you to say to the King that he may always count on my friendship. In the event of a war between Prussia and Austria, I shall preserve absolute neutrality. . . . I desire the union of the Duchies with Prussia, because this is in keeping with the tendencies of the age."[102] Bismarck did not leave the matter there. At the February crown council he argued the importance of securing a clear understanding with France: "An agreement with Napoleon is necessary particularly in the event that the war's aims expand beyond the occupation of the Elbe duchies."[103]

The Italian alliance was the stake with which Bismarck secured French neutrality. For Taylor, "Venetia in the last resort gave Prussia hegemony in Germany."[104] Von Moltke had insisted that such an alliance was essential to ensure a preponderance of manpower against Austria. For their part the Italians were solicitous of an agreement guaranteeing Venetia.[105] Napoleon was supportive of an alliance between the Prussians and Italians not only because it would secure Venetia for Italy, but also because it would foreclose the possibility of an empire of 70 million on his eastern flank.

The agreement negotiated by Bismarck was remarkable in that it pledged Prussia to nothing should Italy find itself at war with Austria, but obliged Italy to attack Austria in the event of an Austro-Prussian war, provided that hostilities commenced within three months.[106] As Napoleon himself advised the Italians to accept Bismarck's terms, and even promised to protect them against Austrian attack, the treaty with Italy served not only to secure a more favorable balance of forces for Prussia in Bohemia but also to ensure French neutrality in the upcoming war. As Italy's protector, it would be difficult for Napoleon to assume a hostile position vis-à-vis its ally, Prussia.[107]

Thus, when on 8 April Prussia concluded the alliance with Italy, Bismarck was confident of the neutrality of the great powers.[108] Unlike the battle over confederate reform in 1850, when Russian troops threatened intervention on the side of Austria and the Confederation against Prussian troops in Hesse-Kassel, Prussia would now achieve its objective of reform in Germany without outside interference.

Response of the Great Powers

Although unwilling to go to war over the dispute, Russia together with the two western powers tried to avert the impending crisis through a new round of diplomatic activity. On 24 May England, France, and Russia invited

Austria, Prussia, and Italy to attend a congress in Paris to discuss European problems. Bismarck accepted, feeling that to do otherwise might compromise the neutrality of the three great powers, which he had worked so hard to ensure. But Bismarck was saved from the prospect of attending, as Austria rejected the proposal fearing it could only come out the loser.[109]

The powers were perpetually late to the game. Although hostilities broke out on 16 June, it was not until 4 July that Gorchakov proposed that France, England, and Russia issue a joint declaration to the effect that insofar as the Confederation was established by a European Congress, no single state could leave or dissolve it without the concurrence of the signatories at Vienna. But Gorchakov's plans had already been outpaced by the progress of the Prussian army: On 3 July the Austrian armies had been routed at Königgrätz.[110]

It had been widely accepted in European circles that the war would be long and would probably lead to a standoff. Thus, the quick and decisive defeat of Austria shocked the leaders of Europe,[111] not least among these Napoleon himself, who had bet on a long conflict from which he could reap gain, intervening at the right moment to structure a peace settlement as neutral arbiter. Recognizing that his moment was about to pass, Napoleon made a half-hearted effort at intervention on 5 July.

Upon their defeat at Königgrätz, the Austrians approached Napoleon and offered to turn Venetia over to him in the event he could secure an armistice from Italy. The Austrians could then redeploy their troops from the Italian front to the Prussian.[112] But Napoleon preferred to play a role in the larger question of German reform. Thus, he sent word to Bismarck that Austria had offered to cede Venetia and requested French mediation "in order to put an end to the whole conflict." Napoleon proposed an immediate armistice to secure the way for negotiations, and the emperor's messenger intimated French military action if he received a negative response.[113] A dispatch also arrived from the Prussian ambassador at Paris, von der Goltz, reporting the content of a conversation he had with Napoleon on 4 July: "[Napoleon III said] the destruction of Austria would cause a gap in the European state system, which could not be filled without a general conflagration. Russia would oppose its destruction, nor could France remain quiet. . . . He, therefore, advises Prussia not to go too far, to show moderation, and to be content with the consolidation of that position in the balance of power which she has justifiably won."[114]

Bismarck was faced with the prospect of French military intervention at the moment the Prussian command was debating a march on Vienna. At one point the Prussian troops were only nineteen kilometers from the imperial capital. Von Moltke's staff and King Wilhelm favored a punitive peace with Austria.[115] But Bismarck recognized that the war's objectives had been secured and were only threatened by excessive demands. Upon the victory at Königgrätz, von Moltke said to the king: "Your Majesty has won not only the battle but the whole campaign." Bismarck quickly added: "The question in dispute is therefore settled. Now it is for us to regain the old friendship of Austria."[116]

Operating in the domain gains, Bismarck was highly sensitive to increases in risk and uncertainty. The uncertainties attendant to French military intervention were for Bismarck greater than those associated with French mediation, and so he urged the king to accept Napoleon's proposal.[117] To his wife Bismarck wrote: "If we are not excessive in our demands and do not believe that we have conquered the world, we will attain a peace that is worth our effort. But we are just as quickly intoxicated as we are plunged into despair, and I have the thankless task of pouring water into the champagne and making it clear that we do not live alone in Europe, but with three other powers who despise and envy us."[118] The king relented, and Bismarck began armistice negotiations with France and Austria at Prussian headquarters in Nikolsburg.[119] Throughout the negotiations Bismarck's demands were limited by the continued fear of French intervention.[120] The "Seven Weeks War" was officially ended with the signing of the Treaty of Prague on 23 August.

Summary

The struggle for supremacy in Germany ended in 1866 with the exclusion of Austria from Germany and the institutionalization of Prussian hegemony north of the Main River. The outcome, however, was not inevitable. Confederate reform could have proceeded along different bases, including the unification of the German states with Austria.

To understand why political reform in Germany corresponded with the *kleindeutsch* solution championed by Bismarck, it is necessary to examine the foreign policies of the great powers. Unlike 1848 and 1850, when threats of Russian intervention in support of the status quo led the Prussian leadership to suspend a course of aggressive expansion, there was a conspicuous absence of great power intervention in the period leading to the Austro-Prussian War. For Britain and Russia, Napoleon was regarded as the principal source of instability in Europe. Napoleon, in turn, feared Austrian power more than Prussian. Thus, seeking to prevent a solution to the German problem that would bring Berlin and Vienna into closer cooperation, Napoleon encouraged Prussian ambition.

As argued in chapter 3, actors operating in the domain of gains are ceteris paribus likely to be risk averse and present appropriate targets for threat-based strategies of deterrence. In 1863–64 and again in 1865–66 Bismarck framed options in terms of the status quo in Germany and clearly sought to make gains at Austria's expense. The evidence strongly suggests that he was deterrable in both cases. Bismarck's diplomacy in the year preceding the war with Austria aimed at securing the neutrality of the great powers; the Italian alliance was an effort to guarantee the neutrality of France. When the rapid success of von Moltke's armies shattered Napoleon's plans, which were dependent for their success on a long war, the emperor considered intervention. The prospect of a two-front war led Bismarck to seek a rapid armistice and a nonpunitive peace with the Austrians.

Even in the exuberance of victory Bismarck was averse to increases in risk. At Nikolsburg he was more determined to secure what he had already gained in the north than he was to press for additional gains in the south. Such behavior is consistent with the expectations of a theory of influence based on assumptions taken from prospect theory as well as some rational choice approaches, but it is at variance with those versions of deterrence theory that see actors emboldened by success.

· 5 ·

Conquest or Consolidation?
The Importance of Motives

When Prussian decision makers were calculating the costs and benefits of aggression in pursuit of gains, threats of force proved effective tools of great power influence. Thus, Russian threats led Friedrich Wilhelm IV to back down in the First Schleswig-Holstein Crisis, and French threats led Bismarck to begin a reverse course in the second crisis over the duchies. Similarly, the threat of French intervention after the battle of Königgrätz led Bismarck to press for a halt to the march on Vienna and to argue for a nonpunitive peace. The pattern corresponds to the expectations generated by the theory of influence developed in chapter 3. To further evaluate the theory's empirical validity the effects of shifting motives or decisional frames on an actor's response to threats, promises, and assurances must be examined.

In 1870 and again in 1875 Bismarck considered waging war on France. In 1870 he was motivated by the perceived opportunity to make gains. In 1875 by contrast, the chancellor of a unified German Reich was fearful that France was preparing for a war of *revanche* and entertained discussions of a preventive war in an effort to reduce the prospect of future loss. In the first case, Bismarck opted for war; in the second, restraint.

Because the motives giving rise to Bismarck's considerations were different in each case, the theory leads us to expect the effects of threats, promises, and assurances to vary across the two cases. Specifically, threats would be expected to produce restraint when Bismarck was gains driven but deepened crisis when he was motivated by security fears and a desire to minimize potential loss. Alone, assurances are not expected to induce restraint in the behavior of gains-seeking actors, but they may be a powerful tool of influence when an actor is facing uncertainty and potential loss. When the prospect of losses looms large in decision makers' calculations, a strategy of influence that incorporates promised rewards is expected to prove most effective.

Bismarck was encouraged to wage war against France in 1870 by assurances of Russian support coupled with the inability of Austria and the unwillingness of Britain to enter the fray. In 1875 Russian assurances served to defuse the War-in-Sight Crisis by convincing Bismarck that the gains of the Franco-Prussian War were not threatened by France.

THE FRANCO-PRUSSIAN WAR

Although the Treaty of Prague ended hostilities between Austria and Prussia, the years immediately following 1866 were characterized by a general sense of unease in European political circles. The Austro-Prussian war made possible the Prussian plan for unification on the basis of the *kleindeutsch* program, but it had not brought that unification about. For Bismarck the natural completion of German unification required the incorporation of the South German states, an outcome opposed by France. Napoleon's policy was guided by the desire for compensation to offset Prussian gains in North Germany, and he looked to the Rhine frontier as an area for French expansion.[1] Bismarck, however, refused to consider the cession of German territory.[2]

The inevitability of a war between Prussia and France was almost universally accepted.[3] However, the immediate challenges of integrating the states north of the Main into a Prussian political system militated against risking an early war with France over South Germany: "We consider our immediate task to be the consolidation of the North German Confederation. We should be afraid to make the performance of this task more difficult for ourselves, and to disturb it by premature attempts to draw south Germany into our political sphere."[4]

Beginning in 1868, when the North was reasonably consolidated into an operating political system, any one of a series of smaller crises could have precipitated the final showdown between Napoleon and Bismarck. It was an unlikely dispute—the question of the Spanish succession—that finally led the two sides into battle.

Despite its seeming inevitability, the Franco-Prussian War might have been deterred. Although war was a possibility, Bismarck would have pursued another route, had he not been able to isolate France and secure Austrian neutrality through an alliance with Russia. In this regard the Luxembourg Crisis of 1866–67 was a significant stop on the road to the Franco-Prussian War.[5]

Bismarck had long indicated a willingness to accept French expansion in Luxembourg and Belgium in exchange for further Prussian gains in Germany.[6] But the announcement in April 1867 that the King of Holland (as Grand Duke of Luxembourg) intended to sell a duchy of the former German Confederation to France produced a cry of outrage in German public opinion that led Bismarck to withdraw his support. Neither Bismarck nor Napoleon was prepared for a war; thus the issue was eventually settled at a European congress held in London during May 1867. In favor of Luxembourg's continued independent existence, the French dropped their plans for annexation, and Bismarck agreed to withdraw Prussian forces from a onetime confederate fortress in Luxembourg that was subsequently destroyed.

Although it brought about no lasting realignment of the European powers, the crisis over Luxembourg forced them to consider the serious prospect of a Franco-Prussian war and gave Bismarck an indication of what the future constellation of powers might be. During the crisis Russia offered to prevent Austrian intervention on the side of France by deploying a contingent of troops along its border with Austria. A formal Russian guarantee against Austria in the event of a Franco-Prussian war was secured through negotiations in March 1868, in exchange for which Bismarck promised to support Russia in the Near East.

By revealing his designs on Belgium during the crisis, Napoleon earned the mistrust of England, foreclosing the option of an Anglo-French alliance, a prospect that Bismarck admitted would preclude a Prussian war with France.[7] French efforts during 1868–69 to negotiate a Triple Alliance with Austria and Italy against Russia and Prussia came to nothing.[8] When it became known to Napoleon on 3 July 1870 that the Spanish government planned to assemble the Cortes to proclaim Prince Leopold of Hohenzollern king of Spain, France was isolated and without allies.

The French viewed the plan to put a German prince on the Spanish throne as an intrigue of Bismarck against France, to be opposed at all costs.[9] On 6 July French Foreign Minister Gramont threw down the gauntlet. If the Hohenzollern candidature went forward, "we should know how to do our duty without hesitation and without weakness."[10]

For Bismarck the time had come for war, a war through which he would finally complete the unification of Germany. Thus, on 14 July Bismarck released the edited "Ems Telegram" through which Europe learned of a purported affront to King Wilhelm perpetrated by the French ambassador Benedetti and the rebuff the king was supposed to have administered.[11] Whether the storm caused in France by the edited telegram provoked the outbreak of hostilities,[12] or whether it was only indicative of the inevitability of war by this point[13] is not important from our perspective. Either interpretation shows that Bismarck realized the other powers would not intervene and was willing to go to war against an isolated France.

On 19 July the French declaration of war was presented at Berlin. The decisive battle took place on 1 September at Sedan. Surrounded by the German third army, Napoleon and Marshal MacMahon were forced to surrender. On 4 September Paris rose in revolt, and a republic was proclaimed.

Decisional Frame

"That German Unity would be furthered by violent events I also hold probable," Bismarck wrote to the Prussian ambassador at Munich, "but it is quite another question to assume the mission of bringing about a violent catastrophe and bear the responsibility for the choice of timing." Bismarck was not adverse to wars of conquest, as the events of 1864 and 1866 made apparent to all, but he first had to be assured that the risks were manageable.

In 1870 Bismarck's goal was unification, but he evaluated the costs and benefits of alternative strategies to this end vis-à-vis the status-quo. Indeed, in 1869 he was not prepared to fight Napoleon: "Arbitrary interference in the course of history, motivated on purely subjective grounds, has never had any other result than the shaking down of unripe fruit. That German unity is not at the moment a ripe fruit is in my mind obvious . . . and the ability to wait, while circumstances develop, is a prerequisite for practical politics."[14] In addition to waiting for the domestic political situation in Germany to mature, Bismarck had to assure himself of Napoleon's acquiescence or the neutrality of the great powers in the event of a war with France. To King Wilhelm he outlined the requisite international conditions: "We can wait for [German unity] in security because the lapse of time and the natural development of the nation, which makes further progress every year, will have their effect. We cannot accelerate it unless out-of-the-way events in Europe, such as some upheaval in France or a war of other Great Powers among themselves, offer us an unsought opportunity to do so."[15]

The crisis over the Spanish succession provided an out-of-the-way event in which Bismarck found his opportunity. The Hohenzollern candidature was seen by Bismarck as a means of promoting the prestige of the Prussian dynasty within Germany, which would in turn promote further integration in the North German Confederation as well as unification with the South. In addition, the presence of a Prussian on the throne of Spain would further contribute to France's strategic isolation:

Your Majesty will, I trust, graciously permit me, with my humble duty to summarize in writing, the motives which, in my modest opinion, favor the acceptance of the Spanish crown by His Serene Highness the Hereditary Prince of Hohenzollern. . . . It is desirable for Germany to have on the far side of France a country on whose sympathy she can rely and with those susceptibilities France would be obliged to reckon. . . . The repute of the Hohenzollern dynasty, the justifiable pride with which not only Prussia regards its Royal House but Germany too . . . forms an important element in self confidence, the fostering and strengthening of which would be of benefit.[16]

Bismarck's motive in promoting the Hohenzollern candidature was German unification, which could not be achieved without a crisis with France. Thus, the candidature must be regarded as an offensive act. As Pflanze concludes, Bismarck hoped to provoke either a war with France, or French internal collapse.[17] French isolation, however, provided a necessary condition that provided a strategic environment of opportunity within which to pursue gains.

Baseline of Expectation

By 1870 Bismarck was confident that none of the other great powers would intervene against him in a war with France. He was equally confident that the German army was up to the task.

The most important piece in the strategy of isolating France was the understanding with Russia. From the Luxembourg Crisis to the outbreak of war in 1870, Bismarck worked to secure Russian support against Austrian intervention. In 1868 he told the Russian ambassador: "We believe ourselves equal to a war against France and have no need to expand it into a general conflict, if Russia covers our rear against Austria."[18] In exchange for supporting Russian proposals for changes in the Black Sea Clauses of the Crimean settlement, Bismarck secured the support of the tsar against Austria and France.[19] On the eve of war Bismarck could declare: "We know from a friendly Power and on the highest authority that Austria will preserve benevolent neutrality towards us. We are sure of Austria's neutrality because of the moral pressure Russia will exert on her."[20]

Under the conservative administration of Disraeli, who became prime minister in February 1868, British policy was pacific and well disposed toward the further consolidation of Prussian influence in Germany. Indeed, to the Prussian ambassador Disraeli admitted: "we do not wish Prussia to be disturbed in her digestion. . . . Tell Count Bismarck, that we do not wish Prussia to be disturbed in her digestion."[21]

Upon the change of administration in England, Clarendon again assumed the position of foreign secretary. He promoted a rapprochement with France and adopted a more assertive policy toward Berlin, cautioning against the incorporation of the South German states into the North German Confederation.[22] But Napoleon's plans for the purchase of the Belgian railways in 1869 raised suspicions as to his ultimate aims and precluded anything resembling entente. Clarendon's long illness in the spring of 1870 and death in June largely removed him from the diplomacy surrounding the Hohenzollern candidature such that Bismarck was able to pursue his policies for Germany without British interference.

Response of the Great Powers

British policy in the period immediately preceding the outbreak of hostilities was limited to securing written assurances from both Prussia and France that in the event of war Belgian neutrality would be respected. Thereafter, Britain stood aloof from the Franco-Prussian conflict, promoting the neutrality of Austria and Russia as well as the smaller states.[23] Russia and Austria likewise abstained from entering the conflict.

After the Battle of Sedan the question emerged of German annexations. Specifically, in a circular dispatch to European capitals, Bismarck demanded the French provinces of Alsace and Lorraine. Unlike the situation after the victory at Königgrätz, however, Bismarck did not confront international opposition to suggestions for a punitive peace. No one wished to play the role assumed by Napoleon in 1866. From Vienna came congratulatory messages.[24] Gladstone, confronting a divided cabinet, refused to intervene unless he could do so in concert with Russia. The Russians were more concerned with conditions in the Near East than in the West and limited their actions to pressing the French to accept an armistice.[25] On 18 January 1871 King Wilhelm I was proclaimed emperor of Germany. Four days later Paris asked for an armistice. The preliminaries of peace, providing for German annexation of Alsace and Lorraine, were completed on 26 February and ratified on 3 March.

Summary

It is more difficult in the case of the Franco-Prussian War than it was in the cases of the wars against Denmark and Austria to make the counterfactual argument that Bismarck was deterrable. In the case of the war with Denmark Bismarck began to retreat when it looked as if Napoleon would intervene after the invasion of Jutland. After the victory at Königgrätz Bismarck showed a remarkable degree of restraint when faced with the threat of Napoleon's intervention. But as the great powers refrained from intervening in the war between Prussia and France, it is more difficult to make an assessment.

Yet the continued focus of Bismarck on the probable position of the European powers in a war with France suggests that he was in fact susceptible to influence. During the Luxembourg Crisis, when the international situation was unclear, Bismarck agreed to great power mediation. Only afterward, when it became clear that Russia and England were unlikely to come to Napoleon's aid, did the Prussian leader aggressively pursue unification with the South, accepting the attendant risks of such a policy for war with France. The strategy Bismarck pursued with regard to the war resembles those he followed in previous engagements: step-by-step progression, always making sure of the ground ahead before moving forward.

Bismarck's stress on the importance of proper timing indicates a sensitivity to managing costs and risks and is consistent with the hypothesis that Prussia was deterrable through the use of coercive threats that would have challenged the expected gains from aggression. Such threats were not forthcoming. Whereas Russian threats led King Friedrich Wilhelm IV to abandon his invasion of Schleswig-Holstein in 1848 and to compromise with Austria in 1850, Russian assurances of neutrality served to promoted Prussian expansion in 1870–71. On the eve of war Bismarck could rest easy, "full of quiet resolution and firm reliance on [Prussian] strength."[26]

THE WAR-IN-SIGHT CRISIS

Quiet resolution was not the description of the German chancellor circulating through European capitals in 1875. Indeed, confessions of sleepless nights produced by security fears, fears regarded by most European leaders as irrational and exaggerated, led many to question Bismarck's mental agility and to ask, "Is war in sight?"

The War-in-Sight Crisis is theoretically interesting for at least two reasons. First, as George Kennan noted, the fact that there was a crisis at all is itself puzzling. Kennan argues that Germany had "no rational motive for wishing to launch a new attack on the recently defeated enemy; and Bismarck, a man highly conscious of the fact that wars, if they were to serve any useful purpose, had to have concrete and realistic objectives, would have been the last to disregard this fact."[27] Yet the Bismarck so capable of rational cost-benefit calculus did precipitate a seemingly irrational crisis, one that might have ended in a second war with France. What accounts for this apparent anomalous behavior? I argue that Bismarck's behavior in the crisis is characteristic of actors facing prospective loss and is consistent with the expectations of prospect theory and the general psychological phenomenon of loss aversion.

Second, insofar as prominent historians have claimed that the crisis was resolved by the threat of Russian intervention in support of France, the case presents something of a "hard test" for the theory developed in chapter 3. If Bismarck was indeed evaluating prospective outcomes in the domain of loss and responded to threats by backing down, we would have less confidence in the empirical validity of our theoretic claims. But as I demonstrate below, the claim that Russian threats deterred a German attack on France cannot be sustained.

With the defeat of France and the negotiation of the Treaty of Frankfurt, the foreign policy challenge for Bismarck was the defense of the new Reich from external challenges so that the balance of his energies could be devoted to the necessary task of internal consolidation. As Raymond Sontag concluded, "During the two decades following the Treaty of Frankfurt, Germany was the staunchest bulwark of the status quo, and Germany to Europe meant Bismarck."[28]

Although intended to be both binding and burdensome for France, the Treaty of Frankfurt inspired calls for *revanche* almost as soon as it was signed. In 1871, however, France was weak at home and without allies abroad. Concluding that France could not contemplate a war on its own, and that a weak France did not present an appealing ally for the other powers, Bismarck's policies were directed at prolonging French weakness as a means for securing and consolidating German gains.[29] Thus, the rapid pace of French economic, political, and military recovery in the years immediately following the Treaty of Frankfurt not only surprised most observers but gave cause for alarm in Berlin.

In May 1873 the government of Thiers fell, and the National Assembly elected a former Napoleonic general and supporter of monarchical restoration, Marshal Patrice MacMahon, to a seven-year term as president of the republic. On 16 September the last German occupation troops withdrew from France upon complete payment of the French war indemnity, eighteen months ahead of schedule. The French military began reorganizing on the basis of the Prussian model and aimed at fielding a force of 600,000 in the near term.[30]

At the very moment a revitalized France presented a possible external threat to the consolidation of the new German Reich, Bismarck was engaged in a near paranoiac battle against the Catholic Church, which he had come to regard as a domestic threat to the Prussian-led, Protestant regime. Bismarck's motives for initiating the *Kulturkampf* arose from "a complex of mutually supporting ideas, prejudices, and circumstances," which led to the "conviction that Prussia was the object of a malevolent crusade on the part of ultramontane clergy and laymen" whose ultimate aim was "domination over all governments, particularly over the Hohenzollern monarchy as the chief Protestant power in Europe." The ostensible objective of the *Kulturkampf* was the separation of church and state in Germany, but the campaign eventually took on proportions such that it "seriously invaded the sphere of the church and rights of the individual."[31] In addition, Bismarck internationalized the conflict, seeking allies for his campaign in London, St. Petersburg, and even Vienna.[32]

The *Kulturkampf* was not without effect in France. In August 1873 the bishop of Nancy, under whose episcopal authority fell a number of churches in German-held Lorraine, called upon the faithful to pray for the return of the lost provinces to France. The appeal was read from the pulpit of all churches in the diocese, including those in Lorraine. In November a number of French bishops criticized anti-Catholic legislation in Germany, calling it immoral. Bismarck protested to the French government and insisted they take action against the bishops.[33]

In response to the threatening tone of Bismarck's demands against France, Queen Victoria wrote a personal letter to Kaiser Wilhelm I expressing her "alarm" with respect to reports that certain parties in Germany favored a new war: "If Germany, through incessant provocations of a fanatical press and priesthood in France (where, however, the Government do all in their power to keep both under control), were at last to resort to renewed war with France, this might lead to lamentable consequences."[34] Although not intended as a threat, the queen's letter was condemned by Bismarck and prompted him to add a paragraph on foreign affairs to the kaiser's speech for the opening of the Reichstag. Asserting Germany's peaceful intentions, the kaiser took issue with the insinuation of others that Germany was pursuing an aggressive policy and warned foreign powers against taking any actions aimed against its interests.[35]

Meanwhile Bismarck began to regard French rearmament with a new sense of alarm. Although French rearmament and military reorganization had begun under Thiers, Bismarck had not regarded it as particularly threatening to Germany. In his analysis continuing political instability would ensure French diplomatic isolation. Radical and republican tendencies inspired continued fear among the most important continental powers, which remained conservative and monarchical. However, the election of a president with clerical and monarchist sympathies increased Bismarck's concern regarding French military recovery. Under MacMahon, Bismarck reasoned, France was a more attractive ally to conservative and Catholic powers. With an Austrian or Russian ally, France might be willing to undertake a war of revenge.

In February Bismarck received word that the French government had placed an order with German traders for 10,000 military horses. Writing to his ambassador in France, Bismarck called the sale of so many horses "a loss that we would still feel if compelled to mobilize in three years."[36] On 4 March the kaiser issued an order prohibiting the export of any horses to France.[37] Eight days later the French National Assembly approved a military reorganization bill that called for the addition of a fourth battalion to each regiment and a fourth company to each battalion of the French army. The German general staff calculated that the move would add 144,000 men to the French forces, eight battalions more than the number then in the German army.[38] For the German government the reorganization left "no doubt" that the French were intent on bringing their army to a point of "tactical readiness" that far exceeded the "demands of a peaceful policy."[39]

Amid rising tensions between Berlin and Paris, and under the pretext of consultations over the status of Serbia, Bismarck dispatched Josef Maria von Radowitz[40] to St. Petersburg in order to ascertain the general attitude of the tsar and his ministry toward Germany.[41] The Radowitz mission was inspired by an apparent warming of relations between Russia and France precisely when relations between the latter and Germany were taking a decided turn for the worse.

In this context the appearance of a German special emissary in St. Petersburg gave rise to speculation that Germany sought to secure Russian neutrality for a new war with France: In exchange for Russian neutrality, Berlin would support Russia's claims in the Balkans. Although there exists no evidence to support this interpretation of the Radowitz mission, it was widely believed by contemporaries including the French ambassador, General Le Flô, and the foreign minister, the Duc Decazes.[42] In the following weeks Decazes issued a series of alarming dispatches to French diplomatic representatives abroad as well as important European capitals in which he claimed a German attack to be in the offing.

The increased suspicions of France might have appeared less ominous had Radowitz returned to Berlin with some indication of continuing Russian fidelity. But here, too, the Radowitz mission was a failure as "he did not succeed in drawing out Gorchakov with respect to the ultimate aims of Russian policy, more particularly as they touched upon France."[43]

The strained state of Franco-German relations became the subject of widespread press speculation in April. On 5 April the *Kölnische Zeitung* published an article that warned of a Catholic conspiracy aimed at creating "new alliances" against the German Reich. Four days later European public opinion was aroused by the publication in the *Berliner Post* of an article with the caption *"Ist der Krieg in Sicht?"* ("Is War in Sight?"). In it the dangers of French rearmament were cited as evidence that war was indeed in sight, but the author concluded that the threatening "clouds might disperse."[44]

But the clouds grew darker when Radowitz, his reserve in retreat after a bibulous dinner party at the British embassy, engaged in a defense of the doctrine of preventive war. If Paris were intent on *revanche*, war was inevitable. Why should Germany wait until France had recovered? Under these circumstances a preventive war was justified on "political, philosophical, and even Christian grounds."[45] Another dinner guest, the Viscount Gontout-Biron, then French ambassador to Germany, promptly relayed these remarks—as well as his conviction that they indicated plans for an early German attack—back to Decazes in Paris.[46]

Five days after Radowitz's rationalization of preventive war, Bismarck himself told the Austrian ambassador that if the French continued to rearm "on the present scale, and their intentions of attacking Germany admitted of no further doubt, it would be manifestly the duty of the German Government to take the initiative."[47] On 2 May Field Marshal von Moltke told the British ambassador that French armaments would force a new war on

Germany. A breach of the peace would not be the responsibility of the party that marched first. Rather, it was "the Power that provoked the necessity of defence in others which must be held responsible for war."[48] The same week Hohenlohe held discussions with Decazes in Paris. The foreign minister concluded that "the emotions brought about by the law of cadres had not been dispelled."[49]

The repeated defense of the concept of preventive war by German officials, their diplomatic representations abroad, as well as the sensational press stories of April combined to produce a flurry of diplomatic activity between Paris and London, on the one hand, and St. Petersburg, on the other. The tsar was scheduled to visit his uncle Kaiser Wilhelm I on his way to take the cure at Bad Ems in mid-May. The French and British governments regarded the visit as an opportune occasion for preventive diplomacy.

Decazes wrote to Le Flô instructing him to request the tsar's intervention on behalf of peace: "[France's] security would be absolute the day his Majesty would declare that he would look on a surprise as on an insult, and that he would not permit such an iniquity to pass. One word like that would simply insure the peace of the world."[50] Queen Victoria likewise wrote the tsar, and Odo Russell was directed to use every means to clear up the misunderstandings that had arisen between France and Germany and to support a Russian peace initiative during the royal visit.[51]

Tsar Alexander II, accompanied by Gorchakov, arrived in Berlin on 10 May. For his part the British ambassador carried out his instructions. During the tsar's visit Russell was unable to meet with Bismarck himself, but related to Bülow, Bismarck's deputy at the foreign ministry, Britain's satisfaction "that France had no aggressive designs, and that H.M.G. would be happy to do all in their power to dispel misunderstandings." Bülow promised to carry the message to Bismarck at once.[52]

Just what was said in meetings between the monarchs and their ministers is not known. There is no official transcript in the documents, and the secondary literature relies almost entirely on a few second-hand reports: Decazes's interpretation as well as Bismarck's own highly suspect account provided much later. I will endeavor to establish the probable content and tone of these discussions below.[53] Afterward, however, Alexander II was able to wire his embassies abroad that "the Emperor is leaving Berlin entirely convinced of the conciliatory disposition which prevails there and which assures the maintenance of peace."[54]

Decisional Frame

Historians have long debated whether Bismarck really intended to start a war with France in 1875, or whether he was only bluffing—the crisis, therefore, artificial.[55] Both positions are erroneous. The crisis was real, but Bismarck did not seek a war with France. Rather, he was willing to risk war in an effort to strengthen the structure supporting the territorial status quo and thereby secure the gains of 1871.[56]

Bismarck's reference point in 1875 was Germany's military and diplomatic position vis-à-vis France, and he regarded the pace of French recovery after the election of MacMahon with a sense of alarm. For the German chancellor the election of MacMahon reflected an important transformation in French domestic politics and a potential threat to Germany: "A weak, civilian, anticlerical, isolated France" had become "a stronger, military, ultramontane France more capable of forming alliances."[57] The German general staff concluded that French policy was aimed at achieving military superiority, a view Bismarck's foreign ministry adopted in its own policy deliberations.[58] But Bismarck regarded French ability to initiate a war of revenge as a function not only of its military strength but also of its ability to attract allies.[59] Austria, Italy, and Russia were all regarded as potential French allies. However, a Franco-Russian alliance was considered the most dangerous possibility, thus the necessity to establish the tsar's disposition through Radowitz's mission.[60]

In retrospect the fear that the pace of French rearmament inspired in the German leadership appears overblown.[61] That France was in no condition to launch a war of *revanche* is now widely accepted.[62] But at the time the fears in Berlin were real, and surprise at the pace of French recovery by no means limited to the German leadership or an alarmist press.

Writing to Queen Victoria, British foreign minister Derby noted: "The truth seems to be that neither Prince Bismarck nor any other German statesman foresaw the rapidity with which France would recover from the blows of 1870–71. The wonderful energy and elasticity of the national spirit has caused the work of a generation to be done in a few years; and it is believed by competent observers that the material losses of the war have been already all but retrieved."[63] The prospect of a Franco-Russian alliance was regarded with concern in London as in Berlin. The British ambassador at Berlin, Lord Odo Russell, remarked to Bülow that he was pleased to hear of the Radowitz mission to St. Petersburg, "as the coquetting between Gorchakov and Le Flô and Decazes had for some time been watched in London with apprehension."[64]

In precipitating a crisis in the spring of 1875 Bismarck was not engaged in aggressive opportunism. Rather, believing that the "end game" of French rearmament was a "military campaign against Germany,"[65] and seeing in MacMahon's election the prospect of French participation in an anti-German alliance, Bismarck's threats against France and Belgium as well as his protestations to European capitals were efforts to raise the issue of German security and its relationship to overall European peace in promotion of the status quo.[66]

Baseline of Expectation

The status quo as defined by the Treaty of Frankfurt was the reference point against which Bismarck judged prospective outcomes during the crisis of 1875. Although Bismarck had not been the most ardent champion of the annexations of 1871, questioning the value of Lorraine in particular,[67] by 1875 his ministry saw the continued attachment of the provinces to Germany as a matter of national security.[68] A Franco-Russian alliance coupled with a reorganized French army would present a threat to the continuation of the territorial status quo.[69] Bismarck reasoned that the French stood to gain in a future war, and such gain could only come at Germany's expense: "If our friends could only realize that Germany has nothing to win in a war, whereas France has much to gain, they might find our mistrust [of French rearmament] justified."[70]

Bismarck further reasoned that time was on the side of France. Its continued progress toward recovery was undoubted and would only increase its attractiveness as an ally for one of the other powers. Thus, if France could be made to slow the pace of rearmament for fear of provoking a German preventive attack, Bismarck could forestall the formation of the "hostile coalition" that so haunted his calculations for the future.[71]

Response of the Great Powers

The belief that Tsar Alexander II used the occasion of his stopover in Berlin to issue a forceful threat against a new German war with France and that this threat prevented a German attack became strongly rooted in the historiography of the crisis and largely persists today.[72] But I cannot find evidence to support this interpretation in the relevant documents.[73] Rather, the evidence suggests that the tsar was sensitive to Bismarck's anxiety and fears regarding German security and sought to reassure the German chancellor of Russia's continued loyalty as an ally and of France's peaceful intentions and true capabilities. Odo Russell's efforts in support of the tsar's mission were similarly reassuring rather than threatening in tone and content and were, at least initially, favorably received by Bismarck.

The tsar outlined the objective of his visit to Berlin in April correspondence. He did not speak of harsh rebukes or threats. Rather, the tsar indicated his intention to try and reassure Bismarck that German security was not in danger: "I hope, during my stopover in Berlin, to somewhat calm the Great Chancellor."[74] The Russian foreign minister likewise briefed his ambassador at Berlin on the approach the Russians would take with Bismarck: "We will adopt the line that although we will never follow a route that is not in our interest, we remain good friends and loyal allies. We will trouble ourselves not to give Bismarck the impression that his erratic and worried behavior has diminished the number of his followers."[75] Oubril supported the approach and urged the foreign minister not to adopt a tone that would increase Bismarck's sense of anxiety.[76] Although sparse, the evidence points to the adoption of a soft line by the Russians.[77]

Before leaving for Berlin, General Le Flô presented a request for a pledge of Russian military support should war break out between France and Germany. The tsar responded: "Oh! That is a bit strong. . . . We will not pull the sword, we will not need that, we will arrive without that."[78] Le Flô confessed "with a tone of sincerity, that it pained him to be compelled to admit that in France all was still in a complete state of dissolution. To admit this was hard for a patriot, but he could give his word of honor that all that was said of French preparations was only on paper, and that much time was needed for the carrying into execution of the new organization."[79] This message was reinforced by Gontaut in Berlin. Gontaut was instructed "to assure the Tsar unequivocally, unconditionally, of France's intention to keep the peace. He was to insist that all its armaments were designed solely for defense, and for the insuring of the maintenance of peace in collaboration with Russia. He should promise, if necessary, that France would take no action without Russia's approval."[80] There is no reason to doubt the tsar and his minister passed this information on to their German counterparts in an effort to ease German fears arising from the military reorganization in France.

In Berlin the tsar met with the kaiser while the two chancellors conferred in a separate session; the meeting between Bismarck and Gorchakov has been the subject of much speculation. Writing his memoirs many years later, Bismarck claimed to have overwhelmed his Russian counterpart with sarcasm, but most historians have come to regard this claim with the same skepticism they accord the work as a whole.[81] In a meeting with the French ambassador immediately following that with Bismarck, Gorchakov said nothing to suggest that the talks had been anything but cordial.[82]

The meeting between the two sovereigns was characterized not only by congeniality but also by agreement on the need to maintain peace based on the status quo.[83] For his part Kaiser Wilhelm I immediately reported the meeting's outcome to his foreign ministry: "The discussion with the Tsar has established an understanding . . . which I could have only wished for."[84]

Russell's communication to Bülow cannot in any way be construed as constituting a threat. Rather, it is best regarded as an offer of mediation and an effort to dispel German fears of French intent. Bülow reported on the British position in a memorandum written after his discussions with Russell:

Her Majesty's Government have observed with great regret that a sullen unrest is permeating Europe; the immediate cause of this is the armaments which France has recently arranged for. It is known that your military authorities look on these armaments as a great danger to peace, and Count Münster has expressed himself to this effect.

The British Government on its side does not believe that the French Government has any warlike intentions or is arming for the recovery of the lost provinces.

It would be very happy if, on its side, it could do anything to abate the unrest and restore the confidence which has been destroyed.[85]

In response to the British offer of mediation, Bismarck instructed his ambassador at London to express his thanks, regarding the offer "a new indication of the friendly disposition of the English cabinet."[86] In a separate communication of the same date, Bismarck added: "If the British Cabinet would speak in a peaceful sense to the French Government and so conduce to calm people's minds, we should be grateful to Lord Derby."[87]

Although there is no complete account of what was said in the meetings of 10 May, there is no evidence to support the contention that the tsar and Gorchakov used the occasion for the issuance of deterrent threats.[88] Presummit diplomatic correspondence as well as post-summit statements and memoranda point to a different conclusion. In addition to the evidence contained in the documentary record, reports contained in the official German press provide some indication of how Bismarck regarded the meetings with the tsar and his minister. In the *Kölnische Zeitung* the meetings were said to represent the renewal of the Three Emperors League and proof that France could hope for nothing from Russia. The *Provinzial-Correspondenz* saw the meetings between the kaiser and the tsar as evidence of a "community of their interests."[89]

The territorial status quo on the Franco-German frontier was the baseline against which Bismarck evaluated prospective outcomes during the crisis of 1875. Insofar as British and Russian signals reinforced the German chancellor's expectations that the status quo would not be challenged by France—alone or in alliance with another power—these signals constituted assurances as defined in chapter 2.[90] The assurances were coupled with a promise, for, with the election of MacMahon, Bismarck feared the possibility of a Franco-Russian alliance. Thus, Russian pledges of continued alliance with Germany constituted an improvement in Bismarck's baseline.

However, Bismarck came to view the conclusion of the War-in-Sight Crisis in negative terms. When he became aware of British attempts to secure the support of Italy and Austria for joint action in the event of a German attack against France, Bismarck concluded that Britain should be listed among the ranks of the Reich's potential enemies.[91] A full appreciation of the potential for a Russian-British alliance in support of France, however, came to Bismarck only well after the crisis had subsided and thus cannot be credited with contributing to its resolution.

Summary

Bismarck's dread of ultramontanism and his conviction that France was engaged in preparations for a war of revenge led him to provoke an international crisis in the spring of 1875. Although he did not contemplate an aggressive war of expansion, Bismarck was willing to risk war with France in order to slow the pace of French rearmament and prevent its recovery as a potential ally for the other powers. According to Fuller, "Bismarck was playing with fire throughout the entire course of events. There is no question in which one government can less safely interfere than in the armaments of another; and it must always recognize the presence of war immediately in the background whenever it undertakes such interference. . . . A single false step on either side might have brought on a conflict, no matter how much against the will of both parties concerned. Bismarck's policy can, therefore, not be acquitted of involving the risk of war."[92]

War would not have been inevitable had either the British or Russians adopted a hard line with Bismarck and threatened intervention in the event of a German move on France. But Bismarck might well have escalated the crisis, responding to such threats with counterthreats. In the course of a descending action-reaction spiral of threats and counterthreats, outcomes are uncertain and events may assume a momentum of their own that is beyond the ability of individual actors to control.

The waters into which Bismarck was willing to sail in 1875 were in large part uncharted. Indeed, in the War-in-Sight Crisis he displayed a tolerance for risk and uncertainty that stands in stark contrast to his behavior in previous diplomatic encounters where he was extremely risk averse. In the conflict with Denmark over Schleswig-Holstein as well as in the run-ups to the Austro-Prussian and Franco-Prussian wars, Bismarck was careful not to move forward until he had convinced himself that the powers would not intervene. The absence of similar caution—for example, after the failure of the Radowitz mission to establish continuing Russian support—is perhaps the most striking feature of Bismarck's diplomacy in 1875.

Most rational choice theories—among them mainstream variants of deterrence theory—assume actors to be of a given type: either risk acceptant or risk averse. Rapid or frequent changes in risk propensity are incompatible with basic assumptions of the rational model. By contrast, a theory of influence based on insights taken from behavioral decision research leads to the expectation that an actor's tolerance for risk and uncertainty will be highly context dependent and subject to change. Specifically, actors are expected to be risk averse with respect to gains, yet risk acceptant when confronting prospective loss. Whereas the shift in Bismarck's behavior—from extreme caution when contemplating expansion to an acceptance of a relatively high degree of uncertainty when contemplating future loss—appears puzzling from the perspective of rational choice theories, it is largely consistent with the expectations of the theory developed in chapter 3.

What appears to have defused the War-in-Sight Crisis was the assurance of the tsar that Bismarck's achievements in the Franco-Prussian War were not at risk. Although the British and Russians were not prepared to see France weakened further, neither were they prepared to see its gain at Germany's expense.[93] The European balance of power after the Franco-Prussian War was perceived as superior to that during the days of Napoleon III in both London and St. Petersburg. Bismarck worried that French rearmament posed a potential threat to Germany sometime in the future and feared that a stronger France would be capable of attracting allies in the short term. The tsar's promise that Russia would remain a loyal friend and ally allowed Bismarck to drop his aggressive policy vis-à-vis France and renew a more balanced foreign policy.

. 6 .

From Europe to Africa:
Threats, Promises, and the Question of Colonies

After dismissing the great chancellor in 1890, Kaiser Wilhelm II announced that the tortuous ambiguities of Bismarckian diplomacy would give way to a simple, open, and straightforward German foreign policy. But the Europe of Wilhelm's reign, already complex, was undergoing unprecedented social, economic, and technological change and demanded a healthy tolerance for ambiguity. The complex interconnections of the international system led statesmen to believe that the fate of seemingly insignificant players in Europe as well as the outcomes of minor disputes in the non-European periphery held significant implications for the relations of the great powers. Consequently, simple policies were unlikely to produce straightforward effects or prove effective at promoting German interests.

It was in large part the failure of Germany's post-Bismarckian leadership to understand, or in some cases even recognize, the complex interrelationships of the international system that allowed for the adoption of policies that contributed to the very outcome Bismarck constantly sought to avoid: the formation of a coalition of great powers hostile to Germany. Thus, concluding that the Reinsurance Treaty with Russia was inconsistent with German obligations to Austria and the Anglo-German entente (a product of the Heligoland-Zanzibar Treaty), the German leadership decided against its renewal in 1890. But this decision, in turn, promoted Franco-Russian rapprochement, which took the form of the Dual Alliance in 1894. Similarly, rather straightforward efforts to defend German interests in the face of French efforts to establish a protectorate in Morocco had the unintended effect of promoting an Anglo-Russian entente as well as the less surprising result of strengthening the Entente Cordiale.

But German leaders were not immune to outside influence. From the crises over African colonies to the Bosnian annexation crisis and even in the tense days of July 1914, German decision making was heavily influenced by the policies of the other powers. The story of European diplomacy from 1890 to 1914 is largely a story of successful crisis management often through immediate deterrence. However, the tragedy of European diplomacy in this period is found in the failure to recognize that German assertiveness was an indication of the political immaturity of the unified German state, a reflection of German fears and insecurities rather than a desire to capitalize on the weakness of others.

With the annexations of 1871 Bismarck's territorial ambitions on the European continent were largely fulfilled. The 1880s, however, saw new impulses for territorial expansion as Germany began efforts to establish an empire overseas.[1] With German explorers and trading companies staking claims to large tracts of territory in Africa and the Pacific, disputes between Germany and the other colonial powers—Britain most important among these—were probably inevitable.

This chapter analyzes three colonial disputes involving imperial Germany. First, the conflict between Britain and Germany over the approaches to the headwaters of the Nile River, a crisis that began during Bismarck's tenure but that was resolved by his successor. Analysis then turns to the First and Second Moroccan Crises, milestones on the road to the First World War.

In all three cases German decision makers were motivated to adopt assertive policies in Africa based on the perception that the status quo was deteriorating and Germany's position among the great powers was at risk. And in each case, German decision making was heavily influenced by the policies of the other powers. To the extent that the German leadership was framing prospective outcomes in terms of loss, the theory of influence presented in chapter 3 would lead us to expect threats to have proved inappropriate—indeed, counterproductive—tools of influence, whereas the use of promises and assurances by the great powers should have been more effective in influencing German decision making.

GERMANY'S SHIFT TO A COLONIAL POLICY

During his first decade as *Reichskanzler,* Bismarck was steadfast in his opposition to colonial acquisitions. When offered French Pondicherry and Vietnam as part of the terms of peace in 1871, Bismarck refused, likening colonies to "sable coats worn by Polish noblemen who don't have any shirts."[2] In 1873 he told Odo Russell that "Colonies . . . would be a sign of weakness, because colonies could only be defended by powerful fleets, and

Germany's geographical position did not necessitate her development into a first-class maritime power."[3] As late as 1880 Hohenlohe noted in his diary that Bismarck would "not hear of colonies. . . . He says we do not have an adequate fleet to protect them and our bureaucracy is not skillful enough to direct their management."[4] Bismarck's sudden adoption of a colonial policy in 1883–84 is in this regard puzzling and has given rise to much historical analysis and debate.[5]

Early scholarship tended to emphasize continuity in the objectives and methods of Bismarckian foreign policy. Thus, Bismarck is portrayed as an aggressive opportunist who decided to pursue a policy of colonial acquisition as early as 1876. Repeated denials of colonial ambitions were intended to conceal his true motives until the propitious moment arrived.[6] Subsequent scholarship has largely discredited this thesis: If true, Bismarck concealed his intentions from not only the other powers but also his closest friends and advisors.[7] Most remaining analyses of the shift to colonialism can be grouped into one of two schools, on the basis of whether they locate the major sources of German foreign policy in the international system or within the German state.

A.J.P. Taylor is the strongest proponent of the notion that the sources for Bismarck's colonial policy are to be found in Germany's relations with the other powers (der Primat der Aussenpolitik). More particularly, Taylor argues that Bismarck's entry into the race for colonies was aimed against Britain: "Bismarck quarrelled with England in order to draw closer to France; and . . . the method of quarrel was the deliberately provocative claim to ownerless lands, in which the Government had hitherto shown no interest. . . . The German colonies were the accidental by-product of an abortive Franco-German entente."[8]

Taylor's creativity would no doubt impress Bismarck himself, but his thesis has been persuasively refuted by Turner.[9] As Turner points out, if Bismarck sought a dispute with Britain, there were simpler, less risky alternatives to the seizure of overseas territory. And the documentary evidence is clear: Bismarck's European policies aimed at the isolation of France, and his early policies in Africa were quite consciously devised to *avoid* conflict with Britain.[10]

Where Taylor emphasizes European factors for Bismarck's decision to seek colonies, the competing school stresses the importance of factors within the German state (der Primat der Innenpolitik). Thus, Bismarck's shift to a colonial policy is explained by the growing public movement for colonies, the pressure of important business interests, and as the natural result of the late, monopoly stage of finance capitalism.[11]

For example, by 1884 the German Colonial Society, comprised of most of Germany's big industrialists, twenty-three chambers of commerce, sixteen city councils, fifteen trade associations, and scores of small and medium-sized businesses, had forty-three branches across the Reich. Large commercial interests had begun establishing profitable ventures in Africa and the Pacific, and with Bismarck's conversion to mercantilism in 1879, these firms represented sources of necessary raw materials and markets for surplus German goods.[12] The Colonial Society was "the most formidable pressure group assembled in Germany," and as such was a desirable addition to Bismarck's political base.[13] Thus, Aydelotte concludes that "Bismarck appears to have inaugurated a colonial program largely for reasons of domestic policy, in the hope of pleasing German public opinion, stimulating national sentiment, and securing by this means a working majority in the insubordinate Reichstag."[14] Imanuel Geiss goes so far as to relegate the preferences of Bismarck to secondary status: "From a certain point onward, the German Chancellor had to conform to dominating trends in German society, whatever his personal views may have been."[15]

Geiss overstates the case. Throughout his career, Bismarck demonstrated a willingness to oppose important domestic constituencies in pursuit of foreign policy objectives (e.g., German Catholics during the *Kulturkampf*). And Bismarck understood the potential for international conflict inherent in a colonial policy. As late as December 1888 he told the German explorer Eugene Wolf: "Your map of Africa is quite beautiful, but my map of Africa lies in Europe. Here lies Russia, and here lies France, and we are in the middle. That is my map of Africa."[16] Why then was Bismarck willing to pursue a course of action in the late 1880s that he had repeatedly rejected because he thought it risked provoking wider disputes with the great powers of Europe?

Although a complete explanation for the shift from a conservative, risk-averse to an assertive, risk-acceptant colonial policy will not be offered here, the documentary evidence supports the hypothesis that the change in policy followed a change in decisional frame or reference point. During the 1870s and early 1880s Bismarck regarded colonies as gains that Germany could forgo. However, by the mid-1880s Bismarck concluded that the failure to acquire colonies would represent a loss. Risk-averse when colonies were framed in the domain of gains, Bismarck displayed a willingness to risk European complications in his effort to prevent a loss in standing vis-à-vis the other great powers.

Bismarck was not immune to the *Torschlusspanik* that took hold of large segments of German society in the 1880s: a fear that the door to African resources and markets was closing and Germany would find itself forever locked out.[17] With the British, Italians, French, Belgians, and even the Portuguese scrambling for Pacific islands and territory in Africa, colonies came to represent not only a benefit for certain parochial interests in German society but also, as Craig notes, "a form of insurance against loss of standing among the nations of the world."[18]

Thus, in response to a request for Imperial protection for a German trading station in the Southwest African harbor of Angra Pequena Bismarck wrote: "If we fail to push our rights with energy, we shall risk, by letting them sink into oblivion, falling into a position inferior to England's, and strengthening the unbounded arrogance shown by England and her Colonies in opposition to us."[19]

Although he probably overstates the case, Dawson highlights the relationship of British actions to Bismarck's adoption of a colonial policy:

Germany never forgot that she obtained hardly one of her early protectorates without having first to overcome resistance from the British Government, and that in nearly every case this opposition was based, not upon any claim of prior occupation, but upon the tacit assumption that territories adjacent to British possessions, which had escaped appropriation, could not properly be claimed by any other country. . . . It is hardly too much to say that the strongest effective impulse to German colonization came from England. . . . It was only when [Bismarck] found himself face to face with opposition that . . . he threw himself into the competition for territory.[20]

In deciding to shift from a purely European foreign policy to one that allowed for efforts to establish an overseas colonial empire, Bismarck was not engaging in the sort of aggressive opportunism that characterized his policies between 1862 and 1871. Rather, he was acting out of a sense of domestic political necessity and a desire to maintain Germany's position relative to the other European powers. Inaction, it was believed, would bring a deterioration of that position.[21] Colonial acquisition, even if halting and tentative, was viewed as a matter of long-range necessity.

Although Bismarck would not remain in office for the balance of the decade, his successor, General Leo von Caprivi, himself a long-time opponent of colonial expansion, was likewise converted to the cause. In his maiden speech before the Reichstag, Caprivi noted: "I . . . believe that those who knew me before I took office know that I was not then an admirer of the colonial policy, but regarded it as dangerous. I am, however, convinced that, as matters now stand, we cannot go back without heavy loss. Nothing is left for us to do but advance."[22]

HELIGOLAND AND THE ANGLO-GERMAN RIVALRY
ON THE UPPER NILE

In the 1880s German traders and explorers became active in the scramble for territory across the African continent. By decade's end an acute Anglo-German rivalry had developed and threatened to disrupt the overall bilateral relationship. In particular, serious differences emerged with respect to German expansion into territories in East Africa that constituted the approaches to the upper Nile. The British feared that foreign control of the Nile's upper waters could endanger Egypt's most important water supply. Critical from the British standpoint were the lake regions in Uganda and the Sudan, which the British had abandoned amid an Islamic insurrection in 1884. Lacking sufficient funds for reconquest because of financial difficulties associated with Egyptian administration, the British prime minister, Lord Salisbury, feared attempts by the other colonial powers to establish themselves in the region.[23]

One of the best approaches to the lakes region was from the East African coast, opposite Zanzibar and north to Mombassa and Witu, where the Germans were firmly entrenched. But as long as Bismarck was directing German affairs, Salisbury did not much fear a German move into the upper Nile, believing that the chancellor would reject a course in Africa that might disturb alignments in Europe.[24] In March 1890, however, Bismarck left the service of the Reich and its new emperor, Wilhelm II, a departure Salisbury characterized as "an enormous calamity of which the effects will be felt in every part of Europe."[25]

Notwithstanding the new emperor's pro-British sympathies, Salisbury viewed the new government as fundamentally unreliable, particularly with regard to colonial affairs.[26] Although British and German claims along the East African coastline had been delimited by an exchange of notes in October 1886, there was no agreement with regard to the territories extending into the interior from these coastal strips.[27] By 1890 German and British colonialists were asserting rival claims to these territories under competing theories of entitlement. The situation in Africa was outlined by Salisbury in a memorandum to his colleagues in the cabinet in June:

The claims of the Germans rest simply upon the doctrine of *Hinterland,* which they have to a great extent invented, and which in their arguments appears to mean that, if you have possession in an uncivilised country, you have a right to extend those possessions to an unlimited distance inland from the sea, until you strike the frontier of another civilised country. On this ground they claim to extend their territory westward, both to the south and the north of Lake Tanganyika, till it abuts on the frontier of the Congo State. . . .The English, on the contrary, rest their claims upon two grounds. In the first place they have a claim, for which it is not very easy to discover any international foundation, that they shall have an unbroken stretch of territory from Cape Town on the south to Lado, the point at which the Nile becomes navigable, on the north, and that this stretch of territory shall only be broken by the waterway of Lake Tanganyika. Secondly, a far more tenable ground of claim consists in the fact that, on the south of Lake Tanganyika the English originally discovered and have now for many years . . . occupied the territory which the Germans claim.[28]

With no agreement to constrain German efforts at expansion into the hinterlands, the news that the German colonialist Karl Peters was leading an expedition from the East African coast into the Sudan led Salisbury to conclude that the security of the Nile was seriously threatened.[29] British concerns were further raised when Baron von Marschall, Bismarck's replacement as foreign minister, denied the existence of any agreement with respect to the hinterlands west of Lake Victoria, territory that the British regarded as part of Uganda and Bismarck had always acknowledged was within the British sphere of influence.[30] Discussing the African situation in the House of Lords, Salisbury admitted that "causes of collision and friction . . . were becoming serious and dangerous."[31]

Decisional Frame

Throughout the scramble for unsettled territory in the African interior, the German leadership judged prospective outcomes in large part as they affected Germany's status relative to the other colonial powers, Britain in particular.[32] That equality of status vis-à-vis Great Britain was important to the German leadership, both for its impact on German domestic politics and on international affairs, is evidenced in documents detailing deliberations over African policy.

For example, in 1885 Bismarck subordinated German interests in Egypt to the larger goal of securing a colonial presence in Africa in a memorandum to his ambassador to Britain: "I beg you . . . not to forget that Egypt in itself is quite indifferent to us and is merely a means of overcoming England's objections to our Colonial aspirations. The smallest corner of New Guinea or West Africa, even if worthless in itself, is just now of greater import to our policy than the whole of Egypt and its future."[33]

The feeling that Britain was obstructing Germany's legitimate rights to empire lingered. In December 1889 Herbert Bismarck[34] complained that the British did not appreciate the "equality of rights" enjoyed by Germany in Africa,[35] and in April 1890 Hatzfeldt suggested to Salisbury that any settlement should include a "general principle" to secure equal rights for the development and expansion of each country's territories in Africa.[36] Insofar as Germany's bid for colonies was driven by a desire to assert and maintain equality of status with the other colonial powers in Africa and prevent Germany's being locked out of the colonial enterprise, any outcome that allowed for the chimera of an expanding, far-flung colonial empire could be sustained as a gain for German prestige.

Up to the point of Salisbury's Heligoland offer, German decision makers promoted reciprocal concessions in the East African hinterlands as the best means for achieving a settlement. However, efforts at arbitration that considered African disputes individually proved unsuccessful in this regard.[37] The British would not accept a settlement that precluded the prospect of an "All-Red Route" from the Cape to Cairo, an outcome the Germans found unacceptable as it would drive a wedge into the back of their possessions and cut them off from the Congo State.[38]

Baseline of Expectation

There is no evidence to suggest that the German leadership expected an offer of European territory as compensation for concessions in Africa.[39] The Heligoland offer was thus unexpected, and it dramatically altered the calculations of the German leadership regarding the utility of restraint and compromise versus continued colonial acquisition in the East African lakes region.

For example, as late as 30 April the German government was steadfast in its opposition to concessions in Witu along the coast of Somalia, a possession they regarded as "full of future promise, which could scarcely be either relinquished or diminished."[40] Two weeks after the Heligoland offer their position was markedly different: "We would, if England cedes Heligoland and promises to support us in acquiring the coastal strip, . . . cede Witu, Manda, Patta, and the Somali Coast, with their Hinterlands to

England."[41] The foreign minister himself acknowledged the reason for the change of policy: "Heligoland having been introduced by Lord Salisbury, this at once becomes our chief consideration, by the side of which our East African interests merely come forward as matters for concession."[42] Why was the Heligoland offer such a powerful means of influencing German calculations and changing German preferences regarding the utility of continued acquisition in East Africa?

The Promise of Heligoland

By May 1890 Salisbury decided that German expeditions into the lake region surrounding the upper Nile could not be ignored, as they challenged important British interests and aroused the consternation of important domestic interest groups.[43] Moreover, he recognized that the unregulated activities of British and German explorers and merchants could lead to hostilities between their respective governments.[44] In addition to disputes over the status of territories on the mainland of Africa, the Germans sought changes in Zanzibar that would diminish British predominance on the island.[45] Thus, Salisbury decided to pursue a comprehensive settlement: to resolve conflicting claims to the African hinterlands as well as disputes over the status of Zanzibar, and, most importantly, to deter German expansion toward the headwaters of the Nile.

Salisbury presented the Germans with an alternative to unrestricted competition in East Africa in a meeting with the German ambassador on 13 May. In exchange for German recognition of British claims to the territories of the upper Nile, the transfer of the Witu province to British control, and the establishment of a British protectorate over Zanzibar, Britain would recognize German rights to a coastal strip opposite Zanzibar and concede German claims to some of the disputed territories surrounding Lakes Nyassa and Tanganyika and in Uganda the territory west of Lake Victoria Nyanza. In addition to these reciprocal concessions in Africa, Salisbury offered the Germans compensation in Europe. By promising to cede the North Sea island of Heligoland to the Reich, Salisbury sought to deter further German expansion in East Africa and more particularly into the territories surrounding the upper Nile.[46]

Although the colonialist Karl Peters dismissed it as nothing more than "a bathtub in the North Sea," for which the Reich had sacrificed "two kingdoms, Witu and Uganda," the island of Heligoland was highly valued

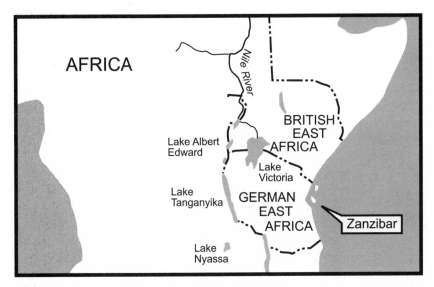

Map 1. Colonial East Africa, circa 1890

by the German leadership, both as a strategic asset and as a tangible reward for foregone expansion in the territory surrounding the upper Nile.[47]

Commanding the mouths of the Elbe and Weser Rivers and the western opening of the *Nord-Ostsee Kanal* (Kiel Canal) then under construction, Heligoland was viewed by Caprivi and the kaiser as a potential source of threat if held by a hostile power. In a war it could provide the British or an allied fleet with a coaling station and convenient shelter. It could be used to enforce a blockade of the northern ports and prevent German ships from leaving the Baltic Sea in a war with Britain or France, or from entering the Baltic for a war against Russia.[48] Thus, Marschall informed Hatzfeldt in London "that the possession of Heligoland is of supreme importance to us and by far the most serious matter in the whole negotiation. His Majesty shares the Chancellor's opinion that without Heligoland the Kiel Canal is useless to our Navy. We shall, therefore, always regard the acquisition of Heligoland as a gain in itself, even against the concessions mentioned in my telegram, or any other similar ones in the colonies."[49] For his part Kaiser Wilhelm II never retreated from the position that the offer of Heligoland was of great importance: "I was firmly resolved to win back Heligoland, that island lying close in front of the great waterways leading to the principal Hanseatic commercial ports. In the hands of the British it was a con-

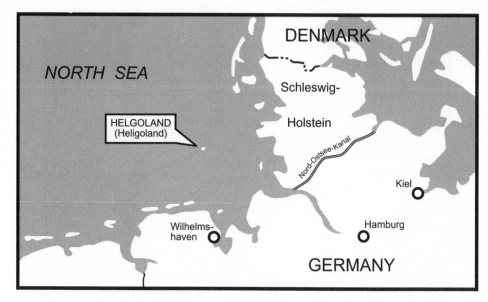

Map 2. German North Sea Coast

stant menace to Hamburg and Bremen, and rendered impossible any project for building up a navy. To exchange Zanzibar was not a loss, but a gain."[50]

In addition to its strategic value, the German leadership saw in Heligoland the domestic political cover necessary to sell concessions in Africa. Marschall noted that the agreement was structured "in a way which will give so little cause of complaint to the Jingos either in England or in Germany."[51] Although colonialists in both Germany and Britain were vocal critics of the agreement—placing greater value on concessions made by their respective governments than those received from the other side[52]—public opinion in Germany was in general quite favorable. Much was made of the fact that former German territory and kindred folk were to be reunited with the fatherland, and the proposition that Heligoland was a strategic asset was widely accepted.[53]

For many people in both countries the importance of the agreement was found less in its impact on immediate conflicts in Africa and more for its implications for a long-term Anglo-German entente. This was especially true for the opposition press in Germany, who pointed to the cession of Heligoland as evidence of England's goodwill and stressed the value of England to the Triple Alliance.[54] In London the *Times* consistently highlighted the benefits of the agreement and of an Anglo-German entente and at one point concluded that "the last of our trifling difficulties with Germany disappeared when the delimitation of the British and German spheres of influence in Africa was finally arranged. . . . The union of England and Germany in the cause of peace and civilization may be as solid and valuable as if it were embodied in a formal treaty."[55] Although motivated to conclude an agreement by the immediate crisis in Africa, Salisbury too recognized the value of an Anglo-German entente and used the prospects for such in his efforts to persuade the queen to accept the cession of British territory.[56] Likewise, Caprivi regarded the agreement as the start of a new period of Anglo-German cooperation.[57]

Summary

By May 1890 Lord Salisbury concluded that German expansion from the East African coast toward the headwaters of the Nile threatened British interests in Egypt and had to be addressed. By conceding German claims to territory around Lakes Nyassa and Tanganyika, granting Germany a strip of coastline opposite Zanzibar, and, most importantly, promising the cession of Heligoland in the North Sea, Salisbury hoped to manipulate the cost-benefit calculus of the German leadership in a way that would deter further expansion. On 10 June Salisbury reported to the queen that the cabinet "unanimously and earnestly" recommended the proposed African settlement: "Under this arrangement the whole of the country outside the confines of Abyssinia and Gallaland will be under British influence up to Khartoum, so far as any European competitor is concerned."[58]

Salisbury's effort was successful, due to the value the German leadership placed on the acquisition of Heligoland, the recognition and guarantee of Germany's status as a colonial power, and the prospect that the agreement presaged a cooperative future and a general Anglo-German entente. Each element of the British offer was an improvement relative to the German leadership's expectations for the future. Thus, each represents a promise as defined in chapter 2. In 1890 British promises deterred German expansion into East Africa, and the agreement led to a period of Anglo-British amity in colonial as well as continental affairs that lasted for at least four years.[59]

THE MORROCAN CRISES

The series of crises in the early part of the twentieth century involving the status of Morocco and the rights of the great powers in that North African state are of long-standing interest to historians and political scientists alike. For many historians the Moroccan question is regarded as a "political barometer" of the European diplomatic scene, a measure of the strength of continental alliances and alignments and the prospect for war among the great powers. The constellation of powers that crystallized at the time of the First Moroccan Crisis (1904–6) was of enduring significance, largely unchanged in July 1914. For political scientists interested in the theory and practice of deterrence, the Moroccan crises have served as case material for the testing of propositions regarding the efficacy of threats,[60] the degree to which the reputations of the protagonists influenced the course of each crisis,[61] and the analysis of bargaining strategies and relative bargaining advantage enjoyed by Germany and France.[62]

This section examines the motives of German decision makers who chose to confront France in 1905 and again in 1911 over unilateral efforts to change the status quo and establish French hegemony in Morocco. The analysis centers on the influence techniques employed by France and Great Britain in their efforts to deter armed intervention by Germany—either in Morocco or against France itself—and to secure German acquiescence to the proposed changes in Morocco. Over the course of the conflict both threats and promises were used in attempts to influence the German decision calculus, with very different results. The Germans were willing to accommodate the French in Morocco provided they were both consulted and given adequate compensation for any losses they might sustain. When confronted with coercive threats, however, the German leadership did not conclude that the costs associated with a firm stand in Morocco were too high; rather, they concluded that the stakes involved were even higher than originally believed. In response to threats from France and Britain, Germany did not back down. Rather, the German leadership most often issued counterthreats that led to increased levels of hostility.

THE FIRST MOROCCAN CRISIS

As Lebow and Stein have demonstrated in their critiques of standard deterrence theory, international conflicts emerge within political contexts that often do not correspond to the scholar's analytic constructs. For example, although Schelling is both persuasive and successful in conceptually differentiating deterrence from compellence, the establishment of a particular instance of coercion as a case of one or the other through empirical observation may prove exceedingly difficult. Similarly, "the attempt to interpret strategies of conflict management within their political contexts . . . introduces a significant element of subjectivity in the selection and coding of deterrence cases. Even if we make the generally unwarranted assumption that a state speaks with only one voice, any deterrence encounter involves two parties, and any extended deterrence encounter involves at least three. Each of these parties is likely to have its own perspective. When those perspectives differ significantly, it may be impossible to assign the roles of challenger or defender with reference to objective criteria."[63]

The First Moroccan Crisis is an example of a case that defies straightforward classification. For instance, in one study Huth and Russett coded Germany as the attacker and France as the defender.[64] In subsequent work they have broken the crisis into two phases. In the first phase they code France as the challenger with respect to Morocco and Germany as the defender. In the second phase Germany is coded as the challenger with respect to France, Britain the defender.[65] Lebow and Stein challenge the status of the case as a deterrence encounter.[66] A review of the documentary record reveals elements of both deterrence and compellence although the case clearly falls within the realm of coercion.

For example, Germany clearly sought to use the prospect of a war with France to compel the French prime minister to abandon the policy of *pénétration pacifique* in Morocco, remove the foreign minister from office, and accede to an international conference to resolve the question of Moroccan reforms. On the other hand, Britain and France sought to deter German aggression through a haphazard strategy that eventually incorporated the use of both threats and promises.

Ultimately, classifications should be judged by the degree to which they prove useful in illuminating causal processes and aid in the establishment of generalizable propositions. In some sense classifications must follow from the questions the analyst asks and the demands of the particular research program he or she is pursuing. This study—which looks at the use of threats and promises by the European powers to influence German behavior across a range of cases—focuses on how France and Britain influenced German calculations regarding resort to force as a means of challenging French plans to establish hegemony in Morocco.

Overview of the Crisis

The origins of the First Moroccan Crisis are to be found in the plans of the French foreign minister, Théophile Delcassé, to establish French hegemony in Morocco. Delcassé had long believed that the acquisition of Morocco would secure French predominance in North Africa as well as its position as a great Mediterranean power.[67] However, the independence of Morocco under the sultan as well as equal commercial rights for foreign powers were guaranteed by the European powers and the United States in a treaty at the Madrid Conference in 1880.[68] Thus, Delcassé set about securing the approval of the signatory powers for a policy of French *pénétration pacifique* in Morocco.

His first target was Italy, with which he reached accord in January 1902. Offering recognition of Italian rights in Tripoli in exchange for Italian recognition of French predominance in Morocco, Delcassé not only promoted his goals in Africa but also weakened the Triple Alliance in Europe.[69]

In the wake of the French defeat at Fashoda, Delcassé negotiated the Entente Cordiale with Great Britain, an agreement that resolved outstanding colonial disputes between the two. Signed on 8 April 1904, the Entente provided for French rights in Egypt to be relinquished in favor of Great Britain, in exchange for which Britain transferred its rights in Morocco to France. The agreement permitted commercial restriction at the end of thirty years and thus violated the open door policy guaranteed at Madrid. The British and French governments further pledged "to afford to one another their diplomatic support, in order to obtain the execution of the clauses of the present Declaration regarding Egypt and Morocco."[70]

With the completion of the Entente Cordiale, Delcassé turned toward Spain, beginning negotiations with the Spanish ambassador at Paris on 19 April. By October agreement was reached, and the two governments issued a public declaration of Spanish adherence to the Anglo-French accords of 8 April. The agreement also contained a secret convention that looked toward the ultimate partition of Morocco between France and Spain, the former to receive the lion's share of the territory.[71]

Thus, through a series of bilateral arrangements, Delcassé sought to extend French influence in Morocco and to change the status quo—equality of rights for foreign powers—as defined by the Treaty of Madrid. Upon the signing of the Anglo-French agreement, Delcassé began to pursue a policy of *pénétration pacifique* and secured a preliminary parliamentary appropriation of 600,000 francs with which to begin that work.[72]

In January 1905 the foreign minister sent Saint-René Taillander to Fez with instructions to convince the sultan to accept a series of reforms, the practical result of which would be the institutionalization of French political and economic preponderance in Morocco.[73] In his discussions with the sultan, Taillander asserted that France had the approval of all interested European powers for the proposed reforms and was acting under their mandate.

The assertion, however, was somewhat misleading. For although Delcassé had secured the support of Italy, Britain, and Spain, throughout the course of his diplomatic initiative he purposefully ignored Germany, whose economic interests in Morocco were overshadowed only by those of Britain and France.[74] Paul Cambon, French ambassador at London, and Bihourd, the ambassador at Berlin, warned of the dangers inherent in neglecting German interests in Morocco, a concern shared by Delcassé's British counterpart, Lord Lansdowne.[75] But Delcassé chose to ignore their advice—and Germany—because he believed that the price of German cooperation in Morocco would be the reaffirmation of the Treaty of Frankfurt and French renunciation of the provinces of Alsace and Lorraine. With the support of Great Britain, Italy, and Spain assured, and the French alliance with Russia in good order, Delcassé believed that Germany was relatively isolated and in no position to challenge French designs.[76] But the perspective of the German leadership was quite different.

With the French representative arrived at Fez and actively pressing the sultan to accept the French reform plan, the German leadership decided that some action was necessary to both defend German interests in Morocco and assert German status as a great power. In February the German representative in Morocco began encouraging the sultan to resist the French demands, assuring him that Germany had a political interest in the Moroccan question and intended to engage the French government over the issue, although he took pains to avoid committing the German government to any particular course of action.[77] Whereas the French foreign minister believed Germany to be diplomatically isolated, the German leadership was convinced that a policy aimed at the preservation of the open door and equality of rights would receive at least the tacit support of the powers, Britain and the United States in particular.[78] Later that February it was announced that the kaiser would stop off at Tangier on a Mediterranean cruise in March. The German chancellor, Bernhard von Bülow, outlined the government's objectives in a letter to the kaiser: "Your Majesty's visit to Tangier will embarrass M. Delcassé, traverse his schemes, and further our business interests in Morocco."[79]

On 31 March 1905 the Germans precipitated a crisis with the kaiser's landing in Tangier. Responding to the public welcome of the sultan's representative, the kaiser announced: "It is to the Sultan in his quality as an independent sovereign that I make my visit today. I hope that under the sovereignty of the Sultan, a free Morocco will remain open to pacific competition of all nations without monopoly and without exclusion, on the footing of absolute equality. My visit to Tangier is intended to make known that I have decided to do everything in my power to safeguard effectively German interests in Morocco, since I consider the Sultan an absolutely free sovereign."[80]

The crisis escalated in the weeks following the kaiser's Tangier declarations, and by mid-April many in the French government feared that the crisis over Morocco would result in another war between France and Germany. Delcassé was urged by the council of ministers to open direct discussions with Germany in order to avoid such an outcome. But instead of seeking an agreement with Germany similar to those he had negotiated with Britain and Spain, Delcassé took the position that he need only resolve any misunderstandings that might have arisen with regard to French policy in Morocco.[81]

For its part the German leadership had succeeded in precipitating a crisis but failed to develop a coherent set of goals, or a strategy for achieving them. In the foreign ministry Holstein came to believe that the kaiser had put German prestige on the line by asserting a German interest in the Moroccan reforms. In a memorandum of 3 April he wrote: "A retreat would stand on the same level with Olmütz and cause Fashoda to be forgotten."[82] But Germany had long denied any territorial ambitions in Morocco; the kaiser himself had foresworn any territorial claims in an interview with the king of Spain at Vigo a year before.[83] Thus, Bülow decided upon a policy that disclaimed any territorial ambitions in Morocco, demanded commercial equality for all nations, and called for an international conference such as that held at Madrid to decide the entire issue of Moroccan reform.[84] The chancellor also pledged German support to the sultan if he should advocate a conference of the powers.[85]

By proposing a conference of the Madrid signatories, the German leadership sought to place France in the wrong, and Germany in the position of defending the rights of the powers and the status quo in Morocco. Germany expected support from a majority of the powers for the conference proposal, and if Britain failed to support France, Germany might contribute to the early demise of the Entente Cordiale.[86]

Although the British government recognized that Delcassé was largely responsible for the crisis, the kaiser's visit to Tangier was regarded as much a challenge to Britain as to France. The British did not believe that Germany's only goal was the preservation of the open door. Rather, they suspected that Germany wanted a port on Morocco's Atlantic coast. As an important component of British foreign policy at this point was the prevention of German expansion in the colonial world,[87] Britain staunchly and publicly supported Delcassé against German demands for a new conference over the status of Morocco.[88]

If Delcassé enjoyed the staunch support of His Majesty's Government in London, it was not so in Paris. Prime Minister Rouvier as well as a large portion of the assembly and public opinion feared another war with Germany and supported a policy of negotiations and concessions. Although he too rejected the idea of another Moroccan conference, Rouvier believed that a bilateral settlement similar to those reached with Britain and Spain would appease Germany. In a bitter parliamentary debate on 19 April, Delcassé was assailed for having ignored Germany's interests and brought the country to the brink of war. In order to quell the uproar and save his government, Rouvier announced that he was assuming personal responsibility for foreign policy and that negotiations were already underway with Berlin.[89]

Delcassé offered his resignation on 22 April, but withdrew it at the request of both President Loubet and Prime Minister Rouvier.[90] The foreign minister's days, however, were numbered. Negotiations between Germany and France continued into May, yet French press attacks against Delcassé and his provocative foreign policy continued. Through a number of sources, Bülow concluded that Rouvier was eager to be rid of Delcassé and that German demands for his dismissal might meet with success.[91] Germany presented such demands in mid-May. On 28 May the sultan rejected French reform proposals and called for an international conference. Bülow warned Rouvier that inasfar as the sultan had accepted the German point of view, Germany "would follow up the consequences if France continued the policy of intimidation and violence hitherto pursued by M. Delcassé."[92] At a cabinet meeting on 6 June, Delcassé defended his Moroccan policy while Rouvier argued that it would result in war. Without a single supporter, Delcassé resigned.

Rouvier had decided that Delcassé's departure was necessary if France and Germany were to reach a bilateral settlement of the dispute. Holstein and Bülow had come to regard Delcassé as the chief obstacle to French acceptance of their proposal for a multilateral conference. Thus, the two sides were no nearer to an agreement than before: Rouvier believing that French acceptance of a conference would be a humiliation, Bülow rejecting offers for a bilateral settlement.

The sense of crisis reached a new high in mid-June. Upon receiving a report that Britain had offered an alliance to France, Holstein arranged to have an article published by an intimate of the kaiser that argued that "Germany can only conduct a war with England . . . in France."[93] Lansdowne denied the offer of an alliance to the German ambassador at London but added that in the event of a Franco-German war he could not be certain of the extent to which British public opinion would demand his government's support of France.[94] In this atmosphere the two sides reached a compromise on the question of a Moroccan conference.

In the "Accord on the Program of the Conference," signed on 28 September, France agreed to attend a conference in Algeciras in exchange for a German guarantee not to pursue any goals that would conflict with any rights France had secured through treaties or other arrangements, provided these rights accorded with the following principles: the independence and sovereignty of the sultan, the integrity of his empire, the open door with commercial equality for foreign powers, the introduction of political and financial reforms regulated by international accord, and the recognition of France's special position in Morocco as created by the contiguity of Algeria with Morocco.[95]

Thirteen states were represented at the Algeciras Conference held from 16 January to 7 April 1906. Germany entered the conference rather confident of the support of a majority of the neutral powers, and both Bülow and Holstein believed that the arrival of Lord Grey in the British foreign ministry had improved the prospects for Anglo-German cooperation.[96] But although Grey was uninterested in the specific issues under dispute in Morocco, the wider political implications of a French defeat led him to support the French—even when he believed them to be in the wrong.[97] Among the other powers only Austria-Hungary and Morocco supported Germany, Austria-Hungary rather begrudgingly.[98]

The principal issues for resolution at the conference were the establishment of a police force, a state bank, and the rights of the powers with respect to trade (the open door). Germany hoped to concede French predominance in the matter of the bank in order to secure international control of the police. France insisted on French and Spanish control of the police in exchange for guaranteeing the open door.

The conference concluded on 7 June with the signing of the "General

Act of the International Conference of Algeciras," which asserted the continued independence and integrity of Morocco under the sultan, and freedom of trade and equal rights for the powers in the economic development of the Sherifian Empire. Monitored by a Swiss inspector-general, the police were to be organized and trained by France in five port towns, by Spain in three, and by officials from both countries in Tangier and Casablanca. The new state bank was to be supervised by France, Germany, Britain, and Spain, with France enjoying a privileged position.

As France clearly emerged from the conference with an enhanced political position by virtue of its control over the police and an economic advantage by virtue of its position in the state bank, the Algeciras agreement has generally been viewed as a victory for France and a diplomatic defeat for Germany.[99] However, if one examines the motives behind Germany's precipitation of the crisis and compares these to the outcome, the result is more ambiguous. Insofar as the independence and integrity of Morocco were again affirmed, and equal commercial rights guaranteed, the Algeciras agreement secured for the German leadership what they most wanted in Morocco and what otherwise might have been threatened had Delcassé's plans gone unchallenged. The German leadership also succeeded in demonstrating that Morocco's fate could not be settled absent German participation. But as Germany emerged more isolated in terms of European alignments, the First Moroccan Crisis was a defeat for the larger strategy of Holstein, who predicted that by standing firm, Germany would force Britain to abandon France and thus weaken the Entente Cordiale.

The German leadership did not want another war with France.[100] However, Germany did threaten war if its interests were ignored in Morocco. Fearing such an outcome, the French and British tried to avert it. The case presents an interesting focus of analysis as both threats and promises were used in an effort to influence German behavior.

Decisional Frame

German decision makers evaluated prospective outcomes in Morocco as they affected the status quo as defined by the Treaty of Madrid (1880). Germany, as a signatory to that treaty, enjoyed the right of most-favored nation. Further, the Treaty of Madrid accorded Germany (and all signatories) the right to veto prospective changes to the terms of the agreement. Thus, any changes that diminished German commercial equality vis-à-vis the other signatory powers in Morocco, or changes that might be undertaken by some grouping of those powers without German consent, were viewed as threats to German interests and prestige. Delcassé's goal of securing French primacy in Morocco through a series of bilateral ententes, ignoring and marginalizing Germany in the process, thus presented the German leadership with a loss on both these dimensions.

Although the erratic course of German strategy during the First Moroccan Crisis probably obscured for contemporaries the underlying motives of German policy, the documentary record is remarkably consistent with regard what those motives were. In an internal foreign ministry memorandum dated 3 June 1904, Holstein wrote:

In acquiring Morocco France entirely ignored the justified interests of third parties, with the exception of Spain, to whom, at England's desire, she is ready to make certain territorial concessions. It is undeniable that the losses which third Powers would suffer through the gradual absorption of Morocco by France would be immensely greater than any injury or loss caused by the new arrangements in Egypt. . . .To-day Morocco is one of the few countries where Germany can compete freely in trade. . . . Even more alarming would be the injury to Germany's prestige. . . . Not only for material reasons, but also in order to protect her prestige, Germany must protest against France's intention to acquire Morocco. The point to be made good is as follows: France's evident scheme to absorb Morocco finishes the free competition of foreign countries and involves sensible injury to the interests of third parties, especially Germany. For long we have clung to the belief that France would seek an understanding with the Powers interested. . . . The German Government intends to oppose the wrong involved when one Power injures the interests of another in neutral territory without that Power's consent.[101]

In instructions for the kaiser's Tangier visit, the chancellor similarly argued "that the systematic exclusion of all non-French merchants and promoters from Morocco according to the example of Tunis would signify an important economic loss for Germany. . . . Delcassé has completely ignored us in this affair."[102] In early April, stressing the equality of rights guaranteed the signatories of the Madrid Treaty, the German government sought support in Washington for a conference and the maintenance of the status quo in Morocco:

It is to be expected that France, if she accepts a conference, will be guided by the hope that she can thereby further her advantage. . . . Germany seeks no gain, but will defend her interests by supporting the equality of rights of all nations. . . . President Roosevelt will surely understand that honor, and that which is connected with it, is more important for us than the matter of interests. Both honor and interests, however, are inextricably linked.[103]

Not only would a conference defend German rights and interests in Morocco, but contrary to the arguments of those who assert that Germany sought a crushing diplomatic defeat of France, the German leadership appears to have believed that a collective solution to the crisis would be less damaging to French prestige, thus making it more likely that France would agree to German demands for equality. "Contractual collectivity," Holstein concluded, "is a principle on which we can take a firm stand without ourselves appearing to harbor aggressive intentions. Moreover, this idea has the advantage that while affecting French interests, it does not affect French pride, just as the collective victories of 1814 were not so great an insult as the German victory, gained alone, in 1870."[104]

Although Bülow remained open to a bilateral arrangement with France that might contain territorial compensation for the relinquishment of German rights in Morocco, territorial gain was not the motive for the policies adopted by the German leadership. The kaiser, it will be remembered, disclaimed any interest in Moroccan territory in his discussions with the king of Spain in March 1904, a position Bülow felt constrained to maintain. Moreover, the bulk of German public opinion was opposed to further colonial expansion in 1905.[105] Consequently, Germany did not seek gain in Morocco; rather it hoped to defend commercial equality by supporting the status quo:

For the present, German policy must be governed by the fact that His Majesty the Kaiser last year at Vigo declared to the King of Spain that he has enough African possessions and wishes no territory in Morocco but only the maintenance of commercial freedom. Such a declaration naturally does not bind one forever, but in the year that has passed since those remarks, the effect of events in Southwest Africa has been of a nature to increase the antagonism to colonial acquisitions by military force with His Majesty as with a great part of the German people. Even if, therefore, France were inclined to permit us to conquer a part of Morocco, we would for the present perhaps not be in a position to take advantage of this overture.[106]

The principal motives for German policy in 1905–6 related to French plans for a protectorate in Morocco, but as the crisis developed, the German leadership recognized the opportunity to strike a blow against the Entente Cordiale and frustrate efforts to extend it to Russia. Believing that the British would be forced to support the maintenance of the open door at a Moroccan conference, Holstein concluded that France would become disillusioned with the Entente and come to recognize the desirability of reconciliation with Germany. In this way Germany could begin to break out of the encircling alliances that had begun to emerge in Europe: France and

Russia connected by the Dual Alliance, France and England through the Entente Cordiale, Italy and Spain each attached with France through colonial arrangements.

A number of historians contend that a desire to strike a blow against the Entente Cordiale was the *principal* motive of German policy in the First Moroccan Crisis.[107] The evidence to support such a claim is not strong. A review of the documentary record shows that a weakening of the Entente was regarded as a welcome side benefit of a strategy that had as its chief aim the defense of German rights in Morocco.[108] For example, in a foreign ministry memorandum of 7 April 1905 it was noted: "Naturally the achievement would be greater if there followed from a conference a break in the Anglo-French accord over Morocco." In response, the chancellor minuted: "We do not desire that at all, or at least we should in no instance show such an aim. We only wish to preserve our rights in Morocco."[109] However, Bülow and Holstein were not unaware that a German success in Morocco would necessarily upset the Anglo-French settlement and thus carried implications for the future development of the Entente.

Delcassé's plans for French *pénétration pacifique* in Morocco threatened German commercial interests. By disregarding German's right under the Treaty of Madrid to be consulted over Moroccan reforms, Delcassé challenged German prestige. Thus, the German leadership's policy during the First Moroccan Crisis, although intended to confront France with the possibility of war, was guided by defensive motives. It aimed at preserving German commercial interests in Morocco and German prestige among the great powers. It was dedicated to defending those rights accorded Germany by international agreement at Madrid. German commercial interests would be defended by support for the status quo in Morocco. German prestige would be defended through the convening of an international conference, a forum wherein Germany could assert its right to be consulted over Moroccan reform as a signatory to the Madrid Treaty. If in the course of defending German rights in Morocco a blow could be struck against the Entente Cordiale, so much the better.

Threats, Promises, and the Resolution of the Crisis

The focus of this section is the effects of French and British signals on German decision making in the Moroccan crisis. Evaluating prospective outcomes in the domain of loss, the arguments presented in chapter 3 would lead us to expect that British and French threats would prove ineffective in moderating German policy toward Morocco because they would reinforce the motives giving rise to the policy. By contrast, we would expect promises and assurances aimed at redressing German fears of loss in Morocco would prove potent tools of influence.

For their part the German leadership settled on a strategy of defending German treaty rights by advocating an international conference to discuss the French proposals for reform in Morocco. There was little doubt in Berlin that the conference proposal would be accepted, and the leadership was quite certain what the alignment of powers at such a conference would be: America would support German demands for the continuation of the open door; England would follow the United States; Spain would support the status quo as the best way to maintain its position in Morocco; Austria would support its ally Germany; Italy would be held in check, if necessary by a promise of progress on the irredentist question; and given its weakened position by virtue of the war with Japan, Russia would remain neutral.[110]

At least until Delcassé's departure, French diplomacy during the First Moroccan Crisis suffered from the effects of divided counsel and consequent lack of consistency. Delcassé was a champion of the Entente Cordiale and had become a committed anglophile.[111] He was determined to achieve his designs in Morocco through the adoption of a hard line with respect to any protests that might emanate from Germany. Rouvier, by contrast, placed a lower value on the British connection and had been an advocate of rapprochement with Germany.

The British were consistent in their policies toward Germany during the First Moroccan Crisis. Most in the government believed that German demands constituted a direct challenge to the Entente, to which Britain was becoming increasingly committed.[112] Delcassé was rightly thought to be the most determined advocate of the Entente in the French government; thus the British settled on a policy of supporting the policies of the French foreign minister. That decision was buttressed by concerns emanating from the admiralty that without firm British support, Delcassé would be forced to bargain, and the price for German acceptance of French preponderance would be a port on the Atlantic coast of Morocco, an outcome they wished to prevent.[113] Despite second thoughts in the aftermath of Delcassé's fall, as well as a change in government in London, British policy remained one of steadfast support for France throughout the crisis.[114]

Holstein clearly miscalculated with regard to the position Britain would adopt. He had been convinced that Britain would abandon France in the

Moroccan affair, especially after Germany reached a separate arrangement with Britain over Egypt in June 1904. And once the conference opened, it became clear that Holstein had made another miscalculation: The United States would not go out on a limb for Germany over the open door in Morocco.

A number of scholars have argued that the German leadership was motivated to adopt an aggressive policy in the Moroccan question based on the belief that Germany could prevail diplomatically and if need be militarily in a war against an isolated France. The explanation for Germany's willingness to agree to a diplomatic solution is thus to be found in the threat of British intervention and absence of diplomatic support from the United States, which forced German decision makers to recognize their miscalculation and back down.

In fact, the German leadership was convinced that they would prevail in a war with France. In April 1905 Bülow asked the General Staff for its estimation of the likely outcome of such a conflict. He was particularly interested in the prospect of Russian participation on the French side. However, having been defeated by Japan in the Far East and facing mounting revolution at home, Russia was in no position provide assistance. Thus, General von Schlieffen, Chief of the General Staff, suggested that Germany might exploit what in 1905 was a favorable military situation.[115]

In January 1906 General von Moltke, Schlieffen's successor at the General Staff, likewise submitted a report to the chancellor on the status of French and German forces and the prospects for another Franco-German war:

In my opinion the French consider that to yield further now in the Morocco question would not befit the dignity of their country, seeing that they have already given way and allowed M. Delcassé to fall.

Nevertheless they fear that, as a result of their firm attitude, the conference may not only be unsuccessful, but may even lead to war complications. . . .

Up till now France was, in fact, not sufficiently prepared for war against Germany. It is now known that last summer a Parliamentary Commission examined the condition of the Eastern fortresses with the result that considerable defects were discovered. . . .

The measures for removing these defects have not yet been completed.[116]

Britain was recognized as a potent naval power, but the probable impact of British participation in a war between Germany and France was regarded by most in the German leadership as negligible. Bülow believed that public opinion in England would keep the British out of a continental war, while

Holstein thought that Britain would take advantage of a Franco-German war to make further gains in the colonial world.[117]

But although confident that they could prevail in a war with France, the German leadership was not motivated by perceived opportunity for gain. The British and French had proceeded to settle the Moroccan affair as if Germany were a *quantité négligeable,* and the German leadership was willing to engage in a risky policy in order to demonstrate that Germany could not be ignored.[118] And it was not the threat of British intervention on behalf of France that led the Germans to back down. The prospect of British support for France did not lead the German leadership to conclude that the risks associated with continuing an assertive policy were too high. Rather, Anglo-French cooperation led them to conclude that the issues at stake were well worth the risk of war: "We stand here before a test of strength; a German retreat before Anglo-French resistance would in no way be conducive to bringing about better German-English relations, but would on the contrary provide the English, the French, and the rest of the world practical proof that one achieves most from Germany through rough treatment, and that after the conclusion of the Anglo-French entente, Germany wants to avoid friction with these to powers at any cost."[119]

Indeed, the crisis escalated when the British and French used threats in an effort to influence the course of German diplomacy. By contrast, the crisis de-escalated when France offered concessions and assurances over Morocco. Compromise was facilitated once the German leadership's essential demands were met; additional gains were not seen to be worth the continued risk of war.

For example, the crisis escalated rapidly during the first weeks of April 1905, following the kaiser's landing at Tangier on 31 March. King Edward VII visited Delcassé in Paris, and the semi-official French press spoke of the formation of a new alliance between Britain and France in response to German demands over Morocco. Speaking with Prince Louis of Battenberg, then director of British Naval Intelligence, the kaiser issued a threat of his own: "We know the road to Paris, and we will get there again if needs be. They should remember, no fleet can defend Paris."[120]

Delcassé did not enter into negotiations with Germany in April, despite pressure to do so from fellow ministers as well as some in the British government. Instead, he pursued the limited objective of clarifying any "misunderstandings" Germany might have with regard to French plans for Morocco. Because it neither addressed German concerns regarding the commercial provisions of the Anglo-French accords, nor indicated recognition of Germany's right under the Madrid Treaty to be consulted over changes in the status quo in Morocco, Delcassé's offer failed to influence the course of German policy. Confident that there was indeed no misunderstanding with respect to French plans, the Germans proposed to discuss the matter at a general conference of the signatories of the Treaty of Madrid.[121]

By contrast, the German leadership was "relieved" by Rouvier's offer in late April to drop the thirty-year limitation on the open door in Morocco and to seek a general settlement of the Moroccan question through an exchange of notes between interested powers and France.[122] Had such an offer been extended to Germany in the previous year, the evidence suggests the leadership would have accepted it.[123] But because the kaiser had already declared German support for the sultan, and because the German government had in fact provided assurances of support to the sultan should he demand a conference, the German leadership felt itself unable to accept Rouvier's April offer or a similar offer of bilateral negotiations after Delcassé's fall in June: "A year ago we were free to have negotiated with France on a basis which would have immediately led to a definitive result. Since then M. Delcassé has forced us to seek another standpoint. We cannot leave the Sultan in the lurch at the very moment when, at our advice, he has sent off invitations to the conference."[124]

Although the German leadership felt constrained by its earlier pledges of support for the sultan, they had no intention of elevating the sultan's interests over their own. At this point Berlin believed that support for the sultan bolstered the prospects for their conference proposal. Support for the sultan was thus a tactical move. The leadership believed that the division of the sultanate into spheres of influence was the most likely outcome of a conference of the various powers.[125]

Although Bülow did not accept the French offer to negotiate a bilateral agreement, neither did he take the occasion of Delcassé's dismissal and Rouvier's offer of accommodation as a sign of French weakness and an opportunity to issue new demands.[126] Rather, the German chancellor reiterated his position on the need for an international conference and assured Rouvier that the German government understood French interests in Morocco: "For that reason we offer our hand in leaving the future open."[127]

On 10 June Rouvier suggested that France might attend an international conference if a prior agreement concerning acceptable reforms was reached with Germany. Bülow agreed to negotiate such an agreement if Rouvier first accepted the sultan's invitation to attend the conference, promising the premier that the conference would afford "no injury to the prospects of

France."[128] Finally, on 8 July the two sides reached the compromise agreement on an international conference.

Further agreement was reached over the program for the conference on 28 September, and Bülow signaled his goals for Algeciras in an interview published by *Le Temps* on 3 October:

I think the conference, far from dividing us, ought to contribute to a *rapprochement* between us. For that *rapprochement*, however, one condition is necessary: that French public opinion thoroughly recognize that the policy of isolating Germany is an object of the past. . . . Today as yesterday, provided your colonial policy respects our commercial interests . . . we will not obstruct you, but in case of need will aid you in Morocco and elsewhere.[129]

If the chancellor hoped through his interview to begin the process of reconciliation with France, the response of the French press was not indicative of success. Anderson reports that "not a single French newspaper spoke well of German policy." *Le Matin* used the occasion to publish an account of the French cabinet meeting of 6 June and asserted that Delcassé had presented his colleagues with a British guarantee to "mobilize her fleet, to seize the Kiel Canal, and to land 100,000 men in Schleswig-Holstein," in the event of a war with Germany.[130]

The implicit threat of a British attack provoked a hostile reaction in Berlin. Rather than reconsider the course of German policy, the leadership once again chose to escalate the crisis. The kaiser wanted to recall his ambassador at London, and Bülow fueled a press war, advising the official press that: "It is important that the German public understand how grave the international situation is, how necessary it is to be armed, and how wretched, in view of the seriousness of the world situation, party conflicts and the usual Philistine pettifogging appear."[131] Holstein too supported a firm stand: "Ever since Delcassé's revelations conjuring up the prospect of English military and naval support, the French have been talking more of rectifying 1870. . . . I still continue to believe in only one danger of war, that is the danger arising from the belief [in France and Britain] that we shall yield to firm pressure."[132] Again, the evidence supports the notion that the German leadership saw the outbreak of war as possible, and Holstein appears to have believed that the surest route to war was a continuation of the Anglo-French policy of threatening Germany militarily and denying Germany's legitimate interests in the Moroccan question.

Faced with another escalation, Rouvier signaled anew his willingness to negotiate a bilateral agreement with Germany. Through the former secretary of the French legation at Tangier and a representative of the *Comité du Maroc,* Rouvier made the following offer: The status quo would be maintained in Morocco for a period of three to four years, after which Germany would accept French control of the police. In return, France would guarantee the open door for all time, German participation in 45 percent of all government undertakings in Morocco, territorial compensation in the French Congo, and the transfer to Germany of French preemption rights of purchase in the Belgian Congo.[133]

The terms of the Rouvier's offer would prove to be better than those Germany would negotiate at Algeciras. Yet the German leadership remained unwilling to give up the conference for a side deal with France. The French offer was appealing to both Bülow and Holstein, but they concluded that it could not be accepted. Holstein argued that Rouvier might leak the contents of any secret agreement in a way that would embarrass Germany before the sultan and the other powers. Germany's public statements in support of the continued sovereignty of the sultan and equality of rights for the powers would then appear cynical.[134] Moreover, there were doubts as to the validity of the French offer.[135] If, however, France were to make such an offer at the conference, they agreed that it would be in Germany's interest to accept it.[136]

As with the French offers in April and June, the offer in November 1905 came too late in the course of the First Moroccan Crisis to change German calculations with respect to the utility of a conference. The Germans came to be constrained by their own rhetoric, believing that they could not back away from their demands for an international conference and repeated denials of territorial ambition without damaging their reputation. Moreover, they doubted the utility of a secret agreement that France could later deny or use to embarrass them. Although Germany succeeded in achieving the conference, this success came at the expense of a secure share of future government enterprises in Morocco and territorial compensation in the Congo.

The German leadership would not sacrifice the conference in order to secure the rewards offered by Rouvier in November; neither did they hold out for such gains when the Algeciras conference deadlocked over the issue of the police in March 1906. Bülow maintained the position that Germany's "only object was the principle of the 'open door', i.e., to secure equal trading rights in Morocco," and he regarded the conference as "the best way of settling the Morocco question suitably and peacefully."[137] Thus, once the continuation of the open door was accepted by the conference, and France prevented from dividing up all of Morocco into spheres of influence with Spain, Bülow considered retreat on the secondary issues of the police and state bank as acceptable.[138] Bülow decided to accept French and Spanish control of the police and to make concessions over the issue of the bank during the second week of March, maintaining that "both politically and economically we [have] achieved everything that mattered."[139] Count Monts, German ambassador at Rome, reported on 24 March that in a conversation with the Italian foreign minister he had adopted the position that if "the Conference finally did show some results [it] was due solely to our giving in and our love of peace." In reply to this message Bülow wrote: "This idea is wrong. We can say this to foreigners, especially in Algeciras, and let them think so. In reality we achieved what we intended from the beginning."[140]

THE SECOND MOROCCAN CRISIS

The issues that gave rise to the Second Moroccan Crisis were those of the first: French efforts to expand political and economic control over the Sherifian empire, and German determination to defend its rights in Africa and prestige among the great powers. The episode is important both as another case where the European powers attempted to influence German calculations on the utility of risking war over Morocco and as a milestone on the road to the First World War. As in 1905–6, assurances and promised rewards played a significant role in allowing for a peaceful resolution to the crisis.

Overview of the Crisis

After the Algeciras conference conditions within Morocco did not improve. The sultan's government was nearly bankrupt, and there was widespread insurrection in the countryside. In an effort to stabilize the internal situation, the European powers agreed at the end of 1908 to recognize Mulay Hafid—who had rebelled against his brother, Abd-el-Aziz—as the new Sultan of Morocco.

Disagreements over Moroccan questions continued to strain relations between France and Germany. For example, in September 1908 a dispute arose between them over the fate of five deserters from the French Foreign Legion, three of whom were German nationals. The dispute was eventually resolved by the Hague Tribunal but served to convince both sides of the inadequacy of the Algeciras agreement and of the need to further clarify the nature of their activities in Morocco.

Bilateral negotiations began in January 1909, and on 8 February both sides initialed an accord wherein Germany declared that it was "pursuing only economic interests" and recognized France's "special political interests" in Morocco. For its part the French government of Clemenceau pledged to "safeguard economic equality" in the Sherifian empire and "not to hinder German commercial and industrial interests there." Both declared "that they [would] not pursue nor encourage any measure of a nature to create in their favor or in the favor of any power whatsoever, an economic privilege."[141]

The German leadership appears to have believed that the agreement of 1909 had eliminated Morocco as an area of political discord in Franco-German relations,[142] but the vague language of the accords made their practical application almost impossible. After a brief honeymoon the two sides found it increasingly difficult to agree on a division of economic interests in Morocco. The distinction between purely economic activity and activity with political implications proved a major issue of contention—France attempting to apply the political restriction widely, Germany insisting on a more limited application. It is generally accepted that German activity after 1909 was consistent with the terms of the accords, but France continued to press for advantage.[143]

The French were provided with a new pretext for expansion in Morocco by the inability of the new sultan to restore fiscal and political order. The tribal revolt continued to grow. In January 1911 members of the Zaer tribe attacked a French army unit, killing one Lieutenant Marchand and four other officers. In March the French consul reported back to Paris that the revolt threatened Fez. The commander of French forces in the region requested reinforcements, whereupon the French leadership decided on a course that promised expansion of their political control beyond the terms of Algeciras and the Franco-German accords of 1909. During the first week of April Jules Cambon, French ambassador at Berlin, informed the German government that France might send troops to Rabat and Fez. On 28 April, citing the need to defend the European population, the French government announced the dispatch of an armed column to Fez and their intention to occupy Rabat in order to punish those responsible for the death of Marchand.[144]

The urgency of the moment was somewhat lost on the German leadership. The German consul at Tangier consistently reported that the situation in Fez was greatly exaggerated by the French and that the resident European population was in no imminent danger.[145] When informed of the possibility of French military action, the German foreign minister, Alfred von Kiderlen-Wächter, cautioned France to move slowly and warned that Germany would regard the occupation of Rabat and Fez as contrary to the Algeciras agreement.[146]

But Kiderlen's intention was not to foreclose all French action in Morocco. For the foreign minister allowed that insofar as the Algeciras agreement was arrived at on the "false basis that Morocco is an organized state," Germany was willing to negotiate a new arrangement for Morocco: "If the sovereignty of the sultan disappears, Germany will leave you free to do what you wish with Morocco provided you give her a share. In the meantime, it is necessary to maintain the state of things as they are."[147]

Cambon informed the German government that French troops had begun their march to Fez on 28 April. Kiderlen responded that if the sultan required French troops to maintain his position, Germany would no longer regard the situation as consistent with Algeciras. With the Algeciras agreement no longer in force, Germany would regain its freedom of action in Morocco.[148]

Germany was not alone in its concern regarding the implications of the French action. Spain concluded that France was intent on partitioning Morocco along the lines of the secret protocols to the Franco-Spanish accords of 1904. In early April the Spanish government warned Paris that an occupation of Fez, even if temporary, would alter the status quo in Morocco and leave Spain free to occupy the zone agreed to in 1904. With the French column arrived at Fez, and despite British efforts to deter any Spanish action, Spanish troops landed at Alcazar and Larache on 8 June.[149]

The British also worried about the French occupation of Fez, but more for the European than Moroccan repercussions. The potential effect on Franco-Spanish, and by consequence Spanish-German, relations was clear. Much as it had in 1905–6, the British government feared that a failure to support France in Morocco would lead the French to seek rapprochement with Germany and negate the benefits of the Entente on the continent. Thus, with the approval of Prime Minister Asquith, Grey decided to support the French occupation of Fez.[150]

During discussions with Cambon on 10 and 11 June, Bethmann-Hollweg encouraged the French ambassador to travel to Bad Kissingen so that he might confer with the foreign minister, who was at that time taking the cure. Kiderlen and Cambon held talks at Kissingen on 20 and 21 June. The

German foreign minister argued that neither the Algeciras agreement nor the bilateral accords of 1909 provided for the establishment of a protectorate such as France was in the process of establishing in Morocco. Cambon suggested the need to reach an agreement on the issues that divided the two sides. Kiderlen agreed, but added that "if we restrict our conversation to Morocco, we will not succeed; it is useless to replaster that which has been done on the subject of Morocco and which seems today to be cracked."[151]

As he had in April, Kiderlen signaled Germany's willingness to agree to a new arrangement in Morocco, provided it receive compensation for any rights it might relinquish. Recalling that Kiderlen had once spoken of Mogador, Cambon cautioned that if Germany wished "to have any part of Morocco, it would be better not to commence the conversation." Although he asserted that French opinion would not support the division of Morocco between Germany and France, Cambon allowed that "one might seek [compensation] elsewhere" and agreed to raise the issue of compensation with his government. On taking his leave, Kiderlen left Cambon with a request: "Bring us back something from Paris."[152]

Cambon had scarcely arrived at Paris when the Monis government fell. A new government, under Joseph Caillaux, was not formed until 28 June. In the interim Hollweg and Kiderlen had secured the kaiser's approval for the dispatch of German ships to the coast of Morocco. Returning to Germany from Southwest Africa, the German gunboat *Panther* appeared at Agadir on 1 July. Its mission, as communicated to European capitals by the imperial government, was "to lend, in case of need, aid and succor to her subjects and protégés as well as the considerable German interests engaged in the environs."[153]

The *coup d'Agadir* caught the new French government by surprise and transformed a colonial dispute into a European crisis that threatened to ignite a great power war. The first instinct of the new and inexperienced foreign minister, Justin de Selves, was to send a French warship to Mogador, and he directed Paul Cambon at London to discuss the idea with Grey. But neither Caillaux nor Delcassé (now the naval minister) supported the plan. Caillaux canceled Selves's directive to London and together with Jules Cambon decided to discuss compensation with Germany.[154]

The initial reaction of the British government was moderate. Grey warned the German ambassador, Metternich, that insofar as Britain had interests in Morocco that were larger than Germany's, it would not recognize any new arrangement in Morocco negotiated without its participation.[155] The foreign secretary assured the French government that Britain would fulfill all its obligations to France, but he encouraged a new round of negotiations wherein Britain, France, Germany, and Spain could reach a new agreement over Morocco. Grey suggested that France might consider compensation for Germany, perhaps even in Morocco.[156]

Ignoring the British call for four-power talks, Cambon renewed bilateral negotiations with Kiderlen on 9 July. Attention soon focused on the Congo as the probable region for compensation, but these negotiations deadlocked over the amount of territory France would have to cede to Germany in exchange for a free hand in Morocco. Kiderlen indicated a desire for the region extending from the ocean to the Sangha River, the bulk of the French Congo. Pointing out that the parcel was larger than the entirety of Morocco, Cambon dismissed the German proposal outright.[157]

At this point the German leadership had to decide how far they were willing to go in their desire to secure the Congo territory. Kiderlen argued that France was unlikely to accede to German demands unless it understood that Germany was "determined on the most extreme measures. . . . Who in advance declares that he will not fight, can attain nothing in politics."[158] Although Kiderlen believed that the best way to ensure adequate compensation was to confront France with the prospect of war, the kaiser was less certain that the issues at stake demanded such a risky policy. Upon reading Kiderlen's recommendations, the kaiser cut short a Norwegian cruise. However, when Bethmann-Hollweg adopted Kiderlen's position, the kaiser yielded.[159]

Meanwhile, concern was growing in the British cabinet that France might reach an agreement with Germany that would compromise British interests in Morocco and weaken the Entente. Thus, Asquith and Grey agreed to allow the inclusion of a warning on Morocco in a speech Lloyd George was scheduled to deliver before the bankers' annual dinner at Mansion House.[160] On the evening of July 21 Lloyd George declared that

it is essential in the highest interests, not merely of this country, but of the world, that Britain should at all hazards maintain her place and prestige among the Great Powers of the world. Her potent influence has many a time been in the past, and may yet be in the future, invaluable to the cause of human liberty. It has more than once in the past redeemed Continental nations, who are sometimes too apt to forget that service, from overwhelming disaster, and even from national extinction. I would make great sacrifices to preserve the peace. I conceive that nothing would justify a disturbance of international good-will except questions of the gravest national moment. But if a situation were to be forced upon us in which peace could only be preserved by the surrender of the great and beneficent position Britain has won by centuries of heroism and achievement, by allowing Britain to be treated, where her interests were vitally affected, as if she were of no account in the Cabinet of nations, then I say emphatically that peace at that price would be a humiliation intolerable for a great country like ours to endure. National honour is no party question.[161]

"The immediate effect of the Mansion House speech was to increase international tension, to make intercourse between the powers difficult, and to prolong the delay in effecting a settlement."[162] Public opinion in both England and France "burst into chauvinistic flames."[163] The French *Journal des Débats* lauded Lloyd George's speech as "worth more than the sending of a cruiser into Moroccan waters."[164] The *Daily Chronicle* head-lined "Britain Warns Germany—National Honour Is at Stake."[165] With both the German and British governments decided on courses of action that ex-plicitly admitted the potential for war, the crisis began a downward spiral that could, quite conceivably, have resulted in that outcome.

Instructed to issue an official protest, Metternich informed Lord Grey that "the more [Germany] received threatening warnings the more deter-mined would be our action."[166] He assured Grey that not a single German had landed at Agadir, but he told the foreign minister that he could not authorize the disclosure of this information to parliament because it would appear as if Germany had given way before a threat. By its actions in Mo-rocco, Metternich argued, France had abrogated the provisions of the Algeciras agreement. Thus, Germany was prepared to secure "by all means . . . full respect by France of German treaty rights."[167] The meeting so shook Lord Grey that he immediately called for Churchill and Lloyd George and reported: "I have just received a communication from the German Ambas-sador so stiff that the Fleet might be attacked at any moment. I have sent for McKenna to warn him!"[168]

While the British admiralty contemplated a German attack at sea, the French grew increasingly anxious that army maneuvers near Metz might be a prelude to a German invasion.[169] When the French army recalled troops from Champagne, rumors of French mobilization spread.[170] This in turn heightened fears in Germany that war was imminent.[171]

With tensions at a level such that one observer concluded that "one step further, and a war between England and Germany would have broken out," Asquith declared before the House of Commons on 27 July that Britain supported Franco-German negotiations.[172] He indicated that while territo-rial compensation for Germany would surely prove difficult in Morocco itself, "in other parts of West Africa, we should not think of attempting to interfere with territorial arrangements considered reasonable by those who are more directly interested."[173] The immediate effect of Asquith's speech was to de-escalate the crisis and allow for bilateral negotiations to proceed.[174]

Caillaux and Cambon lost no time in promising compensation to Germany in the Congo in exchange for a free hand in Morocco.[175] But negotiations were slow,[176] and tensions mounted once again in early August when Ambassador Schön was told that French and British men-of-war would move to Agadir if progress toward an agreement was not evident within eight days.[177]

The French threat backfired. The German leadership responded much as it had after the Mansion House speech. Kiderlen first instructed Ambassador Schön to refrain from further contact with official or non-official agents of the government.[178] He then issued a counterthreat: Unless France withdrew the ultimatum, Germany would break off negotiations.[179] The foreign minister was backed up by the kaiser, at this point the target of a virulent campaign in the right-wing press:[180] "If the French cannot reconcile themselves to respect our rights, we must break off negotiations, throw the Act of Algeciras on the floor, and insist that the French leave Morocco."[181] In addition to pressing for a tough diplomatic line, the kaiser ordered the admiralty to take measures necessary for the mobilization of the fleet.[182] Amid "free discussion in the French press of the possibility of war and the German fleet maneuvers," Caillaux backed down, and tensions were again eased.[183]

Cambon and Kiderlen began to make progress in September, but two points emerged as stumbling blocks to progress: Germany's demand for access to the Congo River and the cession of French option rights to the Belgian Congo.[184] Kiderlen secured access to the Congo River but agreed to place the transfer of French option rights to Belgian territory before the signatories of the Treaty of Berlin (1885). With that, the negotiations were completed.

The Franco-German treaty of 4 November 1911 destroyed the Algeciras agreement as well as the Franco-German accords of 1909. It consisted of two conventions. The first granted France a protectorate over Morocco, although France agreed to a continuation of the open door for trade. The state bank was left unchanged. The convention concerning the Congo followed that on Morocco, and "by reason of the rights of protection over the Sherifian empire recognized to France," provided for "territorial exchange in Equatorial Africa."[185] By this convention Germany gained a narrow strip of territory just south of its possessions in the Cameroon, securing access to the coast, as well as a large section of the French Congo to the east, delimited in such fashion as to give it access to the Congo and Ubangi Rivers.

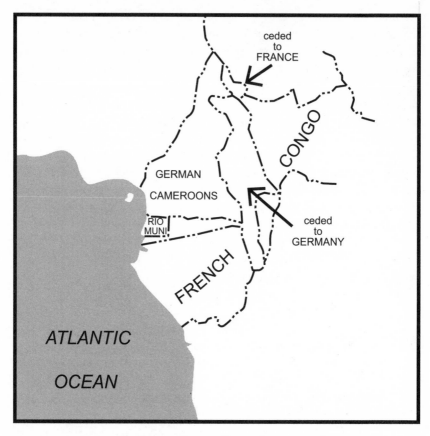

Map 3. The Franco-German Congo Agreement of 1911

In 1911 Germany's decision to challenge French actions in Morocco threatened to ignite a great power war. After first establishing the motives behind the decision to send the *Panther* to Agadir and the baseline against which prospective outcomes were judged by the German leadership as positive or negative, I will turn to an examination of the impact of British and French policies on the course of German actions during the crisis and offer an explanation for its peaceful resolution.

Decisional Frame

The single best statement of German thinking about the crisis is a memorandum written by the foreign minister, Kiderlen-Wächter, on 3 May.

Kiderlen first discusses the deteriorating political conditions in Morocco, the probable response of France, and the implications of such developments for the Algeciras agreement:

In all probability by the force of circumstances sooner or later the provisions of the Act of Algeciras will no longer hold good, however great the pretense. The Sultan who can only maintain his authority in the land with the help of French bayonets, no longer provides guarantees for the independence of his country, and this was the whole object of the Act of Algeciras. Thus, the only course left for us is to recognize the change effected by the force of circumstances and to rearrange our policy as regards Morocco.

The following possibility is indicated: As soon as the French have reached Fez and begun to establish themselves there, we might ask a friendly question in Paris . . . how long they consider it essential to keep troops there. The French could hardly avoid naming some period. After it has lapsed, the return march will naturally be put off on some pretext or other. Then would be the moment for us to declare to the Signatory Powers that we fully comprehend the reasons obliging the French to remain at Fez, but that we cannot any longer regard a Sultan who can only govern with the aid of French troops as the independent sovereign ruler contemplated by the Act of Algeciras; the Act has been torn up by the force of circumstances, and entire freedom of action has been restored to the Signatory Powers. . . . The occupation of Fez would pave the way for the absorption of Morocco by France.

Kiderlen then spells out the basic course of action Germany would pursue:

We should gain nothing by protesting and it would mean a moral defeat hard to bear. We must therefore look for an objective for the ensuing negotiations, which shall induce the French to compensate us. . . . We have large firms at Mogador and Agadir. German ships could go to those ports to protect those firms. They could remain anchored there quite peacefully—merely with the idea of preventing other powers from intruding into these very important harbours of southern Morocco. . . . In possession of such a pledge we should look confidently at the further development of affairs in Morocco and see whether France will offer us proper compensation in her own colonial possessions, in return for which we could abandon the two ports.

Finally, the foreign minister addresses the domestic political implications of the Moroccan question:

Our public opinion, saving only the Social Democratic Party, would reproach the Government severely, if it simply let things in the Sherifian Empire go on as they pleased; whereas it is certain that material results would turn the votes of many dissatisfied electors and perhaps influence not inconsiderably the approaching Reichstag Elections.[186]

The goal of German policy in 1911 was to defend the open door and secure compensation for any rights Germany would be forced to relinquish.[187] The *coup d'Agadir* was thus intended as an assertion of Germany's right to participation in decisions affecting the disposition of colonial territories and a material guarantee of territorial compensation.[188]

Territorial compensation addressed two needs of the German leadership. First, it was seen as a means of maintaining German prestige among the great powers. Second, the leadership believed that territorial compensation was necessary if the government was to successfully defend the surrender of German rights in Morocco before domestic opinion, the pan-Germanists and colonial lobby in particular. Although the German leadership was not guided by purely status quo motives in 1911—they did seek compensatory gains in the French Congo—Germany did not seek to capitalize on the Moroccan anarchy in order to secure unilateral advantage vis-à-vis the other powers.[189]

By early May the German leadership appears to have concluded that Caillaux could be made to offer significant compensation to Germany in exchange for a free hand in Morocco. For example, on 7 May Ambassador Schön reported from Paris:

Recently there have been various suggestions in the Press that Germany should be granted colonial and trade concessions in return for letting France have a free hand in Morocco. Amongst other possibilities it is proposed to satisfy us by handing over the French Congo in return for our giving up Togoland. This idea of an exchange appeared at first in quite vague form; yet it seems to be more than an idle journalistic suggestion; for, as I learn from a Paris financier in close touch with M. Caillaux, the latter . . . appears to be contemplating objects of exchange in the colonies which would be valuable to us, notably on the Congo.[190]

But the German leadership did not believe that France would "spontaneously offer Germany something of value."[191] If left unchallenged, France would absorb Morocco, and Germany would suffer a "defeat hard to bear"[192]—thus the need to send the *Panther* to Agadir.

The choice of Agadir as the site for a German mooring was in part a reflection of Kiderlen's belief that its distance from the Mediterranean would "make it unlikely that England would raise objections."[193] Indeed, the German leadership does not appear to have expected any resistance to its policy from Britain. Kaiser Wilhelm claimed to have discussed Germany's interests in the Moroccan question—the continuation of the open door and a desire for compensation—as well as the possibility of a mooring at Agadir, with King George V during a visit to England in May. Upon his return the kaiser reported to Bethmann-Hollweg: "The King said nothing to this."[194] Thus, the chancellor could include in instructions to Metternich his judgment, "To our satisfaction we gather that the British government appreciates the reasons for our action."[195]

In the spring of 1911 the status quo in Morocco was, from the perspective of the German leadership, deteriorating. The sultan's authority was growing ever less certain, and French political control was on the rise. The German decision makers recognized that the Act of Algeciras was no longer sustainable, but the status quo ante as defined by that treaty provided the reference point against which prospective outcomes were judged as losses or gains.[196]

The arguments presented in chapter 3 would thus lead to the expectation that the German leadership would be relatively risk averse with respect to gains vis-à-vis rights accorded Germany in the Algeciras agreement, but relatively risk acceptant when confronted with outcomes representing a deterioration of Germany's position in Morocco. With regard to the efficacy of threats and promises as tools of influence, one would expect threats to prove most effective at deterring German efforts to secure additional gains, but counterproductive in influencing efforts to minimize losses in Morocco. Insofar as German behavior was motivated by a desire to avoid loss, one would expect promises and assurances to prove potent tools of influence.

French and British Diplomacy and the Resolution of the Crisis

Huth and Russett argue that the threat of British participation on the side of France in a war over Morocco led Germany to back away from the challenge implied by the *coup d'Agadir*.[197] At first glance the conclusion appears reasonable: There is a correlation between the putative cause of German behavior (British threats) and the outcome (Germans back down). However, a closer examination of the course of the Second Moroccan Crisis reveals that when confronted with threats, the German leadership escalated the crisis by issuing threats of its own. By contrast, in periods of acute tension, promises of compensation led the Germans to recalculate the utility of a strategy that risked war over Morocco and facilitated a peaceful resolution of the crisis.

The course and resolution of the Second Moroccan Crisis can only be explained in light of the motives and expectations of the actors involved.

An examination of the course of the crisis in light of the decision to send the *Panther* to Agadir leads to the conclusion that the resolution of the crisis was not the product of British threats, rather of the French assurance of the open door in Morocco and promise of compensation in the Congo.

Most accounts of the crisis attribute a change in German policy to the threat contained in Lloyd George's Mansion House speech on 21 July. Britain was not expected by the German leadership to oppose German demands for compensation. Three weeks had passed since the Germans officially notified London of the *Panther's* mooring at Agadir, and Britain had failed to issue a protest. The Mansion House speech thus caught the German leadership by surprise and challenged their baseline of expectation. It was clearly viewed as a threat. Kiderlen noted: "If it was the British government's intention to complicate and confuse the political situation and bring about a settlement by means of force, they could not have chosen a better way than by the Chancellor's speech, which so ignored the dignity which he claimed for England or the position of a Great Power such as ourselves."[198]

But the response of the German leadership to Lloyd George's speech was not to back down. Kiderlen advised Bethmann: "We have lost our reputation abroad, we must fight!"[199] Metternich warned Grey that British threats would only produce more determination on the part of a German leadership that was prepared to use "all means" to secure German objectives in Morocco.[200] Indeed, the Mansion House speech produced a German response so severe that Britain began to prepare for an attack at sea.

The result of Prime Minister Asquith's speech before parliament on 27 July, however, was quite the opposite. After Asquith withdrew British demands for four-power talks and promised British support for "territorial arrangements considered reasonable by those who are more directly interested,"[201] tensions eased and bilateral negotiations were renewed. Although Asquith placed Britain squarely on the side of France in the Moroccan dispute, the German leadership concluded that the prime minister's speech was a concession and that it would go far toward promoting a peaceful settlement.[202] The reaction of the German press to the prime minister's speech was likewise quite positive. "Peace or war," wrote the *Vossische Zeitung*, "hung upon Herr Asquith's words. His was perhaps the greatest responsibility of any statesman in recent years. It was a peaceful speech."[203]

The cycle repeated itself in August. When, in an effort to speed progress in the bilateral negotiations, the French threatened to engage the *Panther* with British and French men-of-war, the German leadership threatened to break off talks altogether. Kiderlen wrote to Schön: "It should be clear to Mittelsmann and his superior, that we cannot negotiate under the pressure of threats."[204] Even the kaiser, heretofore an advocate of caution, supported breaking off negotiations: "We have now been sitting here for 3 days under this insulting threat, without having achieved even the slightest satisfaction. Until now, no one directly threatened me. I am not disposed to be a spectator to Schön's feeble negotiations in a matter which concern's the honor of the Fatherland."[205] When the French threat was withdrawn, however, talks resumed.

The Second Moroccan Crisis was resolved when France pledged the maintenance of the open door, and reached agreement with Germany on an exchange of territory in the French Congo for recognition of a protectorate over Morocco; that is, the assurance of the open door and promise of compensation in the Congo led the German leadership to recalculate the utility of continuing an assertive policy that risked war with France and Britain. The continuation of the open door would minimize any economic losses Germany might sustain in Morocco, while the Congo territory would compensate Germany for its political loss.

In presenting the Franco-German accords to the Reichstag on 9 November, Bethmann-Hollweg declared: "We drew up a program and carried it out. Nothing, no influence from outside or inside has made us depart one step from it."[206] Germany, he asserted, had secured what it set out to gain and therefore could not be said to have given way before pressure.[207] One would not expect the chancellor to proclaim Germany's defeat in the chambers of the *Reichstag*, but in fact, the German leadership *had* secured the objectives set forth in Kiderlen's memorandum of 3 May. The German plan called for anchoring ships at Mogador and Agadir until France offered "proper compensation in her own colonial possessions, in return for which we could abandon the two ports."[208] With an assurance of the open door for European commerce in Morocco, and the promise of 263,000 square kilometers of territory in the French Congo, the German leadership ordered the *Panther* withdrawn from Agadir at the end of November.

To argue that the German leadership got what they set out for in 1911 is not to argue that they pursued an enlightened foreign policy. Kiderlen's greatest error was his failure to consider the possible intervention of Britain in the crisis, for it was British intervention in July that brought the powers to the brink of war and ultimately led to the charge that the Franco-German treaty of November represented a second Olmütz.[209] British intervention was largely a result of the *coup d'Agadir*. The dispatch of the *Panther* to

Agadir was a blunt instrument of compellence and led many in both England and Germany itself to conclude that German aims were not limited to compensation in the Congo.[210] Britain would have remained out of Franco-German negotiations had they been limited to German compensation in the Congo, but the notion that Britain would be left out of a new partition of Morocco led to the Mansion House speech.

In Germany the *coup d'Agadir* raised the expectations of colonial enthusiasts so high that they were bound to be disappointed when the final territorial settlement made no provisions for a German political entity in southern Morocco.[211] Colonialist propaganda promoted visions of great wealth to be had in the hinterlands of Mogador and Agadir.[212] "Instead of this land of vast riches, which they held almost within their grasp, the foreign secretary offered them a fever-infested, concession-plagued marshland in the Congo."[213] Thus, whereas Kiderlen predicted on 3 May that territorial gain in the Congo would lead to domestic political gain, the Franco-German treaty of 4 November was widely held to be a national humiliation.[214]

· 7 ·

The July Crisis

The Moroccan crises are traditionally viewed as milestones on the road to the First World War. In both cases Germany is said to have shown its implacable lust for expansion, while the alignment of Britain with France is regarded as the death knell to the period of British isolation and the final move in the division of Europe into rival camps.[1] However, as the analysis in the previous chapter demonstrated, the standard interpretations of the Moroccan crises overstate the aggressive intentions of German policy as well as the effectiveness of British threats in deterring recourse to force.

The goal for this chapter is not to proffer yet another explanation for the outbreak of the First World War, but rather to illustrate how the theoretical and methodological foundations of this study allow for the evaluation of existing explanations and interpretations of the July Crisis and the immediate origins of the Great War. After careful establishment of the motives that drove European statesmen in July 1914, the theoretic framework suggests certain hypotheses on the probable effectiveness of threats and promises in strategies designed to influence German decisions over the resort to force.

The July Crisis began with the assassination of the heir to the Habsburg empire, Archduke Franz Ferdinand, by Serbian nationalists in Sarajevo on 28 June 1914. When war broke out in early August, the former *Reichskanzler*, Bernhard von Bülow, asked his successor how it had come to pass. Bethmann-Hollweg is said to have answered, "Oh—if I only knew!"[2] Over eight decades later the search for the deep historical as well as immediate political origins of the First World War continues to generate much scholarship and intense debate.

Was the war the culmination of a long-term German strategy to grab "world power"?[3] Or was the First World War inadvertent—the result of statesmen losing grip on their ability to direct events?[4] Could war have been avoided had Grey issued a credible threat to fight on the side of Russia and France, the outcome explainable as a failure of Britain to deter Germany?[5] Or is the outbreak of hostilities best understood in the framework of the spiral model, a case where threats were inappropriate tools of influence, which, when used, only accelerated movement toward collision?[6]

In his essay on the origins of the First World War, Paul Schroeder notes that "the fact that so many plausible explanations for the outbreak of the war have been advanced over the years indicates on the one hand that it was massively overdetermined, and on the other that no effort to analyze causal factors involved can ever fully succeed."[7] With Schroeder's observations in mind, and given limits of time and space, no comprehensive treatment of the subject will be offered here. Rather, the implications of this study for ongoing debates on the origins of the First World War are briefly presented.

On one level the answer to the question "Was Germany deterrable?" turns on the answer to the question of German motives in 1914. Thus, the debate between the Fischer school and those historians who find the German leadership to have been driven more by security fears than a will to power is central to a discussion of deterrence and World War I.[8]

Returning to the arguments developed in chapter 3, if the German leadership regarded the July Crisis as an opportune moment to secure gains in Europe and the colonial world, the threat of war with Britain on the side of France and Russia should have proven a potent deterrent. But if the German leadership framed the assassination of Franz Ferdinand as a severe threat to the survival of its only reliable ally at a time when Britain and Russia were believed to be nearing completion of a naval treaty, and both Russia and France were thought to be making impressive gains in their military capabilities,[9] then threats would not be expected to deter German support of a firm line in Vienna. Rather, they would increase the sense of strategic vulnerability among the leadership in Berlin and reinforce their determination to minimize loss by risking war in a diplomatic showdown before Germany's relative capabilities diminished further. By contrast, a strategy that incorporated promises and assurances would have had relatively greater impact on German calculations regarding the utility of backing the Habsburg leadership in its efforts to bring Serbia under Austrian domination.

With minimal claims regarding the validity of any conclusions hereby suggested, a brief examination of German calculations during the critical period at the end of July may shed some light on the question of deterrence in 1914. Two incidents are of interest in this regard. First, what was the effect on Bethmann-Hollweg of Grey's meetings with the German ambassador, Lichnowsky, on 27 and 29 July? Second, what was the effect of the Russian decision to order partial mobilization on 28 July?

Up to 28 July Bethmann-Hollweg promoted a hard line in Vienna with regard to Serbia. Since 5 July, when the Austrians were assured of German support in the event of war over Serbia, the chancellor, together with the kaiser and the military leadership, supported swift Austrian action in order to present the world with a fait accompli in Serbia and, it was believed, minimize the chance of Russian involvement.[10] But Bethmann-Hollweg appears to have adopted a very different approach toward Austria by 29 July, a shift in attitude and strategy that has given rise to much analysis. Indeed, during the night of 29–30 July Bethmann-Hollweg sent a series of telegrams to Vienna demanding that Austria agree to negotiations on the basis of the Serbian reply to the Austrian ultimatum of 23 July.

Two explanations have been offered for Bethmann's policy shift. The most widely held view is that it was the threat of British intervention communicated by the prime minister to the German ambassador at London that led Bethmann-Hollweg to recalculate his position.[11] Marc Trachtenberg offers a competing explanation. Arguing that Bethmann-Hollweg could not have known of Grey's statements to Lichnowsky when he sent the first of his telegrams to Vienna, Trachtenberg argues "that it was the news from Russia about partial mobilization that played the key role in bringing about the shift in Bethmann's attitude."[12]

In order to evaluate these competing claims and understand how these developments impacted on Bethmann's decisional calculus, the theoretic framework guiding this study suggests that we must first establish the baseline against which British and Russian signals were judged as positive or negative by the chancellor. What were Bethmann's prior beliefs and expectations regarding British neutrality and how did the Lichnowsky reports modify these? Similarly, what were his prior expectations with regard to the likelihood of Russian mobilization? If he saw mobilization as likely, what form (partial or full) did he anticipate it would take? Once these questions are answered, we can make some judgments as to the likely cause of Bethmann's policy reversal.

Those scholars who believe the war to have resulted from a failure of Britain to deter Germany argue that Bethmann-Hollweg based his policies on the belief that Britain would remain neutral in a continental war.[13] But this argument misses the essence of Bethmann's strategy. For the chancellor *did not* believe Britain would remain neutral in a continental war that involved France but *did* believe Britain would stay out of a localized conflict involving only Austria and Serbia.[14]

At the outset of the crisis Berlin believed that a quick and decisive Austrian move against Serbia held the best prospects for containing the dispute. But Austrian military plans did not allow for so swift an action. Indeed, the Austrian Chief of Staff, General Conrad von Hötzendorf, maintained that his forces would be unable to move against Serbia until 12 August, more than six weeks after the murders in Sarajevo.[15]

As the month of July progressed, the premise on which Bethmann based his belief that the crisis could remain localized became increasingly open to question.[16] Knowing that an Austrian ultimatum would be presented to Serbia on 23 July, the prospect of Russian intervention in support of Serbia became increasingly worrisome for Bethmann.[17] A Russian attack on Austria would require Germany to support its ally through the execution of the Schlieffen Plan, the German war plan calling for a simultaneous war on two fronts—against Russia in the east and France in the west. And Bethmann-Hollweg knew that Britain would not remain aloof in a war involving France. Consequently, as early as 21 July the German chancellor advised St. Petersburg, Paris, and London that the great powers should work toward the "localisation of the conflict, as the intervention of any other Power would, as a result of the various alliance obligations, bring about inestimable consequences."[18]

Bethmann believed that if the war could remain localized, Britain would not intervene. Thus, Grey's comments to Lichnowsky on 27 July did not constitute a threat. Rather, they confirmed the basis on which he would develop his policy. Lichnowsky reported to the chancellor that Grey regarded Serbia's 25 July reply to the Austrian ultimatum as a basis for negotiation and that the prime minister made

a sharp distinction between the Austro-Serbian and Austro-Russian conflict, i.e. he would not interfere in the Austro-Serbian, as long as it did not develop into an Austro-Russian conflict. But now he finds himself obliged to intervene, since it threatens to develop into an Austro-Russian and hence a European conflict. . . . If an agreement between Vienna and St. Petersburg on the basis of the Serbian note were attainable without the use of military measures against Serbia, Sir E. Grey would have achieved all that he desires. What he wants to avoid is an Austrian passage of arms with Serbia because he fears this will disturb the peace of Europe. He confirms, to-day, that no Russian call-up of reserves has taken place.[19]

Bethmann-Hollweg was unwilling to advise the Austrian leadership on whether or not to accept the Serbian reply as satisfactory.[20] But in response to Grey's message, and in an effort to keep the conflict confined to Austria and Serbia, Bethmann-Hollweg backed away from his support of a fait accompli and advised the Austrians to initiate discussions with St. Petersburg and was prepared to serve as an intermediary.[21]

To keep the conflict localized, Bethmann-Hollweg needed to keep the Russians at bay. This would require a political agreement between Austria and Russia and military restraint on all sides. Concluding that the German military leadership would demand mobilization in response to a full mobilization of Russian forces, and knowing that for Germany mobilization meant war, Bethmann-Hollweg cautioned St. Petersburg against a full mobilization. For example, on 26 July he instructed the German ambassador Pourtalès to inform the Russian leadership that

preparatory military measures on the part of Russia directed in any way against ourselves would force us to take counter measures which would have to consist in mobilizing the army. Mobilization, however, means war, and would moreover have to be directed simultaneously against Russia and France, since France's engagements with Russia are well known. We cannot believe that Russia means to unloose a European war of this kind. In view of Austria's territorial *désintéressement* we rather take the view that Russia can adopt a waiting attitude towards the issue [*Auseinandersetzung*] between Austria-Hungary and Serbia. Russia's desire not to have the territorial integrity of the Serbian Kingdom called into question can receive our support, the more as Austria-Hungary has stated that she does not intend to call this integrity into question. This might provide a common basis of agreement also in the further course of the affair.[22]

The basis on which Bethmann was conducting policy in the critical closing days of July is clear. Recognizing that a full mobilization of Russian forces would force a counter-mobilization in Germany, that German mobilization meant war, that war would be fought against both France and Russia in accordance with the Schlieffen Plan, and that war with France meant the loss of British neutrality, Bethmann-Hollweg sought to localize the conflict by encouraging a limited mobilization in Russia and supporting Austro-Russian negotiations on a plan for achieving Austrian satisfaction against Serbia.

Thus, the tsar's decision to order a partial mobilization of Russian forces on 28 July *did* influence Bethmann-Hollweg's calculations, but not in the manner Trachtenberg asserts. Rather than forcing him to confront the prospect of world war, the Russian move reinforced his belief that the crisis could be contained, and world war avoided, provided Austria and Russia could be persuaded to reach some sort of modus vivendi.

Trachtenberg himself presents the evidence that calls into question his interpretation of events. For example, he writes: "It is striking that neither Conrad nor Moltke nor the Russians took it for granted that mobilization by Austria and Russia against each other would in itself lead to war." He then presents evidence to refute "the argument that Germany could not tolerate even a partial Russian mobilization directed only against Austria."[23]

If the chief military leadership did not feel that a partial mobilization of Russian forces against Austria demanded a counter-mobilization in Germany, why should Bethmann-Hollweg have concluded differently? Indeed, even on 30 July, a day after word reached Berlin of the Russian partial mobilization, Bethmann-Hollweg refused to issue the *Kriegsgefahrzustand,* the declaration of "threatening danger of war," although by this time von Moltke had joined Falkenhayn in pressing for military preparations.[24]

Trachtenberg is probably correct in his conclusion that Bethmann-Hollweg learned of partial mobilization in Russia before he learned of the substance of Grey's discussions with Lichnowsky on 29 July.[25] But the sequence is not critical to the analysis presented here. For Lichnowsky's telegram contained nothing new in terms of substance. The difference appears to be one of urgency; Grey had concluded that the situation was acute. While again warning the German ambassador that Britain would not remain neutral in a general European war, Grey once more held out the prospect of a negotiated settlement: "Sir E. Grey said that, if mediation is agreed to, he thinks he could procure every possible satisfaction for Austria; there could be no further question of a humiliating withdrawal by Austria, because in any case the Serbs would receive chastisement and with the consent of Russia be forced to bow to Austrian wishes. Austria could obtain surety for the future without a war which would jeopardize the peace of Europe."[26]

If Bethmann-Hollweg had decided as early as the 28th that the best means for localizing the conflict was restraint in Russian and German mobilization coupled with Austro-Russian negotiations, then word of the partial mobilization in Russia and the renewed efforts of Grey to force negotiations did not challenge Bethmann's expectations. Both developments served to reinforce his belief that war could be averted, and Austrian grievances against Serbia addressed, but only through negotiations between Austria and Russia. For negotiations to proceed, Austria had to be restrained.

That the threat of European war was a constant corrective to any opportunistic behavior on the part of Berlin is not in dispute. But by comparing British and Russian actions to Bethmann-Hollweg's expectations, we see that his shift of 28–29 July was not a shift in goals, but in means. It was not British threats or Russian mobilization that provoked the chancellor's change of course, rather his realization that the Austrian mobilization schedule had rendered his earlier strategy of a fait accompli untenable. Localization remained the goal, Austro-Russian negotiations became the means.

The relevant counterfactual question is not "What would Bethmann-Hollweg have done absent British and Russian threats?" Rather, "What would Germany policy have been had the Tsar ordered a full mobilization on July 28, and Grey shown no hope for localizing the conflict and a negotiated settlement when he met with Lichnowsky on July 27 and 29?" The result most likely would have been the very response that followed full mobilization in Russia: the rapid onset of hostilities across the continent. Instead, what Bethmann-Hollweg perceived as assurances that the conflict could be contained and world war avoided prompted his urgent efforts to slow Austrian preparations for war against Serbia and compel the Vienna leadership to begin negotiations with Russia.

But by the end of July events were beyond the ability of one person to control. Indeed, it is doubtful whether *any* effort at immediate deterrence would have succeeded in July 1914, for reasons directly related to the theoretic framework presented in chapters 1 and 3. For it was not only the German leadership that, concluding that the status quo was deteriorating, was willing to pursue a risky course of action, but virtually all of the great powers saw their position at risk and were highly motivated to prevent or minimize any loss. None were likely to back down in the face of coercive threats.

By 1914 the precarious position of Austria-Hungary in the constellation of great powers was recognized by all, most importantly by Austria itself. As Schroeder demonstrates, the great power most directly threatened by the effects of entente diplomacy in the decade preceding the war was not Germany, but Austria.[27] And Russian efforts to establish a new Balkan League would only exacerbate the problem posed by Austria's own South Slavs. Thus, in a letter dated 22 June 1914, the Austrian diplomat Czernin outlined the imminent dangers facing the Habsburg monarchy:

Before our eyes, in broad daylight, openly and obviously, as clear as the sun, with shameless impudence, the encirclement of the Monarchy is being completed; under Russian-French patronage a new Balkan League is being welded together, whose purpose, today still apparently complicated, will soon appear in astonishing simplicity—against the Monarchy.[28]

The same conclusion was reached by the Chief of the Austrian General Staff, General Conrad von Hötzendorf:

The course of political events . . . has led to the encirclement of the Monarchy on its North-East, East, and South-East fronts by openly aggressive foes (Russia, Roumania, Serbia, Montenegro), all pursuing positive aims, it has to the South-West an unreliable ally (Italy) and only on its North-West frontier a reliable ally, who, however, is threatened by two powerful neighbors (Russia and France) even if I do not take England into account.[29]

Regarding itself encircled by hostile powers, supported by allies of questionable value, and facing internal collapse owing to the rise of ethnonationalism, the Austrian leadership came to believe that an assertive policy toward Serbia was the only possible response to the assassination of the archduke and his wife if the Austrian state was to survive.[30] Given the Austrian leadership's sense of isolation and encirclement, Bethmann-Hollweg's efforts in the final days of July to force a moderation in Austrian policy toward Serbia and encourage Austro-Russian negotiations probably only heightened the sense of vulnerability in Vienna. Now even their German ally was wavering![31]

In Russia memories of military defeat in Manchuria (1904) and diplomatic defeat in the Bosnian annexation crisis (1908–9) led the leadership to adopt a hard line against Vienna in 1914. William Fuller stresses the point: "The ministers of state believed that Russia could not afford another humiliation on that scale. Passivity in the face of the Austrian destruction of Serbia was not an option. If Russia did not respond to the provocation, it would vacate its position as a Great Power. The Russian Empire would be dishonored, and its prestige would dwindle away into insignificance. The internal consequences of such a fiasco might be incalculable. Even if worse came to worst and Russia went down in defeat, that would be better than skulking away in shame."[32]

Russian behavior was contingent on Austria's stance vis-à-vis Serbia, but as in St. Petersburg, leaders in Vienna had concluded that the risk of military defeat was preferable to the political risks attendant to diplomatic retreat. Thus, neither Russia nor Austria-Hungary was receptive to the idea of a negotiated settlement.[33] And once the Russians had ordered a general mobilization on 30 July, the universal belief in first-strike advantage and the rigid nature of European mobilization plans led to rapid preparations for war across the continent and rendered the war inevitable.[34]

Summary

The complex interconnections governing the international system in 1914 made any effort at deterrence problematic. Yet even amid the heightened tensions of late July, assurances appear to have convinced Bethmann-Hollweg that events might still be brought under control. But the policies each state saw as vital to the maintenance of its position in the system were seen by others to threaten their own. Thus, although Bethmann-Hollweg came to regard Austrian restraint and a negotiated settlement as the best outcome from Germany's perspective, the Austrian leadership regarded a policy of restraint as suicidal. But St. Petersburg regarded an Austrian victory over Serbia as a threat to Russia's position as a great power. As Schelling pointed out, some degree of common interests is a prerequisite for successful coercive diplomacy.[35] Although in retrospect we might identify interests common to the ruling elites of prewar Europe, in 1914 those same elites saw none.

Conclusions

How can desirable changes in the international status quo be effected, and undesirable change prevented, without recourse to war? Threats of punishment and promised rewards are central to international politics at the start of the twenty-first century.

Consider, for example, the questions raised by North Korea's nuclear program. What can the United States do to deter the proliferation of weapons of mass destruction? One answer was provided in a *Wall Street Journal* column entitled "Rewarding Virtue Is a Good Policy in Curbing Nukes." *New York Times* columnist William Safire appeared to offer another when he wrote: "We must now decide whether to continue the protracted runaround, hoping vainly that Kim Il Sung wants only to be bought off, or to enforce international law—which would require the credible threat of war."[1] Similar questions were raised in an article on how to promote the restoration of democracy in Haiti: "A military junta must go. But are threats or treats the best tactic?"[2] In 1999 Western leaders confronted a similar choice in the former Yugoslavia. U.S. Secretary of State Madeleine Albright supported threats of NATO air strikes to compel Serbia to grant autonomy to the Kosovo Albanians, whereas former British Foreign Minister, Lord David Owen, supported a plan to compensate Serbia for the loss of territory in Kosovo with Serbian-populated territory in Bosnia.[3] When threats failed to stop a Serbian drive to expel ethnic Albanians from the province, NATO launched a bombing campaign that lasted for seventy-two days.

Although decision makers are routinely confronted with a choice between threats or promises, scholarly analysis has to date focused almost exclusively on the role of threats in coercive diplomacy. Few have systematically studied the role of promises and assurances in international politics. Yet the evidence presented in this book indicates that threats—even when credible—are often ineffective and counterproductive. Moreover, under certain conditions promises and assurances appear to be potent tools of influence.

This book has had three goals. The first is to develop a definition of promises that distinguishes them from threats and assurances, and to more fully explore the ways in which these three tools of influence relate to one another. A second is to integrate threats, promises, and assurances into a broader theory of influence. Finally, in pursuit of a more accurate explanation of past events and better policy making in the future, the implications of that theory have been explored in a series of case studies.

LESSONS FOR THEORY AND PRACTICE

As the cases examined in this study demonstrate, the effects of threats, promises, and assurances on the calculations of decision makers are not uniform. Therefore, the question "Which is the better tool of influence?" is misguided. The crucial task is to identify the conditions under which each is most likely to prove effective.

Motives

The cases examined here support the argument that the target's motives are important determinants of whether threats, promises, or assurances are more likely to promote compliant behavior.

Thus, in the crises over Schleswig-Holstein, where German decision makers were encouraged to pursue expansionist foreign policies because they perceived the moment opportune, threats proved to be effective deterrents. In the first crisis over Schleswig-Holstein, King Friedrich Wilhelm backed down from an invasion of Jutland in response to Russian threats. Similarly, Bismarck backed away from an invasion of Jutland when confronted with the threat of French intervention.

However, when the German leadership was motivated by loss aversion, threats proved ineffective tools of influence. In the 1880s Bismarck sought to minimize loss in Germany's standing among the European powers through the creation of an overseas empire. But in contrast to the Second Schleswig-Holstein Crisis where French threats produced moderation, British threats in colonial disputes only reinforced Bismarck's determination to assert German equality. In the Moroccan crises British and French threats confirmed the fears of Bismarck's successors that Germany faced a hostile coalition intent on violating German rights in Morocco and diminishing German prestige among the powers. In both cases threats led to increased hostility and deepened crisis. By contrast, promises and assurances produced de-escalation and facilitated the peaceful resolution of the conflicts.

The finding that motives are important to explaining behavior should not surprise the social scientist. But establishing motives—even post hoc—is always difficult. Owing to the problems associated with gauging what are in effect psychological processes internal to the decision maker, analysts have shied away from explanations that rest on an assessment of actors' motives even though statesmen appear to place a high premium on estimations of their adversaries' motives.[4]

In principle, one could deduce an actor's likely motives from a theory of international politics. In this respect it is odd that most deterrence theorists have assumed that aggressors are most often motivated by opportunism and have neglected to consider aggression motivated by fear or a sense of vulnerability, since the dominant theory of international politics holds states to exist in an anarchic system and argues that fear for survival is the principal motive for state action.[5] Indeed, most Realist scholarship finds the international system to be a realm of compulsion, one where statesmen's range of choice is severely constrained.[6] To the extent that the balance of power operates efficiently, opportunities for gains seeking should be rare in international politics.

But deductions of this sort are made difficult by the fact that motives are not entirely a function of the international system. For example, Bismarck's adoption of a colonial policy was motivated by both domestic and international concerns. Jack Snyder has found that the origins of expansionist foreign policies are often traceable to societal interest groups with concentrated interests.[7] When and how domestic interests will be aggregated into a "national" interest is usually path dependent and cannot be predicted a priori.

If motives cannot be identified by means of deductive entailment, neither can they be directly inferred from state behavior. This is because behavior is likely to reflect the influence of strategy and lower-order means-ends beliefs.

Even with access to the relevant documentary evidence, post hoc assessment of an actor's motives is not entirely straightforward and is likely to be influenced by the scholar's theoretic predilections. The task is even more difficult for decision makers who seek to assess an adversary's motives in the formulation of policy, as information is generally ambiguous and would support a variety of conclusions. Consequently, decision makers' assessments are generally strongly biased by preexisting beliefs.[8]

Since Munich, where promises were inappropriate tools of influence given that Hitler was either opportunistic or undeterrable,[9] decision makers have tended to base policy on the assumption that all aggressors are similarly motivated.[10] The assumption that all aggressors are Hitler-like opportunists of unbounded ambition is probably more often implicit than explicit in policy deliberations.[11] But even when explicit, policy makers frequently fail to consider what kinds of behavior would provide evidence that their assessments of the adversary's motives are incorrect.[12]

Because many fail to recognize the operation of the security dilemma and do not appreciate the pernicious effects of threats on the perceptions and behavior of statesmen acting out of fear and/or a belief that the status quo is deteriorating, policy makers often conclude that a threat-based strategy dominates all others[13]—that is, it is better than a policy based on promises and assurances no matter what the adversary's motives may be.[14] "Better safe than sorry!" the argument goes. But the dichotomy is often more apparent than real, for the inappropriate use of threats may leave the state unsafe and the decision maker quite sorry.

Although the motives of an adversary may be uncertain, it might still be possible to specify conditions under which it makes more sense to err on the side of overreliance on threats—at times provoking an unnecessary spiral, or risk encouraging an opportunist to increase its appetite for gain through inappropriate use of promises. For example, after the Cold War the overwhelming military capability and favorable geographic location of the United States provide a great deal of latitude for American leaders; the costs of mistaking an opportunist for a state motivated by security fears are for most scenarios very low.

The situation would be very different for contiguous states of roughly equivalent capability, especially when geography and/or technology favor offensive over defensive military strategies. Under such a scenario the risk of fighting an unnecessary war provoked by the inappropriate use of threats may be preferable to the risk of having to pay the costs of reversing a successful conquest that resulted from the failure to deter an opportunistic aggressor.

Sometimes capability and geography combine in such fashion that a decision maker can take the measures necessary to defend the state's vital interests yet still probe the adversary's motives or offer incentives to forgo a challenge. For example, in October 1994, when the concentration of 60,000 Iraqi troops along the Kuwaiti border raised fears that Saddam Hussein might repeat his invasion of 1990, the Iraqi leader's motives were unclear and gave rise to much speculation in U.S. foreign policy circles. But the situation did not demand premature closure. A reasonable response for the United States would have been to reinforce Kuwaiti and Saudi defenses with a rapid deployment of troops to the region and still initiate a dialogue with Iraq in an effort to uncover the motives behind what appeared a threatening act.

Because most students of deterrence have failed to problematize motives for aggression, a stark and rather artificial distinction between actors motivated by opportunity and those motivated by vulnerability is drawn here. This has allowed for hypothesis generation and the fruitful reexamination of a number of international crises. In most situations, however, actors will be motivated by a mixture of opportunism and vulnerability. If the identification of opportunism and vulnerability is difficult when these motives exist in isolation, determining the relative weight of each when they exist simultaneously will be even harder. But, as Lebow and Stein argue, the determination is critical, as it speaks to the appropriate mix and timing of threats and promises.[15] In this regard future research should focus on the interaction between threats and promises in different sequences and contexts in an effort to devise strategies for coping with actors of mixed motives.[16]

Framing Signals and Outcomes

Decision makers evaluate the signals of others as they relate to a baseline of expectation. Similarly, prospective outcomes are evaluated as gains or losses relative to a reference point.

Analyzing influence attempts in light of the target's baseline not only provides for conceptual clarity but also leads to the reinterpretation of historical events. For example, many scholars have assumed that Grey's statements to Lichnowsky in late July 1914 constituted a British threat: The British, Grey told Lichnowsky, would not stay out of a war between the Triple Alliance and one or more members of the Entente. But Bethmann had already come to this conclusion; his was a policy of localization. In addition to signaling Britain's intention to enter a war that involved Russia and France, however, Grey indicated a willingness to stay out of a purely Austro-Serbian conflict. Thus, Grey's signals confirmed Bethmann-Hollweg's estimations of Britain's interests in the conflict and therefore constituted assurances, not threats.

Across the range of cases examined here, prospective outcomes were most often framed around the actor's subjective appraisal of the status quo. Even when gains seeking, the salient referent was generally the status quo and not an aspiration level. For example, in the First Schleswig-Holstein Crisis, King Friedrich Wilhelm IV judged prospective outcomes as gains and losses not in terms of his goal of detaching the duchies from Denmark, but rather as they related to Prussia's security and relations with the great powers. In the Moroccan crises the reference point was based on existing treaties that either defined a territorial status quo or conferred upon Germany certain economic and political rights.

The notion that treaties give rise to expectations and promote stable interaction among states has long been asserted by students of international law and more recently advanced by the literature on international regimes.[17] However, most Realists accord formal treaties and less formal regimes only limited status in explanations of state behavior. Seen at most as epiphenomenal reflections of underlying relationships of power, Realism accords regimes and their associated norms significance only to the extent that they constrain short-term self-interested behavior.[18]

Although French policies in the Moroccan crises clearly violated the terms of existing treaties, German behavior is not explicable merely in terms of short-run material calculations. The loss of Moroccan trade would have had a very small impact on Germany's economic position at the time of the First Moroccan Crisis, when trade with Morocco constituted less than 1 percent of aggregate foreign trade.[19] But the French threat to the "open door" and the right to equal status accorded Germany under the Treaty of Madrid led Germany to adopt an assertive policy that appears out of proportion to the short-run material stakes involved.

In Morocco German behavior was closer to the characterization of international politics as a discourse wherein norms provide vehicles for states to challenge the legitimacy of the behavior of others.[20] German actions were not based on short-run calculations of interest, but rather were in large measure a response to French (and British) actions that challenged a normative framework (equality of rights for the European powers) with which the German self-image was intimately connected.[21] But a more considered judgment with respect to the importance of the norms codified in the Treaty of Madrid to the final outcome of the two Moroccan crises would require a more detailed analysis of French and British policy deliberations than that offered here. Moreover, the fact that a bilateral agreement between France and Germany in 1911 shattered the multilateral Algeciras agreement suggests that the processes by which some treaties retain their moral force whereas others appear subject to rapid decay are complex and poorly understood.

In the case of Anglo-German competition for colonies in Africa, the territorial status quo did not present a compelling reference point against which German leaders could evaluate prospective outcomes. In 1889–90 the German leadership's frame of reference was strongly affected by comparisons of Germany's colonial position relative to Britain. Equal status vis-à-vis Britain was important to the German leadership for both its impact on domestic politics and its perceived impact on international affairs. But status was not defined strictly in terms of the amount of territory controlled. Rather, by the late 1880s the German leadership appears to have been content with a limited empire, one that nonetheless allowed it to promote the image of Germany as a colonial power.

The cases provide direct evidence to support the hypothesis that reference points are subject to rapid shift when actors achieve gains, and indirect evidence indicating that the reference points are resistant to shift when actors are confronted with losses. In at least two cases Bismarck's frame of reference appears to have shifted immediately upon victory in battle: first, after driving Austria from Germany and consolidating Prussian military control north of the Main River in 1866; second, upon the annexations of Alsace and Lorraine in 1871. However, Franco-German cooperation over Morocco was impeded in 1904 by Delcassé's desire to regain the lost provinces of Alsace and Lorraine, behavior suggesting French decision makers had yet to renormalize to the loss in endowment.

The Manipulation of Risk

An individual's tolerance for risk is to some degree idiosyncratic. However, as the foregoing discussions of motives and framing indicate, the cases analyzed in this study provide evidence to support the laboratory findings of psychologists that risk propensity is also highly context dependent. Specifically, statesmen appear risk seeking when prospective outcomes are framed as losses, but risk averse when outcomes are framed as prospective gains.

Bismarck provides an example. After the invasion of Jutland during the second crisis over Schleswig-Holstein, a simple inquiry from Paris as to the extent of Prussian war aims prompted Bismarck's immediate retreat; he was unwilling to risk the entry of France into the crisis to secure gains in Denmark. Similarly, after the victory at Koniggrätz Bismarck was unwilling to seek additional gain when it became clear that further advance increased the risk of French entry into the war on the side of Austria. But his unwillingness to risk war with France over gains in the Danish and Austrian wars stands in stark contrast with his behavior during the War-in-Sight Crisis.

In 1875 the fear that France was engaged in a rapid military recovery that threatened German control of Alsace and Lorraine led Bismarck to adopt a belligerent policy and provoke a continental crisis. However, whereas threats were powerful tools of deterrence when Bismarck contemplated gains in 1864 and 1866, British threats did not lead him to abandon his efforts to prevent German losses in 1875. Rather, when Britain threatened to support France in another war with Germany, Bismarck escalated the crisis with a bellicose speech and counterthreats. The crisis was resolved when the tsar assured the chancellor that Russia was a loyal ally and that French recovery presented no real threat to Germany.

The finding that statesmen display a high tolerance for risk and uncertainty when confronting the prospect of loss has important implications for deterrence theory. Since Schelling, scholars of deterrence have stressed the "manipulation of risk" as a method of deterrence, as statesmen are held to undertake aggressive challenges only when they are confident that the attendant risks are manageable.[22] Through what Schelling calls the "threat that leaves something to chance," statesmen can threaten an adversary with an outcome that appears beyond the ability of anyone to control; the threat of uncontrolled escalation is held to be a potent deterrent.[23] This is probably true for cases where statesmen can manipulate the risk that the adversary's homeland will be destroyed.[24] But in cases where such threats are incredible, either because the state does not have the capability to destroy the other's homeland or because international norms would make such an all-out attack extremely costly for the state,[25] the motives behind a challenge will strongly condition the impact of increases in risk. For if statesmen facing loss are relatively insensitive to risk, then threats that manipulate risk are unlikely to deter.

Thus, in 1905 Bülow was not deterred from his efforts to minimize German losses in Morocco by British threats. Nor was Bethmann-Hollweg deterred by Lloyd George's Mansion House Speech in 1911. Indeed, with French troops engaged in the Moroccan interior, a German ship at Agadir, the British Admiralty on alert for a German attack at sea, and the French army recalling troops to their barracks near the Franco-German frontier, the Second Moroccan Crisis threatened to ignite a great power war not because of the plans of any one party to the conflict, but as the unintended resultant of the policies of many. Churchill was characteristically sensitive to suspense when he wrote of the crisis that "the Germans . . . were prepared to go to the very edge of the precipice. It is so easy to lose one's balance there: a touch, a gust of wind, a momentary dizziness, and all is precipitated into the abyss."[26]

Although he admitted that French compensation played a part in the peaceful resolution of the Second Moroccan Crisis,[27] Churchill maintained that it was the threat of a war with Britain on the side of France that ultimately led Germany to accept a French protectorate in Morocco.[28] But in both cases the evidence suggests that French assurances of the open door in Morocco and promises of territorial compensation led the Germans to back away from their challenge.

Even when statesmen confront an opportunist, successful deterrence requires the ability to issue both threats and assurances, a point noted by Schelling.[29] But if the ability to make credible promises and assurances is as important to strategies of deterrence as the ability to manipulate risk, statesmen face a dilemma. Many of the means by which statesmen can manipulate the risk of war diminish their capacity to make credible assurances and promises. Brinkmanship strategies may facilitate the issuance of threats that credibly leave something to chance, but in relinquishing control over the course of events, decision makers also diminish their ability to reassure the adversary that the threatened punishment will be withheld in the event of compliance. The threat that leaves something to chance means that the corresponding assurance of peace is only a probability. The need to make credible promises and assurances also arises when deterrent threats fail, for unless a war is to be fought to the finish, war termination will require the making and accepting of promises, a component of strategy that is too often overlooked.[30]

Reputation and Precedent

Both statesmen and scholars argue that reputation is fundamental to international politics in general, and to the outcomes of crises in particular. Thus, former U.S. National Security Advisor and university professor Zbigniew Brzezinski argued that the Soviet invasion of Afghanistan "was a vindication of my concern that the Soviets would be emboldened by our lack of response over Ethiopia."[31] By failing to stand firm in one crisis, states are said to risk gaining a reputation for weakness and thereby invite further aggression. Following this intuition, deterrence theorists have asserted the interdependence of threats and have devoted inordinate energy to developing strategies whereby threats will gain credibility and states can earn a reputation for resolve.

Although intuitively plausible and extremely influential, the proposition that threats are interdependent is based on neither logical necessity nor a firm empirical foundation. In the only systematic study of reputation in international politics, Jonathan Mercer found that states rarely gained a reputation for weakness after backing down from an assertive position.[32] Indeed, although it is hard to earn a reputation for resolve, the problem appears to lie not in the interdependence of threats, rather in their independence. And as Jervis has noted, if threats are independent, much of the logic driving the arguments of deterrence theorists breaks down.[33]

At first glance a reputation for keeping promises would appear to be a precondition for securing compliance and cooperative outcomes. And in neglecting promises in general, students of international politics have devoted little thought to whether and how states can develop a reputation for keeping their word.

But do statesmen seek such a reputation? Again, the answer is not straightforward. When confronted with the prospect of exchanging Heligoland for German claims in Africa, Queen Victoria feared the reputational repercussions: "It is a very bad precedent. The next thing will be to propose to give up Gibraltar; and soon nothing will be secure."[34] Indeed, Salisbury succeeded in gaining the queen's acquiescence only after he persuaded her that there was "no danger of this case being made a precedent, for their is no possible case like it."[35]

A decision maker's willingness to adopt a strategy that incorporates the use of promised rewards may depend on the extent to which the crisis is seen as representative of future contingencies. To the extent that a given case is regarded as unique, a decision maker will probably be more willing to employ promises in his or her strategy. When a case appears representative of future contingencies, decision makers will probably examine the likely long-term costs associated with setting a precedent.[36]

The offer of Heligoland does not appear to have led the German leadership to conclude that it could demand further concessions, nor does it appear to have encouraged the Germans to challenge other British interests.

German restraint was perhaps a function of the type of reward promised. Salisbury incorporated both concessions and compensation in his strategy, but the central feature of the agreement was compensation: for example, Heligoland for Zanzibar, Witu, and other related territory in Africa.

A firm posture on the part of the source with respect to the territory under dispute coupled with a willingness to grant some form of compensation may be a stronger position from which to bargain than a posture that relies chiefly on concessions. As with Heligoland, compensatory rewards can probably be structured in such fashion as to convey the uniqueness of a given situation and suggest limits on the resources available to the source for exchange.

BEYOND DETERRENCE

Most deterrence theorists define immediate deterrence encounters as a class of international engagements where decision makers in one state (the "challenger") are considering attacking another state's ("defender") values, and where the defender tries to prevent the attack. Extended immediate deterrence is characterized by a challenger threatening a third state (the "protégé") that is formally allied to or deemed important by the defender, and where the defender tries to prevent an attack.[37] Lebow and Stein are only slightly broader in their definition of immediate deterrence as "a challenge to a commitment."[38]

Because immediate deterrence encounters are defined in terms of prior commitments, such encounters are commonly regarded as indicative of a general deterrence failure.[39] However, many of the cases examined in this study suggest that this image of international crises is too narrow and leaves out a range of important encounters. For example, German expansion toward the headwaters of the Nile was not reflective of a failure of general deterrence; it arose from the scramble of European states for unclaimed territory in Africa. Yet Salisbury came to regard German expansion as a threat to British interests and concluded that further expansion had to be deterred.

The requirement that commitments be known in advance of a crisis rules these cases out of a data set of immediate deterrence encounters even though they clearly fall under the rubric of coercive diplomacy outlined by Schelling. These *meeting engagements* are often characterized not only by lack of prior commitment by the defender, but also by the absence of any explicit consideration of an attack by the challenger.

Such findings point not only to the limited utility of many standard rational deterrence models, but also to more recent efforts to model immediate deterrence encounters as games of incomplete information. For example, James Fearon models immediate deterrence as a game where the challenger is uncertain about the value the defender places on the status quo.[40] Crisis bargaining is seen as a game of "costly signals" whereby the defender can convince the challenger of a willingness to fight. But in many of the cases presented here, neither the challenger nor defender had a clear conception of the conditions under which war was preferable to compromise. Thus, at the outset of the First Moroccan Crisis, Britain was committed to no more than diplomatic support for French ambitions in Morocco. Indeed, Lansdowne warned Delcassé of the dangers inherent in ignoring German interests and suggested he seek a bilateral agreement with Germany much as he had with the other powers. However, British commitments escalated during the course of the crisis. The extent to which Britain would come to support France was unknown at the outset, not just by the Germans, but by the British themselves.

In the Second Moroccan Crisis the German leadership did not weigh the costs and benefits of a war with France before sending the *Panther* to Agadir. Rather, they were willing to pursue a course of action that held the potential for war. If Schelling is correct in arguing that wars may result from inadvertent escalation, then holding fast to the requirement that statesmen have contemplated an attack rules another broad class of crises out of our data set. The end result of a narrow interpretation of deterrence encounters may be a data set so small as to miss much of what constitutes international crises and render useful generalization impossible.

COPING WITH FAILURE

Although debate continues as to whether nuclear deterrence succeeded in preventing a war between the United States and the Soviet Union, few would argue that it was a demonstrable failure (although it may have been irrelevant). Owing perhaps to the absence of a nuclear war between the superpowers—or indeed major-power war—in the second half of the twentieth century, or perhaps owing to the fact that what is threatened in pursuit of nuclear deterrence would in many respects be irrational should nuclear deterrence fail, the question of how to deal with deterrence failures has been in large part neglected by students of international politics and military strategy.[41]

The arguments developed here stress the need to establish an adversary's motives prior to the formulation of strategy. Because the task is extremely demanding, it would be unreasonable to expect that statesmen will always, or even generally, get things right. But is war the necessary result of a failed strategy of deterrence? And when promised rewards fail to produce the intended results, is one forced to admit defeat? How should decision makers cope with failure?

Notwithstanding some prominent exceptions—such as the launching of nuclear-armed intercontinental ballistic missiles—most "moves" in international politics are either "reversible" or of only limited importance to the eventual outcome of political disputes. Even when characterized by short time horizons, most crises provide multiple opportunities for a change of course. Thus, having failed to employ a strategy of immediate deterrence in the first crisis over Schleswig-Holstein, the tsar was able to reverse Prussian advances on Denmark through the issuance of compellent threats. Similarly, Bismarck was compelled to reverse the invasion of Jutland when confronted with the threat of French intervention. In the Second Moroccan Crisis Lloyd George's Mansion House speech produced so hostile a response in Berlin that the British fleet was instructed to prepare for an attack at sea. However, a week later Prime Minister Asquith succeeded in dramatically reducing tensions by promising British support for territorial compensation.

Because international crises are rarely characterized by, or resolved through, a single, simultaneous interaction, failure to secure one's goals in one stage need not imply defeat in the endgame. But whereas earlier contributions to the deterrence literature—primarily by "second wave" theorists such as Brodie, Schelling, Snyder, and Wohlstetter—viewed strategy as central to the outcome of deterrence encounters, in much of what falls under the rubric of rational deterrence theory as elaborated in the 1980s, skill and strategy are curiously absent as important contributors to success.[42] In the most extreme manifestations of this development, capabilities or interests appear to produce outcomes (and thereby derive their meaning) independent of the behavior of political actors. In this regard game theoretical models of international crises, which allow for sequential moves through which actors can signal one another, are clearly superior to deterrence models that characterize crises in terms of a single decision to either "attack" or "back down," or that seek to predict outcomes in terms of an objective and quantifiable "balance" of interest or resolve.[43]

As the cases examined above demonstrate, the goals and interests at stake in international crises are often neither objective nor fixed. Indeed, through the iterative process of signaling—of threatening and promising—actors' goals and interests are formed and transformed. Thus, Salisbury's offer of Heligoland transformed the entire character of the Anglo-German dispute in East Africa. When set in a wider context, German claims to the African interior were no longer seen as essential to the maintenance of Germany's position in the balance of power, but rapidly came to be regarded "merely . . . as matters for concession."[44]

Because interests and objectives can rapidly change in the course of crisis bargaining, even sophisticated game theoretic models, which usually require relatively stable preferences, will be unable to capture important possibilities for action. But such possibilities exist and give rise to optimism, for even in the wake of failure, all is rarely lost. Creative statecraft can identify *or create* common interests on the basis of which crises can be resolved and political relations reconstituted. To do so, however, requires a conceptual move beyond deterrence and a recognition that promises and assurances are as important to the conduct of international politics as threats.

◆

NOTES

1 ◆ *Threats and Promises*

1. John J. Mearsheimer, "The False Promise of International Institutions," *International Security* 19 (winter 1994–95): 11.

2. Exceptions include David Baldwin, "Thinking about Threats," *Journal of Conflict Resolution* 15, no. 1 (1971): 71–78; Baldwin, "The Power of Positive Sanctions," *World Politics* 24 (October 1971): 19–38; Thomas W. Milburn and Daniel J. Christie, "Rewarding in International Politics," *Political Psychology* 10, no. 4 (1989): 625–45; Janice Gross Stein, "Deterrence and Reassurance," in Philip Tetlock et al., eds., *Behavior, Society and Nuclear War*, vol. 2 (New York: Oxford University Press, 1990), pp. 9–72; and Richard Ned Lebow, *The Art of Bargaining* (Baltimore: Johns Hopkins University Press, 1996), ch. 7.

3. For Kennan's original articulations of containment see Kennan to the State Department, 22 February and 20 March 1946, U.S. Department of State, *Foreign Relations of the United States, 1942–1952/54*, vol. 6 (Washington, D.C.: 1971), pp. 696–709; and "X" [George F. Kennan], "The Sources of Soviet Conduct," *Foreign Affairs* 25 (July 1947): 566–82. For the history of containment understood in terms of strategies of deterrence, see John Lewis Gaddis, *Strategies of Containment: A Critical Appraisal of Postwar American National Security Policy* (New York: Oxford University Press, 1982).

4. The classic works on deterrence include Bernard Brodie, *The Absolute Weapon: Atomic Power and World Order* (New York: Harcourt Brace, 1946); Brodie, *Strategy in the Missile Age* (Princeton: Princeton University Press, 1965); Thomas C. Schelling, *The Strategy of Conflict* (Cambridge: Harvard University Press, 1960); Schelling, *Arms and Influence* (New Haven, Conn.: Yale University Press, 1966); Herman Kahn, *On Thermonuclear War* (Princeton: Princeton University Press, 1960); Kahn, *Thinking the Unthinkable* (New York: Horizon, 1962); William W. Kaufmann, *The Requirements of Deterrence* (Princeton: Center for International Studies, 1954); and Glenn H. Snyder, *Deterrence and Defense* (Princeton: Princeton University Press, 1961). Later works of note include Patrick Morgan, *Deterrence: A Conceptual Analy-*

sis (Beverly Hills: Sage, 1979); Richard K. Betts, *Nuclear Blackmail and Nuclear Balance* (Washington, D.C.: Brookings Institute, 1987); Alexander George and Richard Smoke, *Deterrence in American Foreign Policy: Theory and Practice* (New York: Columbia University Press, 1974); and Robert Jervis, *The Meaning of the Nuclear Revolution* (Ithaca, N.Y.: Cornell University Press, 1989).

5. The classic remains Robert Jervis, "Cooperation under the Security Dilemma," *World Politics* 30 (January 1978): 167–214.

6. See, for example, Glenn H. Snyder and Paul Diesing, *Conflict among Nations: Bargaining, Decision Making, and System Structure in International Crises* (Princeton: Princeton University Press, 1977).

7. Christopher H. Achen and Duncan Snidal, "Rational Deterrence Theory and Comparative Case Studies," *World Politics* 41 (January 1989): 151.

8. George and Smoke, *Deterrence in American Foreign Policy*, p. 590.

9. For variations on this theme, see Robert O. Keohane and Joseph Nye, *Power and Interdependence,* 2d ed. (Glenview, Ill.: Scott Foresman, 1989); Joseph Nye, *Bound to Lead: The Changing Nature of American Power* (New York: Basic Books, 1990); Robert Jervis, "The Future of International Politics: Will It Resemble the Past?" *International Security* 16 (winter 1991): 39–74; and Daniel Deudney and G. John Ikenberry, "The Logic of the West," *World Policy Journal* 10 (winter 1993–94): 17–25.

10. For example, Jack Snyder, "Averting Anarchy in the New Europe," *International Security* 14 (spring 1990): 5–42.

11. Deterrence theorists have made this point but failed to develop it. See, for example, Kaufmann, *Requirements of Deterrence,* and Paul Huth and Bruce Russett, "Testing Deterrence Theory: Rigor Makes a Difference," *World Politics* 42 (July 1990): 471.

12. Robert Jervis, "Rational Deterrence: Theory and Evidence," *World Politics* 41 (January 1989): 183. For an extended discussion of what Jervis calls the "spiral model" see his *Perception and Misperception in International Politics* (Princeton: Princeton University Press, 1976), pp. 58–113.

13. Here I follow the work of Robert Jervis, Richard Ned Lebow, and Janice Gross Stein. See Jervis, *Perception and Misperception in International Politics,* ch. 3; Lebow and Stein, "Rational Deterrence Theory: I Think, Therefore I Deter," *World Politics* 41 (January 1989): 208–24; Jervis, Lebow, and Stein, eds., *Psychology and Deterrence* (Baltimore: Johns Hopkins University Press, 1985); and Stein, "Deterrence and Reassurance."

14. This observation flows directly from the logic presented by proponents of rational deterrence theory. See, for example, Barry Nalebuff, "Rational Deterrence in an Imperfect World," *World Politics* 43 (April 1991), especially p. 313.

15. On the method of focused comparison, see Alexander George, "Case Studies and Theory Development: The Method of Structured, Focussed Comparison," in Paul Lauren, ed., *Diplomacy: New Approaches in History, Theory and Policy*

(New York: Free Press, 1979), pp. 51–52; and Arendt Lijphart, "Comparative Politics and the Comparative Method," *American Political Science Review* 65 (September 1971): 682–93.

16. For scholarship reflective of this tradition, see, for example, David Calleo, *The German Problem Reconsidered* (Cambridge: Cambridge University Press, 1978); Ludwig Dehio, *Germany and World Politics in the Twentieth Century* (New York: Alfred A. Knopf, 1959); Andreas Hillgruber, *Die Deutsche Frage im 19. und 20. Jahrhundert* (Munich: E. Vogel, 1983); Hillgruber, *Die Zerstörung Europas* (Frankfurt: Propylaen, 1988); Otto Hintze, "Military Organization and the Organization of the State," in Felix Gilbert, ed., *The Historical Essays of Otto Hintze* (New York: Oxford University Press, 1975), pp. 178–215; and Max Lenz, "Ranke und Bismarck," *Kleine Historische Schriften* (Munich: R. Oldenbourg, 1910), pp. 383–408.

17. The main proponents of these views are Alexander Gerschenkron, *Bread and Democracy in Germany*, 3d ed. (Ithaca, N.Y.: Cornell University Press, 1989); Eckard Kehr, *Economic Interest, Militarism, and Foreign Policy* (Berkeley: University of California Press, 1977); and Hans-Uhlrich Wehler, *Das Deutsche Kaiserreich: 1871–1918* (Göttingen: Vandenhoeck und Ruprecht, 1988). See also Hajo Holborn, *A History of Modern Germany, 1840–1945* (Princeton: Princeton University Press, 1969). For a similar argument from a sociological perspective see Ralf Dahrendorf, *Society and Democracy in Germany* (Garden City, N.Y.: Doubleday, 1967).

18. Fritz Stern has characterized the Bismarckian Reich as "a system of checks and imbalances designed not to work"; "Bethmann-Hollweg and the War: The Limits of Responsibility," in Leonard Krieger and Fritz Stern, eds., *The Responsibility of Power: Essays in Honor of Hajo Holborn* (New York: Doubleday, 1967), p. 255. For a theoretic examination of why the German system worked as it did see Jack L. Snyder, *Myths of Empire: Domestic Politics and International Ambition* (Ithaca, N.Y.: Cornell University Press, 1991), pp. 66–111.

19. Fritz Fischer, *Griff nach der Weltmacht: Die Kriegszielpolitik der Kaiserlichen Deutschland, 1914–1918* (Düsseldorf: Droste Verlag, 1961); and Fischer, *Krieg der Illusionen: Die deutsche Politik von 1911 bis 1914* (Düsseldorf: Droste Verlag, 1969).

20. See George F. Kennan, *The Decline of Bismarck's European Order: Franco-Russian Relations, 1875–1890* (Princeton: Princeton University Press, 1979); and Otto Pflanze, *Bismarck and the Development of Germany. Vol. 2: The Period of Consolidation* (Princeton: Princeton University Press, 1990).

21. For a sampling of the debate see Alexander V. Kozhemiakin, "Democratization and Foreign Policy Change: The Case of the Russian Federation," *Review of International Studies* 23, no. 1 (1999): 49–74; Charles L. Glaser, "Why NATO Is Still Best: Future Security Arrangements for Europe," *International Security* 18 (summer 1993): 5–50; and Ted Hopf, "Managing Soviet Disintegration: A Demand for Behavioral Regimes," *International Security* 17 (summer 1992): 44–75.

22. Sherman Garnett, "Ukraine's Decision to Join the NPT," *Arms Control Today* (January-February 1995): 7–13.

23. James Cotton, "The North Korea/U.S. Nuclear Accord: Background and Consequences," *Korea Observer* 26 (autumn 1995): 321–44. Cotton suggests that security fears best explain the North Korean nuclear program.

2 ♦ *Tools of Influence*

1. David Baldwin, "The Power of Positive Sanctions," *World Politics* 24 (October 1971): 27.

2. The framework is taken from James T. Tedeschi, "Threats and Promises," in Paul Swingle, ed., *The Structure of Conflict* (New York: Academic Press, 1970), p. 159.

3. Ibid.

4. David Baldwin, "Thinking about Threats," *Journal of Conflict Resolution* 15, no. 1 (1971): 71–78. On power as a relational concept, see Robert A. Dahl, "The Concept of Power," *Behavioral Science* 2 (1957): 201–15. See also Harold D. Lasswell and Abraham Kaplan, *Power and Society: A Framework for Political Inquiry* (New Haven, Conn.: Yale University Press, 1950).

5. Thomas W. Milburn and Daniel J. Christie, "Rewarding in International Politics," *Political Psychology* 10, no. 4 (1989): 634.

6. Tedeschi, "Threats and Promises," p. 159. In his study of inter-state crisis behavior, Russell Leng operationalizes threats and promises based on the structure of the signal rather than its relationship to the target's expectations. See Russell J. Leng, *Interstate Crisis Behavior, 1816–1980: Realism Versus Reciprocity* (Cambridge: Cambridge University Press, 1993), pp. 35, 39, 117. Interestingly, despite the differences between the two approaches, the two research designs yield similar results.

7. Thomas C. Schelling, "Promises," *Negotiating Journal* (April 1989): 115. Schelling credits J. R. Searle, *Speech Acts* (Cambridge: Cambridge University Press, 1969), pp. 54–64, as the inspiration for his analysis.

8. The concept of a baseline used to distinguish threats from promises appears in Peter M. Blau, *Exchange and Power in Social Life,* 2d ed. (New Brunswick, N.J.: Transaction Publishers, 1986), pp. 116–17.

9. Again, Baldwin provides the pioneering application of the concept to international relations theory. See "The Power of Positive Sanctions," pp. 25–27.

10. Ibid., p. 26, emphasis in the original.

11. Barry O'Neil, "Conflictual Moves in Bargaining: Warnings, Threats, Escalations, and Ultimatums," in H. Peyton Young, ed., *Negotiation Analysis* (Ann Arbor: University of Michigan Press, 1991), p. 89; Martin Patchin, *Resolving Disputes between Nations* (Durham, N.C.: Duke University Press, 1988), p. 2; and Schelling, "Promises," p. 114.

12. Text of Article V, "Treaty between the United States of America and the Union of Soviet Socialist Republics on the Limitation of Anti-Ballistic Missile Systems," *Arms Control and Disarmament Agreements* (Washington, D.C.: U.S. Arms Control and Disarmament Agency, 1982), p. 140.

13. Some of these are refinements of the hypotheses presented by Baldwin, "The Power of Positive Sanctions," pp. 28–36.

14. Because they may be difficult or impossible to detect, decision makers may fear small and incremental defections from agreements that promise longer-term joint gain, especially when it is believed that unilateral advantages gained through defection will cumulate and confront the state with a large threat sometime in the future.

15. On indices and the strategic use of these, see Robert Jervis, *The Logic of Images in International Relations,* 2d ed. (New York: Columbia University Press, 1989), ch. 2.

16. Charles Osgood, *An Alternative to War and Surrender* (Urbana: University of Illinois Press, 1967), ch. 5.

17. I. William Zartman and Maureen R. Berman, *The Practical Negotiator* (New Haven, Conn.: Yale University Press, 1982), p. 7; Tedeschi, "Threats and Promises," p. 183; Charles G. McClintock, Frank J. Stech, and James K. Beggan, "The Efficacy of Commitment to Threats and Promises upon Bargaining Behavior and Outcomes," *European Journal of Social Psychology* 17 (1987): 455.

18. W. J. Mommsen, "The Debate on German War Aims," *Journal of Contemporary History* (July 1966): 63; Volker R. Berghan, *Modern Germany,* 2d ed. (Cambridge: Cambridge University Press, 1987), ch. 1; James Joll, *The Origins of the First World War* (London: Longman, 1984), ch. 6.

19. William Rose, *U.S. Unilateral Arms Control Initiatives: When Do They Work?* (Westport, Conn.: Greenwood Press, 1988), pp. 92–100; Arkady Shevchenko, *Breaking with Moscow* (New York: Knopf, 1985), pp. 201–2.

20. For example, see the statement by Secretary Kissinger, "Detente with the Soviet Union: The Reality of Competition and the Imperative of Cooperation," 19 September, *State Bulletin* 71 (14 October 1974): 518.

21. Schelling, "Promises," pp. 115–16.

22. Schelling, *Arms and Influence* (New Haven, Conn.: Yale University Press, 1966), p. v.

23. Kenneth E. Boulding, "Towards a Pure Theory of Threat Systems," *American Economic Review* 53 (1963): 290.

24. Thomas W. Milburn, "What Constitutes Effective Deterrence?" *Journal of Conflict Resolution* 3 (1959): 139.

25. McClintock et al., *Efficacy of Commitment to Threats and Promises,* p. 451.

26. On the norm of reciprocity and how it promotes cooperation, see James K. Esser and S. S. Komorita, "Reciprocity and Concession Making in Bargaining," *Journal of Personality and Social Psychology* 31, no. 5 (1975): 864–72; Alvin W.

Gouldner, "The Norm of Reciprocity: A Preliminary Statement," *American Sociological Review* (April 1960): 161–78; Patchin, *Resolving Disputes between Nations*, p. 266. The difficulty of inducing cooperative reciprocity is discussed by Daniel Druckman, "The Social Psychology of Arms Control and Reciprocation," *Political Psychology* 11, no. 3 (1990): 553–81.

27. Schelling, *Strategy of Conflict* (Cambridge: Harvard University Press, 1960), p. 18.

28. See Paul M. Kennedy, "The Tradition of Appeasement in British Foreign Policy 1865–1939," *British Journal of International Studies* 2 (1976): 195.

29. Alexander George and Richard Smoke, *Deterrence in American Foreign Policy: Theory and Practice* (New York: Columbia University Press, 1974), p. 604.

30. See Marc Trachtenberg, *History and Strategy* (Princeton: Princeton University Press, 1991), ch. 5.

31. See George C. Homans, *Social Behavior: Its Elementary Forms* (New York: Harcourt, 1961); Peter M. Blau, "Social Exchange," in David L. Sills, ed., *International Encyclopedia of the Social Sciences* (New York: Macmillan and Free Press, 1968), pp. 452–58; David Baldwin, "Power and Social Exchange," *American Political Science Review* 72 (December 1978): 1229–42.

32. This point is made in Jervis, *The Logic of Images*, pp. 198–99. For an analysis of precedents in international politics, see Elizabeth Kier and Jonathan Mercer, "Setting Precedents in Anarchy: Military Intervention and Weapons of Mass Destruction," *International Security* 20 (spring 1996): 77–106.

33. The best study of the role of reputation in international politics is provided by Jonathan Mercer, *Reputation and International Politics* (Ithaca, N.Y.: Cornell University Press, 1996).

34. Schelling, *Arms and Influence*, p. 124.

35. See James Fearon, "Domestic Political Audiences and the Escalation of International Disputes," *American Political Science Review* 88 (September 1994): 577–92.

36. For experimental work that suggests the same, see Madeline E. Heilman and Katherine A. Gerner, "Counteracting the Boomerang: The Effects of Choice on Compliance to Threats and Promises," *Journal of Personality and Social Psychology* 31, no. 5 (May 1975): 911–17; Madeline E. Heilman and Barbara Ley Toffler, "Reacting to Reactance: An Interpersonal Interpretation for the Need for Freedom," *Journal of Experimental Social Psychology* 12, no. 6 (November 1976): 519–29.

37. See Zartman and Berman, *The Practical Negotiator*. See also Patchin, *Resolving Disputes between Nations*, p. 269. For related research in a different context, see Douglas Easterling, "Fair Rules for Siting a High Level Nuclear Waste Repository" (unpublished ms., Risk and Decision Process Center, University of Pennsylvania, 1991), pp. 36–38; and Howard Kunreuter et al., "Public Attitudes toward Siting a High Level Nuclear Waste Repository in Nevada," *Risk Analysis* 10, no. 4 (December 1990): 469–84.

38. Amos Tversky and Daniel Kahneman, "The Framing of Decisions and the Psychology of Choice," *Science* 211 (January 1981): 458.

39. Schelling, *Arms and Influence,* p. 69.

40. I am aware that referring to promises as deterrent or compellent is odd, but I employ the terms here for ease of comparison and because I cannot think of anything better. George and Smoke speak of inducements that forestall crisis, by which they mean deterrence, and those intended for political "trade," by which they mean compellence. See George and Smoke, *Deterrence in American Foreign Policy,* pp. 604–10.

41. Schelling, *Arms and Influence,* pp. 69–91.

42. Ibid., p. 72.

43. Ibid.

44. Quotation found in Richard M. Nixon, *No More Vietnams* (New York: Arbor House, 1985), p. 157.

45. Schelling, *Arms and Influence,* p. 75.

46. In fact, there is no consensus on whether a strategy of firmness would have deterred Hitler. See, for example, Ernest R. May, ed., *Knowing One's Enemies: Intelligence Assessment before the Two World Wars* (Princeton: Princeton University Press), p. 520; John Hiden and John Farquharson, *Explaining Hitler's Germany: Historians and the Third Reich* (London: Batsford, 1983); and J.L. Richardson, "New Perspectives on Appeasement: Some Implications for International Relations," *World Politics* 40 (April 1958). Historically appeasement represented a strategy rather than an outcome. See Kennedy, "The Tradition of Appeasement in British Foreign Policy, 1865–1939."

47. The methodological debate on this point is intense. For a sample, see Richard Ned Lebow and Janice Gross Stein, "Deterrence: The Elusive Dependent Variable," *World Politics* 42 (April 1990): 336–69; Paul Huth and Bruce Russett, "Testing Deterrence Theory: Rigor Makes a Difference," *World Politics* 42 (July 1990): 466–501; and Robert Jervis, "Rational Deterrence: Theory and Evidence," *World Politics* 41 (January 1989): 183–207.

48. In the summer of 1992 such a mix of promises and threats was the basis of a U.S. plan for the return of deposed President Jean-Bertrand Aristide to Haiti. The initiative required opposition forces in Haiti to allow for Aristide's return in exchange for army participation in the selection of the prime minister and the lifting of an OAS embargo. Simultaneously an international force was sent into the country to deter further unrest. See "U.S. is Discussing an Outside Force to Stabilize Haiti," *New York Times,* 6 June 1992, p. A1. Similarly George and Smoke argue that Eisenhower should have provided inducements (promises) immediately following the successful maintenance of deterrence in the Taiwan Straits and Quemoy crises of 1954–55 and 1958 (*Deterrence in American Foreign Policy,* p. 608).

49. Schelling, *Arms and Influence,* p. 82.

50. Of course, rewarding a representative of an adversarial nation may have the unintended effect of raising doubts as to his loyalty among his constituents.

51. Milburn and Christie, "Rewarding in International Politics," p. 634.

52. In order to understand the Japanese decision to surrender in August 1945 one cannot overlook the importance of the American decision to allow retention of the emperor: "Whatever effect the bombing of Hiroshima and Nagasaki may have had on the thinking of the Japanese political and military leadership, the choice between last-ditch resistance and capitulation did not depend on it. That choice was governed by the political payment on which the Japanese insisted and had to insist—the retention of the Emperor"; Paul Kecskemeti, *Strategic Surrender: The Politics of Victory and Defeat* (Stanford, Calif.: Stanford University Press, 1958). See also Robert J.C. Butow, *Japan's Decision to Surrender* (Stanford, Calif.: Stanford University Press, 1954), p. 132. The issue was contentious in American political circles as well. Those wanting complete reform of the Japanese system cried "Appeasement!" at those who sought retention of the emperor; see Butow, *Japan's Decision to Surrender*, pp. 189—90; On the integral relationship between threats and promises represented by the atomic bombs and the emperor's status, see Henry L. Stimson and McGeorge Bundy, *On Active Service in Peace and War* (New York: Harper & Brothers, 1948), pp. 626–33.

53. See Robert Carswell and Richard J. Davis, "Crafting the Financial Settlement," in Paul H. Kreisberg, ed., *American Hostages in Iran: The Conduct of a Crisis* (New Haven, Conn.: Yale University Press, 1985), pp. 201–34.

54. McClintock et al., "The Effects of Commitment to Threats and Promises," pp. 447–64.

55. In the only systematic study Jonathan Mercer finds that it is quite easy for states to develop a reputation for breaking promises. By contrast, he finds states do not easily acquire reputations for keeping them. See Mercer, *Reputation and International Politics*.

3 ♦ A Theory of Influence

1. Robert Jervis, "Deterrence Theory Revisited," *World Politics* 31 (January 1979): 289. See also Christopher H. Achen and Duncan Snidal, "Rational Deterrence Theory and Comparative Case Studies," *World Politics* 41 (January 1989): 153.

2. For one example, see Achen and Snidal, "Rational Deterrence Theory and Comparative Case Studies," especially p. 153.

3. Robert Jervis, "Cooperation under the Security Dilemma," *World Politics* 30 (January 1978): 178. For a discussion of Chicken see Thomas Schelling, *Arms and Influence* (New Haven, Conn.: Yale University Press, 1966), pp. 116–25; and Glenn H. Snyder and Paul Diesing, *Conflict among Nations* (Princeton: Princeton University Press, 1977), 44–45 and 118–22.

4. See, for example, Paul Huth and Bruce Russett, "What Makes Deterrence Work? Cases from 1900 to 1980," *World Politics* 36 (July 1984): 496–526 ; Huth and Russett, "Testing Deterrence Theory: Rigor Makes a Difference," *World Politics* 42 (July 1990): 466–501.

5. Bruce Bueno de Mesquita, *The War Trap* (New Haven, Conn.: Yale University Press, 1981). For similar critiques of decision-theoretic models, see Frank Zagare, *The Dynamics of Deterrence* (Chicago: University of Chicago Press, 1987), pp. 17–28; Robert Jervis, *System Effects: Complexity in Political and Social Life* (Princeton: Princeton University Press, 1997), pp. 82–87; and James D. Fearon, "Rationalist Explanations for War," *International Organization* 49 (summer 1995): 379–414.

6. The claim is made in Achen and Snidal, "Rational Deterrence Theory and Comparative Case Studies," p. 164.

7. For example, John Mueller, "The Essential Irrelevance of Nuclear Weapons: Stability in the Postwar World," *International Security* 13 (fall 1988): 55–79; and Mueller, *Retreat from Doomsday: The Obsolescence of Major War* (New York: Basic Books, 1989).

8. Richard Ned Lebow and Janice Gross Stein, *When Does Deterrence Succeed and How Do We Know?* (Ottawa: Canadian Institute for International Peace and Security, 1990); and Lebow and Stein, "Deterrence: The Elusive Dependent Variable," *World Politics* 42 (April 1990): 336–70.

9. For discussions of the difficulties associated with explaining international outcomes when complex interconnections exist, see Jervis, *Systems Effects,* especially chs. 1 and 2; and Kenneth Waltz, *Theory of International Politics* (Reading, Mass.: Addison-Wesley, 1979), especially chs. 3 and 4.

10. See Achen and Snidal, "Rational Deterrence Theory and Comparative Case Studies," p. 151. For similar arguments see George W. Downs, "The Rational Deterrence Debate," *World Politics* 41 (January 1989): 228–29; Snyder and Diesing, *Conflict among Nations,* pp. 66–67; and George H. Quester, "Some Thoughts on 'Deterrence Failure,'" in Paul C. Stern et al., eds., *Perspectives on Deterrence* (New York: Oxford University Press, 1989), p. 54.

11. Achen and Snidal, "Rational Deterrence Theory and Comparative Case Studies," pp. 145–46. See also Huth and Russett, "Testing Deterrence Theory."

12. Schelling, *Arms and Influence,* p. 74, emphasis in the original. See also Schelling, *The Strategy of Conflict* (Cambridge: Harvard University Press, 1960), pp. 6–7.

13. See, for example, Bruce Russett, "Pearl Harbor: Deterrence Theory and Decision Theory," *Journal of Peace Research* 4 (1967): 89–105, especially p. 99; Janice Gross Stein, "Calculation, Miscalculation, and Conventional Deterrence I: The View from Cairo," in Robert Jervis, R. Ned Lebow, and Janice G. Stein, eds., *Psychology and Deterrence* (Baltimore: Johns Hopkins University Press, 1985); and Jack L. Snyder, "Perceptions of the Security Dilemma in 1914," in *Psychology and Deterrence.*

14. Schelling, *Arms and Influence*, p. 75, emphasis in the original.

15. See Christoph Bertram, "Im Banne Saddams: Amerika muß notfalls Gewalt anwenden—aber nur eine neue Irakpolitik kann die nächste Krise verhindern," *Die Zeit* 47 (14 November 1997), p. 1. In a speech some months before the crisis, U.S. Secretary of State Madeleine Albright had apparently rejected the lifting of sanctions prior to the emergence of a successor to Saddam Hussein in Baghdad. See Jim Hoagland, "In the Iraq Affair, Washington Caved in to the Allies," *International Herald Tribune*, 27 November 1997, p. 8. The crisis was defused when the Russian foreign minister secured the reentry of American arms inspectors in exchange for a promise to work for the lifting of the economic sanctions. See Francis X. Clines, "Clinton to 'Wait and See' after Iraq Backs Down," *International Herald Tribune*, 21 November 1997, pp. 1 and 12; Joseph Fitchett, "Accord's Easy Test: Will It Work?" *International Herald Tribune*, 21 November 1997, pp. 1 and 12; and Daniel Williams, "Russia's Balancing Act," *International Herald Tribune*, 22–23 November 1997, p. 7.

16. For the argument that deterrence theory stunted postwar U.S. foreign policy, see Michael McGwire, "Drain the Bath but Spare the Child," *Journal of Social Issues* 43, no. 4 (1997): 135–42.

17. Alexander L. George and Richard Smoke, *Deterrence in American Foreign Policy: Theory and Practice* (New York: Columbia University Press, 1974), pp. 590–91.

18. Alexander L. George and Richard Smoke, "Deterrence and Foreign Policy," *World Politics* 41 (January 1989), p. 181.

19. Janice Gross Stein, "Deterrence and Reassurance," in Philip Tetlock et al., eds., *Behavior, Society and Nuclear War*, vol. 2 (New York: Oxford University Press, 1990), p. 32; see also Richard Ned Lebow and Janice Gross Stein, "Rational Deterrence Theory: I Think, Therefore I Deter," *World Politics* 41 (January 1989): 208–24.

20. See, for example, Richard Ned Lebow and Janice Gross Stein, "Beyond Deterrence," *Journal of Social Issues* 43 (winter 1987): 5–72; Stein, "Deterrence and Reassurance"; Lebow and Stein, "Rational Deterrence Theory"; Lebow and Stein, *We All Lost the Cold War* (Princeton: Princeton University Press, 1994), especially ch. 12.

21. Huth and Russett argue that contingent rewards are logically within the rubric of deterrence theory, but they correctly note that in both academic writings and policy debates they have generally been excluded. See Huth and Russett, "Testing Deterrence Theory," p. 471.

22. See Robert Jervis, *Perception and Misperception in International Politics* (Princeton: Princeton University Press, 1976), ch. 3.

23. For examples, see George and Smoke, *Deterrence in American Foreign Policy*, especially ch. 15; Stein, "Calculation, Miscalculation and Conventional Deterrence"; and Lebow and Stein, *We All Lost the Cold War*, chs. 2–4.

24. Stein, "Deterrence and Reassurance," p. 58.

25. See Lebow and Stein, "Beyond Deterrence"; and Stein, "Deterrence and Reassurance."

26. Lebow and Stein, "Rational Deterrence Theory," p. 222; and Stein, "Deterrence and Reassurance," p. 59.

27. Risky choice situations are defined as those for which the probabilities associated with prospective outcomes are well defined. Under uncertainty probabilities are subjectively given.

28. The most important studies include Daniel Kahneman and Amos Tversky, "Prospect Theory: An Analysis of Decision under Risk," *Econometrica* 47 (March 1979): 263–91; Tversky and Kahneman, "The Framing of Decisions and the Psychology of Choice," *Science* 211 (30 January 1981): 452–58; Tversky and Kahneman, "Rational Choice and the Framing of Decisions," *Journal of Business* 59, no. 4 (1986): S251–75; Kahneman and Tversky, "Choices, Values and Frames," *American Psychologist* 39 (1984): 341–50; Daniel Kahneman, J. Knetsch, and R. Thaler, "Experimental Tests of the Endowment Effect and the Coase Theorem," *Journal of Political Economy* 98, no. 6 (1990): 1325–48; Kahneman, Knetsch, and Thaler, "The Endowment Effect, Loss Aversion, and Status Quo Bias," *Journal of Economic Perspectives* 5 (winter 1991): 193–206.

29. The example is taken from Tversky and Kahneman, "Rational Choice and the Framing of Decisions," pp. S258–59; see also Tversky and Kahneman, "The Framing of Decisions and the Psychology of Choice," pp. 453–58; and Paul Slovic and Sarah Lichtenstein, "Preference Reversals: A Broader Perspective," *American Economic Review* 73 (1983): 596–605. Not all violations of expected utility theory represent violations of rational choice, but rapid shifts in preferences are inconsistent with basic axioms of the rational model, namely, consistent and transitive preferences and invariant choice.

30. Tversky and Kahneman, "Rational Choice and the Framing of Decisions," p. S258.

31. Richard Thaler, "Toward a Positive Theory of Consumer Choice," *Journal of Economic Behavior and Organization* 1 (1980): 39–60; Kahneman, Knetsch and Thaler, "Experimental Tests of the Endowment Effect and the Coase Theorem," pp. 1325–48; Jack L. Knetsch and J.A. Sinden, "Willingness to Pay and Compensation Demanded: Experimental Evidence of an Unexpected Disparity in Measures of Value," *Quarterly Journal of Economics* 99 (1984): 507–21; and Jack L. Knetsch, "The Endowment Effect and Evidence of Nonreversible Indifference Curves," *American Economic Review* 79 (1989): 507–21.

32. Kahneman, Knetsch, and Thaler, "Experimental Tests of the Endowment Effect and the Coase Theorem," p. 1344; Robin Gregory, Sarah Lichtenstein, and Donald MacGregor, "The Role of Past States in Determining Reference Points for Policy Decisions," *Organizational Behavior and Human Decision Processes* 55 (July 1993): 195–206; William Samuelson and Richard Zeckhauser, "Status Quo Bias in

Decision Making," *Journal of Risk and Uncertainty* 1 (1988): 7–59; and Robert Jervis, "The Political Implications of Loss Aversion," *Political Psychology* 13 (June 1992): 187–204.

33. The general pattern tends to break down for very small probabilities and catastrophic losses. As prospective losses approach the extreme, actors' tolerance for risk begins to decline.

34. Tversky and Kahneman, "Rational Choice and the Framing of Decisions," p. S259. Loss aversion and risk acceptance are analytically distinct concepts. The former is reflected in the steep slope of the curve in the domain of losses, the latter in the convexity.

35. See, for example, Barbara R. Farnham, "Roosevelt and the Munich Crisis: Insights from Prospect Theory," *Political Psychology* 13 (June 1992): 205–35; Farnham, *Roosevelt and the Munich Crisis: A Study of Political Decision-Making* (Princeton: Princeton University Press, 1997); Jervis, "The Political Implications of Loss Aversion"; Jack S. Levy, "Prospect Theory and International Relations: Theoretical Applications and Analytic Problems," *Political Psychology* 13 (June 1992): 283–310; Levy, "Loss Aversion, Framing and Bargaining: The Implications of Prospect Theory for International Conflict," *International Political Science Review* 17 (1996): 177–93; Rose McDermott, *Risk Taking in International Politics: Prospect Theory in American Foreign Policy* (Ann Arbor: University of Michigan Press, 1997); and Janice G. Stein and Louis W. Pauly, eds., *Choosing to Cooperate: How States Avoid Loss* (Baltimore: Johns Hopkins University Press, 1993).

36. See Jack S. Levy, "Prospect Theory, Rational Choice and International Relations," *International Studies Quarterly* 41 (March 1997): 93–94.

37. Janice Gross Stein, "International Co-operation and Loss Avoidance: Framing the Problem," in Stein and Pauly, *Choosing to Cooperate*, p. 21.

38. Both the internal and external validity of the laboratory findings have been questioned. The debates are not uninteresting. However, the real issue is whether models incorporating assumptions taken from prospect theory generate explanations for behavior that survive rigorous empirical testing. For the student of international politics the important issues include whether collective decision making over political goods resembles individual decision making over private goods, and whether prospect theory provides leverage over "real-world" situations in which choices may appear equally risky. For criticism of the laboratory designs employed by psychologists, see David S. Brookshire and Don L. Coursey, "Measuring the Value of a Public Good: An Empirical Comparison of Elicitation Procedures," *American Economic Review* 77 (September 1987), pp. 554–66; and Don L. Coursey, John L. Hovis, and William D. Schulze, "The Disparity between Willingness to Accept and Willingness to Pay Measures of Value," *Quarterly Journal of Economics* 102 (August 1987): 687–90. For discussions of the challenges of moving from laboratory findings to explanations of political decision making see William A. Boettcher III, "Context, Methods, Numbers, and Words: Evaluating the Applicability of Prospect

Theory to International Relations," *Journal of Conflict Resolution* 39 (September 1995): 561–83; and Jack Levy, "Prospect Theory, Rational Choice, and International Relations," especially pp. 94–100.

39. See Schelling, *Arms and Influence,* p. 92–125, and his *Strategy of Conflict,* pp. 187–203.

40. See Jervis, "The Political Implications of Loss Aversion," and Stein, "International Co-operation and Loss Avoidance," pp. 21–22.

41. The term comes from Jervis, "The Political Implications of Loss Aversion," p. 199.

42. For a discussion of the spiral model, see Jervis, *Perception and Misperception in International Politics,* pp. 58–113.

43. Because of the lower slope in the domain of gains, promised rewards (or threatened punishments) bring lower marginal utility than in the domain of losses.

44. See Daniel Kahneman, "Reference Points, Anchors, Norms and Mixed Feelings," *Organizational Behavior and Human Decision Processes* (1992): 296–312.

45. For discussions of the security dilemma, see John H. Herz, "Idealist Internationalism and the Security Dilemma," *World Politics* 2 (January 1950): 157–80; Herz, *Political Realism and Political Idealism* (Chicago: University of Chicago Press, 1951), pp. 209–10; Jervis, "Cooperation under the Security Dilemma"; Jervis, *Perception and Misperception in International Politics,* pp. 62–76; Schelling, *The Strategy of Conflict,* ch. 9; Schelling, *Arms and Influence,* ch. 6; and George Quester, *Offense and Defense in the International System* (New York: John Wiley, 1977).

46. Jervis, *Perception and Misperception in International Politics,* pp. 67–72 and 349–55.

47. This was appreciated by classical realists but has been forgotten by Kenneth Waltz and his students. See, for example, Hans J. Morgenthau, *Politics among Nations: The Struggle for Power and Peace,* 3d ed. (New York: Knopf, 1966), ch. 4. Compare to John Mearsheimer, "The False Promise of International Institutions," *International Security* (winter 1994/95): 5–49.

48. See McGeorge Bundy, *Danger and Survival: Choices about the Bomb in the First Fifty Years* (New York: Random House, 1988), ch. 9, especially pp. 432–33.

49. See Henry A. Kissinger, *White House Years* (Boston: Little, Brown, 1979), pp. 632–35.

50. The connection between the Nixon assurance and the Cienfuegos Bay incident remains unclear, but see Raymond Garthoff, *Reflections on the Cuban Missile Crisis* (Washington, D.C.: Brookings Institution, 1987), pp. 94–100.

51. German motives during the July Crisis are discussed in chapter 7.

52. For discussions of Khrushchev's motives see Aleksandr Fursenko and Timothy Naftali, *"One Hell of a Gamble": Krushchev, Castro, and Kennedy, 1958–1964* (New York: W.W. Norton, 1997); Bundy, *Danger and Survival,* pp. 415–27; Garthoff, *Reflections on the Cuban Missile Crisis,* pp. 5–22; and Lebow and Stein, *We All Lost the Cold War,* pp. 19–50.

53. For a discussion of these, see Jervis, *Systems Effects,* especially pp. 21–28 and 32–39.

54. See Thomas Ehrlich, *Cyprus, 1958–1967* (London: Oxford University Press, 1974), pp. 61–89; George Harris, *The Troubled Alliance* (Washington, D.C.: American Enterprise Institute, 1972), especially pp. 114–17; Henri Barkey, "Turkish-American Relations in the Post-War Era," *Orient* (September 1992): 447–64; and Sharon Weiner, *Turkish Foreign Policy* "Decision-Making on the Cyprus Issue: A Comparative Analysis of Three Crises" (Ph.D. diss., Duke University, 1980).

55. See Ali E. Hillal Dessouki, "The Primacy of Economics: The Foreign Policy of Egypt," in Bahgat Korany and Ali. E. Hillal Dessouki, eds., *The Foreign Policies of Arab States,* 2d ed. (Boulder: Westview, 1991); and John Watterbury, *The Egypt of Nasser and Sadat: The Political Economy of Two Regimes* (Princeton: Princeton University Press, 1983), ch. 8.

56. See Jervis, *Perception and Misperception in International Politics;* and Jervis, *The Logic of Images in International Relations.*

57. For details, see Ernest May, *Imperial Democracy* (New York: Harcourt, Brace, 1961), p. 161.

58. For a discussion of public opinion formation in cases where the public lacks sufficient contextual information, see John R. Zaller, *The Nature and Origins of Mass Opinion* (Cambridge: Cambridge University Press, 1922), ch. 3.

59. For an analysis of the European domestic politics of the period see Thomas Rochon, *The Politics of the Peace Movement in Western Europe* (Princeton: Princeton University Press, 1988). For data on public opinion in the Federal Republic of Germany, where opposition to INF deployments was most intense, see Stephen Szabo, "West European Public Perceptions of Security Issues" (Washington, D.C.: United States Information Agency, July 1988). German domestic politics is analyzed in Thomas Risse-Kappen, *Die Krise der Sicherheitspolitik: Neuorientierungen und Entscheidungsprozesse im politischen System der Bundesrepublik Deutschland, 1977–1984* (Mainz: Grünewald-Kaiser, 1988). For a general discussion of mixed strategies and doing things "in twos," see Jervis, *Systems Effects,* pp. 271–75.

60. Morgenthau, *Politics among Nations,* pp. 540–41.

61. See Tversky and Kahneman, "The Framing of Decisions and the Psychology of Choice," p. 211; Kahneman and Tversky," Prospect Theory: An Analysis of Decision under Risk," p. 286; Kahneman and Tversky, "Choices, Values and Frames," *American Psychologist* (April 1984): 341–150; Daniel Kahneman, "Reference Points, Anchors, Norms and Mixed Feelings," *Organizational Behavior and Human Decision Processes* 51 (March 1992): 296–312; William Samuelson and Richard Zeckhauser, "Status Quo Bias in Decision Making," *Journal of Risk and Uncertainty* 1 (1977): 7–59; and Gregory, Lichtenstein and MacGregor, "The Role of Past States in Determining Reference Points for Policy Decisions."

62. For a discussion of decision making and the levels of analysis question in

international politics, see Jervis, *Perception and Misperception in International Politics*, pp. 13–31.

4   ◆   Confronting Prussian Ambition

1. For a full discussion of the social and economic precursors to the German revolutions, see Rudolph Stadelmann, *Soziale und politische Geschichte der Revolution von 1848* (Munich: F. Bruckman, 1948); Veit Valentin, *Geschichte der deutschen Revolution*, 2 vols. (Cologne: Scientia Verlag, 1968); and Theodore S. Hamerow, *Restoration, Revolution, Reaction: Economics and Politics in Germany, 1815–1871* (Princeton: Princeton University Press, 1958). For a discussion of the lack of unity among the disaffected classes, see Friedrich Meinecke, "The Year 1848 in German History," *Review of Politics* 10 (1948): 475–88.

2. See Lewis Namier, "Frankfurt, 1848: Start of Germany's Bid for World Power," in Otto Pflantze, ed., *The Unification of Germany, 1848–1871* (Huntington, N.Y.: Krieger, 1979), pp. 85–87; Otto Pflantze, *Bismarck and the Development of Germany: The Period of Unification, 1815–1871* (Princeton: Princeton University Press, 1963), pp. 39–44; and W. H. Dawson, *The German Empire, 1867–1914*, vol. 2 (Hamden, Conn.: Archon Books, 1966), ch. 2.

3. Quoted in Dawson, *The German Empire*, p. 37. See also Erich Eyck, *Bismarck and the German Empire* (New York: W.W. Norton, 1968), p. 22; and H.W. Koch, *A History of Prussia* (London: Longman, 1978), pp. 234–35.

4. Recall Palmerston's statement on the question was the following: "Only three men have understood it. One was the Prince consort, and he is dead. The second was a German professor, and he went mad over it. I am the third, and I have forgotten all about it."

5. For discussions of the Eider-Danes and their political movement, see William Carr, *The Origins of the Wars of German Unification* (London: Longman, 1991), pp. 39–41, 66–67. See also Lawrence D. Steefel, *The Schleswig-Holstein Question* (Cambridge: Harvard University Press, 1932), pp. 6–7.

6. For discussions of the development of competing bodies of law in Europe see Gerald Strauss, *Law, Resistance, and the State: The Opposition to Roman Law in Reformation Germany* (Princeton: Princeton University Press, 1986), and Harold J. Berman, *Law and Revolution: The Formation of the Western Legal Tradition* (Cambridge: Harvard University Press, 1983). The Salic Law may be found in Ernest F. Henderson, ed., *Select Historical Documents of the Middle Ages* (London: G. Bell, 1925), pp. 176–89.

7. The death of Christian VIII in December 1847 did little to ease tensions as his successor, Friedrich, continued to support the Danish succession for Schleswig.

8. F. Darmstaedter, *Bismarck and the Creation of the Second Reich* (London: Methuen, 1948), pp. 88–89.

9. See Hajo Holborn, *A History of Modern Germany, 1840–1945* (Princeton: Princeton University Press, 1982), pp. 65–66; Keith Sandiford, *Great Britain and the Schleswig-Holstein Question, 1848–1864: A Study in Diplomacy, Politics, and Public Opinion* (Toronto: University of Toronto Press, 1975), pp. 24–25; and A.J.P. Taylor, *The Struggle for Mastery in Europe, 1848–1918* (Oxford: Oxford University Press, 1971), p. 12.

10. Cowley, the British representative at Frankfurt, was receiving instructions "to recommend to the Germans that liberal and enlightened system of Commercial Policy which the Progressive Diffusion of Political Knowledge has convinced all reflecting men is sound in Theory and which the experience of late years has proved to be advantageous in Practice." Quoted in W.E. Mosse, *The European Powers and the German Question, 1848–1871* (New York: Octagon, 1966), p. 23.

11. Bastide to Arago, 31 July 1848, quoted in Taylor, *The Struggle for Mastery in Europe*, p. 16.

12. The position was adopted for awhile by Palmerston. Neither Prussia nor Denmark could be made to accept it. See Mosse, *The European Powers and the German Question*, p. 20; and Sandiford, *Great Britain and the Schleswig-Holstein Question*, p. 31.

13. There is widespread agreement among historians that the Russian threat was a bluff. It did, however, serve to deter the Prussians from continuing their invasion of Jutland and compelled them to seek a negotiated settlement. See Theodor Schiemann, *Geschichte Russlands unter Kaiser Nikolaus I*, vol. 4 (Berlin, 1904–19), p. 164; Carr, *The Origins of the Wars of German Unification*, p. 40; and Taylor, *The Struggle for Mastery in Europe*, pp. 15–16. A different impression of the tsar's feelings regarding the invasion of Prussia is conveyed in Heinrich von Sybel, *The Founding of the German Empire*, vol. 1 (New York: Crowell, 1890), pp. 448–49. Taylor is inconsistent in his explanation for the Prussian withdrawal. He variously locates the chief influence on Friedrich Wilhelm in domestic and international politics. Compare, for example, *The Struggle for Mastery in Europe*, pp. 14 and 38.

14. Poorly written and full of potential loopholes for both the Danes and the Germans, the London Treaty established the constitution of 1849 for Denmark. The duchies would each have their own constitution, and the estates would retain deliberative authority over local matters. The succession issue was settled in favor of the House of Glücksburg. The Duke of Augustenburg surrendered his estates in the duchies for a cash payment and agreed to live outside of Danish dominions. He promised that he and his heirs would never undermine the new succession although he did not officially renounce his rights. His promise, however, had no legal status in the German Confederation, as his son had attained majority and was not considered bound by his father's representations. The Confederation itself was not a signatory to the treaty, an omission that was not without consequence for the future of German policy toward the duchies.

15. See Winfried Baumgartz, "Zur Außenpolitik Friedrich Wilhelms IV., 1840–

1858," in Otto Büsch, ed., *Friedrich Wilhelm IV. in Seiner Zeit* (Berlin: Colloquium, 1987), pp. 132–56.

16. This is the conclusion reached by Friedrich Meinecke in *Radowitz und die deutsche Revolution* (Berlin: Mittler und Sohn, 1912), pp. 241 ff. See also Alexander Scharff, *Die europäische Grossmächte und die deutsche Revolution: Deutsche Einheit und europäische Ordnung 1848–1851* (Leipzig: Koehler & Amelang, 1942), pp. 29–31.

17. My translation. Diary entries can be found in Walter Möring, ed., *Josef von Radowitz: Nachgelaßene Briefe und Aufzeichnungen zur Geschichte der Jahre 1848–1853* (Osnabrück: Biblio Verlag, 1967), pp. 86–87.

18. See Helmutt Diwald, ed., *Von der Revolution zum norddeutschen Bund: Politik und Ideengut der preußischen Hochkonservativen 1848–1866. Aus dem Nachlass von Ernst Ludwig von Gerlach*, 2 vols. (Göttingen: Vandenhoeck & Ruprecht, 1970), vol. 1, p. 318.

19. Walter Bußmann, *Zwischen Preußen und Deutschland: Friedrich Wilhelm IV: Eine Biographie* (Berlin: Siedler Verlag, 1990), p. 273.

20. See ibid., p. 275; and David E. Barclay, *Friedrich Wilhelm IV and the Prussian Monarchy, 1840–1861* (Oxford: Clarendon Press, 1995), pp. 161–62.

21. Palmerston to Prince Albert, 16 September 1847, in T. Martin, *The Life of H.R.H. the Prince Consort* (London, 1875), vol. 1, pp. 447 ff.

22. Palmerston to Strangways, 23 March 1848, in Mosse, *The European Powers and the German Question*, p. 16.

23. My translation. Freiherr von Arnim to King Friedrich Wilhelm IV, 2 April 1848, in *Revolutionsbriefe 1848: Ungedrucktes aus dem Nachlass König Friederich Wilhelms IV. von Preussen* (Leipzig: Koehler, 1930), no. 30. See also same to the same, 17 April 1848, no. 38.

24. My translation. King Friedrich Wilhelm IV to Alexandra Feodorowna, tsarina of Russia, 21 April 1848, in *Revolutionsbriefe 1848*, no. 42, p. 82.

25. Meyendorff to Nesselrode, 19 March 1848, in Mosse, *The European Powers and the German Question*, pp. 16–17.

26. Emphasis in the original. "Jetzt ist Hamlet kriegsdurstig, rechnet auf russische und schwedische Truppen und Schiffshilfe." King Friedrich Wilhelm IV to Alexandra Feodorowna, tsarina of Russia, 22 June 1848, *Revolutionsbriefe 1848*, no. 64, p. 113.

27. See, for example, Mosse, *The European Powers and the German Question*, p. 20; René Albrecht Carrié, *A Diplomatic History of Europe since the Congress of Vienna* (New York: Harper & Row, 1958), p. 77.

28. My translation. Nesselrode to Meyendorff, 26 April 1848, in Mosse, *The European Powers and the German Question*, p. 19.

29. My translation. Alexandra Feodorowna, tsarina of Russia, to Friedrich Wilhelm IV, date uncertain, *Revolutionsbriefe 1848*, no. 50. On the problem with dating this letter, see note 2, page 92, which accompanies the document.

30. See Steefel, *The Schleswig Holstein Question*, p. 7; Carr, *The Origins of the*

Wars of German Unification, p. 40; and Sandiford, *Great Britain and the Schleswig-Holstein Question,* pp. 23–24.

31. "Une rupture complète avec Francfort, la paix avec le Denmarc, telles sont à mes yeux les conditions indispensables." The text of the tsar's letter is reprinted in Otto Hoetsch, *Peter von Meyendorff, Politischer und Privater Briefwechsel, 1826–1863,* vol. 2 (Berlin: Gruyter, 1923), pp. 197–98.

32. See Mosse, *The European Powers and the German Question,* pp. 28–29. The effect of the tsar's communications on the king's demeanor is noted in the diary entries of his Court President, Ludwig von Gerlach. See Hellmut Diwald, ed., *Von der Revolution zum Norddeutschen Bund: Politik und Ideengut der preußischen Hochkonservativen, 1848–1866. Aus dem Nachlaß von Ernst Ludwig von Gerlach* (Göttingen: Vandenhoeck & Ruprecht, 1970), p. 182.

33. King Friedrich Wilhelm IV to Tsarina Alexandra Feodorowna, Sanssouci, 22 June 1848, *Revolutionsbriefe 1848,* no. 64, pp. 112–15.

34. See, for example, the tsar's letter of 2/14 June 1848 to Friedrich Wilhelm: "Je suis fier et heureux de pouvoir me dire que nos coeurs se comprennent malgré les distances qui nous séparent." *Revolutionsbriefe 1848,* no. 69.

35. Quoted in Steefel, *The Schleswig-Holstein Question,* pp. 94–95.

36. For an analysis of the Hesse-Kassel crisis and its relationship to the two crises over Schleswig and Holstein and to the larger question of German unification, see James W. Davis Jr., "The Forgotten Variable: The Role of Promises in Deterrence" (Ph.D. diss., Columbia University, 1995), pp. 142–51.

37. For more on the content of the March Patent, see Steefel, *The Schleswig-Holstein Question,* ch. 3.

38. See Otto Pflanze, *Bismarck and the Development of Germany,* 2 vols. (Princeton: Princeton University Press, 1990), vol. 1, *The Period of Unification, 1815–1871,* p. 234; Steefel, *The Schleswig-Holstein Question,* pp. 79–81, 99–100. Friedrich, it will be remembered, was of legal age when his father resigned his right of succession. Thus, the claim was made that having never acceded to the conditions of the Treaty of London himself, he could not be bound by it. Further, the ducal estates argued that they had never ratified the new right of succession and considered Augustenburg to be their duke. See Eyck, *Bismarck and the German Empire,* p. 82.

39. See Carr, *The Origins of the Wars of German Unification,* pp. 72–76; Eyck, *Bismarck and the German Empire,* pp. 85–87; Pflanze, *Bismarck and the Development of Germany,* vol. 1, pp. 242–43; Steefel, *The Schleswig-Holstein Question,* pp. 99–109; and Heinrich von Sybel, *The Founding of the German Empire,* 7 vols. (New York: Crowell, 1890), vol. 3, pp. 185–86.

40. Carr, *The Origins of the Wars of German Unification,* p. 80.

41. Goltz to King Wilhelm, 9 February 1864, in Hermann Oncken, *Die Rheinpolitik Kaiser Napoleons III von 1863 bis 1870 und der Ursprung des Krieges von*

1870/71 (hereafter RKN) (Stuttgart: Deutsche Verlags-Anhalt, 1926), no. 13. "Er sagte mir, wir sollen Schleswig-Holstein und einige andere in der näheliegende Länder annexieren." Taylor asserts that the French interest was "the district of the Saar which France had retained by the first treaty of Paris (1814) and lost by the second (1815)" (Taylor, *The Struggle for Mastery in Europe*, p. 148, n. 3).

42. Quoted in Mosse, *The European Powers and the German Question*, p. 152.

43. See ibid., pp. 150–52; Pflanze, *Bismarck and the Development of Germany*, vol. 1, p. 244; and Sandiford, *Great Britain and the Schleswig-Holstein Question*, pp. 70–72.

44. Sandiford, *Great Britain and the Schleswig-Holstein Question*, pp. 144–45.

45. The sources of Britain's estrangement from France were recognized at the time. In Paris Drouyn de Lhuys told Cowley that "the question of Poland had shown that Great Britain could not be relied upon when war was in the distance." See the memorandum from Cowley to Russell, 3 January 1864, reprinted in Steefel, *The Schleswig-Holstein Question*, pp. 166–67. See also Cowley to Russell, 15 January 1864, reprinted in Mosse, *The European Powers and the German Question*, p. 164.

46. See Mosse, *The European Powers and the German Question*, p. 153.

47. Sandiford, *Great Britain and the Schleswig-Holstein Question*, p. 142.

48. Napier to Russell, 11 May 1864, quoted in Mosse, *The European Powers and the German Question*, p. 195, n. 1. Napier grasped the essence of the Russian position: "The interest of Russia on behalf of Denmark is sincere, but it is secondary. The interest of Russia in maintaining an alliance with Austria and Prussia against France on account of Paris is capital and predominant."

49. Steefel, *The Schleswig-Holstein Question*, p. 130.

50. Quoted in Heinrich Friedjung, *The Struggle for Supremacy in Germany, 1859–1866* (London: Macmillan, 1935), p. 48.

51. Quoted in Steefel, *The Schleswig-Holstein Question*, p. 107.

52. Pflanze, *Bismarck and the Development of Germany*, vol. 1, p. 238.

53. However, in *Reflections and Reminiscences* Bismarck writes: "If the utmost we aimed at [annexation] could not be realized, we might have, in spite of all Augustenburg renunciations, gone as far as the introduction of the dynasty and the establishment of a new middle state" (Bismarck, pp. 125–26), the documentary evidence to the contrary is quite convincing. See Arnold O. Meyer, "Die Zielsetzung in Bismarcks Schleswig-Holsteinischer Politik von 1855 bis 1864," *Zeitschrift der Gesellschaft für Schleswig-Hosteinische Geschichte* 53 (1923), pp. 106, 108, and 113. See also Steefel, *The Schleswig-Holstein Question*, p. 107. Historians generally agree that in his memoirs Bismarck was trying to secure his place as a champion of German (rather than Prussian) nationalism, a cause he first adopted in 1866.

54. To the Prussian ambassador at Paris, Robert von der Goltz, Bismarck remarked, "Seeing things from the Schleswig-Holstein angle must never cloud for us the European angle" (Carr, *The Origin of the Wars of Unification*, p. 70).

55. See Darmstaedter, *Bismarck and the Creation of the Second Reich*, p. 233; Steefel, *The Schleswig-Holstein Question*, p. 160; and Pflanze, *Bismarck and the Development of Germany*, vol. 1, pp. 240–41.

56. Quoted in Chester Wells Clark, *Franz Joseph and Bismarck: The Diplomacy of Austria before the War of 1866* (Cambridge: Harvard University Press, 1934), p. 65.

57. Quoted in Mosse, *The European Powers and the German Question*, p. 168.

58. Redern to Bismarck, 2 February 1864, in Herman von Petersforff et al., eds., *Bismarck: Die gesammelten Werke* (Berlin: 1923–33), vol. 4, no. 243, pp. 297–98.

59. Steefel, *The Schleswig-Holstein Question*, p. 166.

60. See Count Redern to Bismarck, 3 February 1864, in ibid., appendix VII, p. 349. The Prussians were not the only power informed of the limits to Russian support. After meeting with Russian foreign minister Gorchakov, the British ambassador reported to Lord Russell: "From his present expressions I understood that not only he had resolved in no case to go to war in this quarrel, but that he believed no other Government would ever go to war" (Napier to Russell, 24 May 1864, Steefel, *The Schleswig-Holstein Question*, pp. 353–54). The tsar saw a strong Prussia as a necessary counterbalance to the revisionist France of Napoleon III. See the report of Napier quoted in Mosse, *The European Powers and the German Question*, p. 165.

61. See Mosse, *The European Powers and the German Question*, p. 167, n. 3.

62. Steefel, *The Schleswig-Holstein Question*, p. 141.

63. See Bismarck to von Werther, 21 December 1863, GW, vol. 4, no. 193.

64. Taylor, *The Struggle for Mastery in Europe*, p. 150.

65. The position was supported by his diplomats abroad. Napier (ambassador at St. Petersburg) argued for a naval presence in the Baltic and Buchanan (ambassador at Copenhagen) insisted that "a little decided language" would induce the Prussian king to "abstain from military operations." See Sandiford, *Great Britain and the Schleswig-Holstein Question*, chs. 5 and 6, quotation on p. 89.

66. Quoted in Steefel, *The Schleswig-Holstein Question*, p. 171.

67. For example, ibid., pp. 162–63; Sandiford, *Great Britain and the Schleswig-Holstein Question*, p. 91.

68. Quoted in Steefel, *The Schleswig-Holstein Question*, p. 172.

69. On Christmas Eve 1863, Bismarck wrote to his ambassador at Paris that "he was not in any way frightened of war" with Denmark but that Prussia must not turn its back to the great powers. See Carr, *The Origins of the Wars of German Unification*, p. 69.

70. Pflanze, *Bismarck and the Development of Germany*, vol. 1, p. 240.

71. Ibid., p. 239.

72. Steefel, *The Schleswig-Holstein Question*, pp. 170–71. Although it appears that the frontier had been crossed not on orders from the governments but rather as a result of events in the field, it was determined that it was undesirable to give up the

position in Kolding and the threat to all of Jutland it conveyed (Mosse, *The European Powers and the German Question*, pp. 179, 189).

73. Mosse, *The European Powers and the German Question*, p. 179.

74. Quoted in Steefel, *The Schleswig-Holstein Question*, p. 187.

75. Ibid., pp. 189–90.

76. Talleyrand to Drouyn, 23 February 1864, quoted in Mosse, *The European Powers and the German Question*, p. 181. For Austro-Prussian discussions regarding the expansion of military activity into Denmark proper, see Clark, *Franz Joseph and Bismarck*, ch. 2.

77. Mosse, *The European Powers and the German Question*, p. 186.

78. There exists much speculation, if little solid research, on the determinants of Napoleon's shifting policies in this period. Most accounts center on the influence at court of the Austrian ambassador Metternich and his admirer, the pro-Austrian Empress Eugénie.

79. Prussia and Austria had signed a protocol agreement on 17 January 1864, at the time of their ultimatum to Denmark over Schleswig-Holstein. Article 5 held, in part, that the question of ducal succession would be decided only by mutual agreement. See Clark, *Franz Joseph and Bismarck*, pp. 62–64.

80. At Napoleon's insistence a condition was added with respect to Schleswig: "the populations of the northern districts of Schleswig, if they give evidence in a free vote of their desire to be united with Denmark, shall be ceded to Denmark." Bismarck succeeded in postponing the plebescite, which was not held until 1920. See Steefel, *The Schleswig-Holstein Question*, pp. 261–62.

81. See Sybel, *The Founding of the German Empire*, vol. 4, pp. 136–37; Dawson, *The German Empire*, vol. 1, p. 198; Carr, *The Origins of the Wars of German Unification*, pp. 122–23. For a statement of the political objectives of the third Germany by one of its proponents, see the letter of Prince Chlodwig von Hohenlohe-Schillingsfürst to Queen Victoria of England dated 4 May 1864 in *The Memoirs of Prince Chlodwig of Hohenlohe-Schillingsfürst*, 2 vols. (New York: Macmillan, 1906), vol. 1, pp. 132–35.

82. See the discussions of Schönbrunn in Taylor, *The Struggle for Mastery in Europe*, p. 154; Mosse, *The European Powers and the German Question*, pp. 215–16; Steefel, *The Schleswig-Holstein Question*, p. 258; and Carr, *The Origins of the Wars of German Unification*, pp. 120–21.

83. My translation. *Preussisches Kronratsprotokoll* (Crown Council Transcript), Berlin, 29 May 1865, *Die Auswärtige Politik Preussens, 1858–1871* (hereafter APP) (Berlin: Historische Reichskommission, 1939), vol. 6 (April 1865–March 1866), doc. 100, p. 177.

84. Helmuth von Moltke to Adolf von Moltke, 24 June 1865, in *Letters of Field-Marshal Count Helmuth von Moltke to His Mother and His Brothers* (New York: Harper & Bros., 1892), p. 176.

85. My translation. *Preussisches Kronratsprotokoll,* 29 May 1865, APP, vol. 6, p. 178.

86. My translation. Ibid., p. 179.

87. *Preussisches Kronratsprotokoll,* Berlin, 28 February 1866, APP, vol. 6, pp. 611–19; Carr, *The Origins of the Wars of German Unification,* p. 127; Pflanze, *Bismarck and the Development of Germany,* vol. 1, pp. 284–85; Dawson, *The German Empire,* vol. 1, p. 205.

88. My translation. *Preussisches Kronratsprotokoll,* 28 February 1866, APP, vol. 6, p. 615.

89. My translation. Ibid. p. 616. See also von Moltke's notes on the council, ibid., pp. 617–18.

90. Writing to the Austrian representative in London, Count Mensdorff argued that by pursuing "strict neutrality between Austria and Prussia, England in fact tilts the balance in favor of the latter." My translation. Quoted in the original French by Mosse, *The European Powers and the German Question,* pp. 222–23.

91. Ibid., pp. 229–30.

92. See Clarendon to Cowley, private, 11 April 1866, cited in ibid., p. 230.

93. Clarendon to Loftus, private, 7 March 1866, *The Diplomatic Reminiscences of Lord Augustus Loftus 1863–1878* (London, 1894), 2d series, vol. 2, p. 43. See also Loftus to Clarendon, most confidential, Berlin, 17 March 1866, APP, vol. 6, pp. 689–90.

94. Mosse, *The European Powers and the German Question,* p. 229.

95. See ibid., p. 237.

96. Taylor, *The Struggle for Mastery in Europe,* p. 156.

97. Quoted in Mosse, *The European Powers and the German Question,* p. 218.

98. Quoted in Sybel, *The Founding of the German Empire,* vol. 4, p. 299.

99. "Vous ne doutez certainement pas de la sollicitude affectueuse avec laquelle je comprends et partage les sentiments que doivent Vous causer l'état présent des affaires et en particulier la tension de Vos rapports avec la cour de Vienne." Tsar Alexander II to King Wilhelm I, St. Petersburg, 19 March 1866, APP, vol. 6, no. 592.

100. Taylor, *The Struggle for Mastery in Europe,* p. 156.

101. Ministère des Affaires Etrangères, *Les origines diplomatiques de la guerre de 1870/71: Recueil des documents officiels,* Lefebvre de Béhaine to Drouyn de Lhuys, 27 September 1865, vol. 7, no. 1590.

102. Quoted in Sybel, *The Founding of the German Empire,* vol. 4, p. 316.

103. My translation. *Preussisches Kronratsprotokoll,* 28 February 1866, APP, vol. 6, p. 615.

104. Taylor, *The Struggle for Mastery in Europe, 1848–1918,* p. 160.

105. For a study of the Italian-Prussian negotiations see Friedrich Beiche, *Bismarck und Italien: Ein Beitrag zur Vorgeschichte des Krieges 1866,* no. 208 of the series *Historische Studien* (Berlin: Ebering, 1931).

106. The text of the treaty can be found in Sybel, *The Founding of the German Empire*, vol. 4, pp. 354–55.

107. Napoleon had in fact concluded a secret convention with Austria on 12 June 1866, in which he secured a promise of the cession of Venetia, even in the event of an Austrian victory, in exchange for French neutrality. There is some debate as to whether Bismarck deserves credit for Napoleon's neutrality. Sybel and Taylor appear to attribute Napoleon's position to Bismarck's diplomatic skill and the Italian alliance. Clark and Gall argue that Napoleon preferred neutrality in any case so as to maximize his maneuverability in postwar deliberations. See Taylor, *The Struggle for Mastery in Europe*, pp. 160–62; Sybel, *The Founding of the German Empire*, vol. 4, p. 356; Clark, *Franz Joseph and Bismarck*, p. 439; and Lothar Gall, *Bismarck: The White Revolutionary*, 2 vols. (London: Allen & Unwin, 1986), vol. 1, p. 285.

108. Von Moltke shared the assessment. When it became clear that war was inevitable, he wrote his brother: "Fifty years of peace have shown that union can never be achieved by means of a peaceful understanding; the German mind is too unpractical and too easily carried away by phrases. If it is God's will that Prussia should solve the problem, the general European situation is not unfavorable." Helmuth von Moltke to Adolf von Moltke, 26 May 1866, in *Letters to His Mother and His Brothers*, pp. 177–78.

109. See Eyck, *Bismarck and the German Empire*, pp. 122–23; Gall, *Bismarck*, vol. 1, p. 296; Mosse, *The European Powers and the German Question*, pp. 237–38; and Taylor, *The Struggle for Mastery in Europe*, p. 166.

110. For an excellent account of military operations, see Gordon Craig, *The Battle of Königgrätz: Prussia's Victory over Austria 1866* (Princeton: Princeton University Press, 1964).

111. When told of the massive battle and Prussia's speedy victory, the papal secretary of state, Cardinal Antonelli, cried, "Casca il mondo!" (The world is collapsing). Quoted in Fritz Stern, *Gold and Iron: Bismarck, Bleichröder and the Building of the German Empire* (New York: Vintage Books, 1979), p. 88.

112. Ironically, the Austrians had beat back the Italian attack and defeated the Italian army at Custoza.

113. See Gordon A. Craig, *Germany: 1866–1945* (New York: Oxford University Press, 1978), pp. 4–5; Darmstaedter, *Bismarck and the Creation of the Second Reich*, pp. 292–93; Taylor, *The Struggle for Mastery in Europe*, pp. 167–68; Mosse, *The European Powers and the German Question*, pp. 239–41. The relevant documents are in *Die gesammelten Werke*, vol. 15, p. 271 ff.

114. My translation. Goltz to Wilhelm I, Paris, 4 July 1866, in Oncken, RKN, 1926, vol. 1, p. 301.

115. See Eyck, *Bismarck and the German Empire*, pp. 132–33; Craig, *Germany, 1866–1945*, pp. 2–4.

116. Quoted in Darmstaedter, *Bismarck and the Creation of the Second Reich*, p. 290.

117. Bismarck recounts the debates over expanding war aims and his appraisal of the French threat in his memoirs: "After the battle of Königgrätz the situation was such that a favorable response on our part to the first advances of Austria with a view to peace negotiations, was not only possible, but seemed demanded by the interference of France" (*Reflections and Reminiscences*, pp. 137–52). In an interview with the historian Heinrich Friedjung in 1890, Bismarck claims to have feared a force of 40–60,000 French troops on the Rhine frontier as well as a French-directed assault from the south with the assistance of troops from the South German states; see Heinrich Friedjung, *Der Kampf um die Vorherrschaft in Deutschland, 1859–1866* (Stuttgart: Cotta, 1913), vol. 2, appendix 1, p. 581.

118. My translation. Hermann Gaupp, ed., *Bismarck: Briefe an seine Braut und Gattin* (Stuttgart: Cotta, 1944), p. 572.

119. Bismarck also began negotiations for defensive alliances with the South German states aimed at strengthening his hand for further talks with Napoleon.

120. Pflanze, *Bismarck and the Development of Germany*, vol. 1, p. 309, n. 70, p. 370.

5 ◆ Conquest or Consolidation?

1. Hermann Oncken, *Die Rheinpolitik Kaiser Napoleons III von 1863 bis 1870 und der Ursprung des Krieges von 1870/71* (hereafter RKN) (Stuttgart: Deutsche Verlags-Anhalt, 1926), vol. 1, pp. 331, 340, 353; vol. 2, pp. 82–96; Gordon A. Craig, *Germany: 1866–1945* (New York: Oxford University Press, 1978), p. 16; E. Malcolm Carroll, *Germany and the Great Powers, 1866–1914* (Hamdon, Conn.: Archon, 1966), p. 29; and A.J.P. Taylor, *The Struggle for Mastery in Europe, 1848–1918* (Oxford: Oxford University Press, 1971), pp. 171–75.

2. See Bismarck to Goltz, Berlin, 8 March 1867, in Herman von Petersforff et al., eds., *Bismarck: Die gesammelten Werke* (hereafter GW) (Berlin: 1923–33), vol. 6, no. 702, pp. 293–95.

3. Robert H. Lord, *The Origins of the War of 1870: New Documents from the German Archives* (New York: Russell & Russell, 1966), pp. 10–12; Craig, *Germany: 1866–1945*, p. 114; Carroll, *Germany and the Great Powers*, p. 28; and Erich Eyck, *Bismarck and the German Empire* (New York: W.W. Norton, 1968), p. 157.

4. Bismarck to Bernstorff, 14 January 1867, in Helmut Böhme, ed., *The Foundation of the German Empire: Select Documents* (Oxford: Oxford University Press, 1971), no. 125, p. 183. See also Otto Pflanze, *Bismarck and the Development of Germany* (Princeton: Princeton University Press, 1990), vol. 1, pp. 368–70; Wilhelm Busch, "Bismarck und die Entstehung des Norddeutschen Bundes," *Historische*

Zeitschrift 103 (1909): 73–78; A.J.P. Taylor, *Bismarck: The Man and the Statesman* (London: Hamish Hamilton, 1955), pp. 92–102; Otto von Bismarck, *Reflections and Reminiscences* (New York: Harper & Row, 1968), pp. 153–76; and Craig, *Germany: 1866–1945*, pp. 11–22.

5. For detailed accounts of the crisis, see William Carr, *The Origins of the Wars of German Unification* (London: Longman, 1991), pp. 156–61; W.E. Mosse, *The European Powers and the German Question, 1848–1871* (New York: Octagon, 1969), pp. 262–70; and Carroll, *Germany and the Great Powers*, pp. 31–42.

6. See, for example, Bismarck to Goltz, Berlin, 8 August 1866, GW, vol. 6, no. 539, pp. 111–12, and Bismarck to Goltz, Berlin, 20 August 1866, GW, vol. 6, no. 579, pp. 135–38. See also Pflanze, *Bismarck and the Development of Germany*, vol. 1, p. 372.

7. Writing to Goltz, Bismarck allowed that a triple alliance between France, Austria, and Italy was a danger, but " a greater danger [would be] a closer alliance of France with England, whose predominant sea power could destroy our trade, and would provide support to French ground operations" (Bismarck to Goltz, Berlin, 15 February 1867, secret, *Die Auswärtige Politik Preussens, 1858–1871* [hereafter APP] [Berlin: Historische Reichskommission, 1939], vol. 8, no. 241, p. 392). British mistrust of France only deepened during a crisis over Belgian railways in 1869.

8. See Oncken, RKN, vol. 2, ch. 8; Taylor, *The Struggle for Mastery in Europe, 1848–1918*, pp. 192–95. See also Mosse, *The European Powers and the German Question*, pp. 275, 280–81.

9. Lord, *The Origins of the War of 1870*, p. 27.

10. Ibid., p. 42.

11. Bismarck's diplomatic activities as well as his maneuvering within Prussian political circles during this period are fascinating. For a good account see Pflanze, *Bismarck and the Development of Germany*, vol. 1, pp. 433–57. The relevant documents from the Sigmaringen archives are collected in Georges Bonnin, *The Hohenzollern Candidature for the Spanish Throne* (London, 1957). The Ems Telegram in its original and edited versions may be found in Böhme, *The Foundation of the German Empire*, no. 177, pp. 228–29.

12. This is Lord's position. See *The Origins of the War of 1870*, p. 113.

13. Mosse takes issue with Lord's interpretation. See *The European Powers and the German Question, 1848–1871*, p. 305, n. 6.

14. My translation. Bismarck to Werthern, 26 February 1869, GW, vol. 6Ib, no. 1327, p. 2.

15. Bismarck to Wilhelm I, 20 November 1869, translation in Böhme, no. 152, pp. 203–4.

16. Bismarck to Wilhelm I, 9 March 1870, GW, vol. 6b, no. 1521, p. 271. Found in translation in Böhme, *The Foundation of the German Empire*, pp. 218–19.

17. Pflanze, *Bismarck and the Development of Germany,* vol. 1, p. 449. For the opposite position, see Rudolph Morsey, "Die Hohenzollernsche Thronkandidatur in Spanien," *Historische Zeitschrift* 186 (1958): 573–88.

18. Quoted in Pflanze, *Bismarck and the Development of Germany,* vol. 1, p. 423.

19. The Russo-Prussian entente was not lost on the Austrians. The Austrian ambassador at St. Petersburg wrote Vienna that on Germany, the tsar was completely "Prussian." See Chotek to Beust, 12 January/31 December 1870/1869, in Mosse, *The European Powers and the German Question,* p. 294.

20. Münch to Beust, Berlin, 16 July 1870, in Böhme, *The Foundation of the German Empire,* no. 182b, p. 233. Taylor downplays the significance of the Russian threat for Austrian neutrality arguing that Austria preferred neutrality in any event. See *The Struggle for Mastery in Europe, 1848–1918,* p. 208.

21. Albrecht von Bernstorff, *Im Kampf für Preussens Ehre,* ed. K. Ringhoffer (Berlin, 1906), p. 609. Quoted in Mosse, *The European Powers and the German Question,* p. 295.

22. See Mosse, *The European Powers and the German Question,* pp. 295–300.

23. Ibid., pp. 312–19.

24. See Taylor, *The Struggle for Mastery in Europe,* p. 212.

25. Mosse, *The European Powers and the German Question,* pp. 338–55.

26. Extract from the diary of the Baroness Spitzemberg, R. Vierhaus, ed., *Das Tagebuch der Baronin Spitzemberg* (Göttingen, 1960), p. 94.

27. George F. Kennan, *The Decline of Bismarck's European Order: Franco-Russian Relations, 1875–1890* (Princeton: Princeton University Press, 1979), pp. 11–12.

28. Raymond J. Sontag, *European Diplomatic History, 1871–1932* (New York: Appleton-Century-Crofts, 1961), pp. 6–7.

29. See E. Malcolm Carroll, *Germany and the Great Powers, 1866–1914: A Study in Public Opinion and Foreign Policy* (Hamden, Conn.: Archon, 1966), pp. 90–91; Allan Mitchell, *Bismarck and the French Nation: 1848–1890* (New York: Pegasus, 1971), ch. 5.

30. For discussions of the French recovery see William L. Langer, *European Alliances and Alignments, 1871–1890* (New York: Alfred A. Knopf, 1939), pp. 26, 31, 37; Mitchell, *Bismarck and the French Nation,* pp. 84–86; Otto Pflanze, *Bismarck and the Development of Germany,* vol. 2 (Princeton: Princeton University Press, 1990), p. 261; Gerhard Ritter, *The Sword and the Scepter: The Problem of Militarism in Germany,* 4 vols. (Coral Gables, Fla.: University of Miami Press, 1969), vol. 1, p. 227, and vol. 2, p. 20; Taylor, *The Struggle for Mastery in Europe,* p. 223.

31. See Pflanze, *Bismarck and the Development of Germany,* vol. 2, ch. 7; quotations from pp. 196 and 202. For background on the dynamics of political Catholicism in this period, see Jonathan Sperber, *Popular Catholicism in Nineteenth Century Germany* (Princeton: Princeton University Press, 1984). For a discussion of church-state relations in the new empire, see William Harbutt Dawson, *The Ger-*

man Empire, 1867–1914, vol. 1 (Hamden, Conn.: Archon Books, 1966), pp. 401–41.

32. See, for example, Winifred Taffs, *Ambassador to Bismarck: Lord Odo Russell, First Baron Ampthill* (London: Frederick Muller, 1938), pp. 26–29. See also Pflanze, *Bismarck and the Development of Germany,* vol. 2, pp. 263–64. Langer turns the argument around. Rather than internationalizing a domestic struggle, he argues that "the Kulturkampf was part and parcel of Bismarck's policy to isolate France and prevent the formation of a coalition against Germany" (Langer, *European Alliances and Alignments,* p. 37).

33. Charles Lowe, "A Famous War Scare," *Contemporary Review* 84 (July-December 1903), p. 93; Langer, *European Alliances and Alignments,* pp. 37–38; Pflanze, *Bismarck and the Development of Germany,* vol. 2, pp. 262–63. Criticism of the *Kulturkampf* emanating from the bishops of Belgium provoked similar threats from Bismarck. See Winifred Taffs, "The War Scare of 1875," *Slavonic Review* 9 (1930–31), p. 339.

34. Queen Victoria to the kaiser, 10 February 1874, in George Earle Buckle, ed., *Letters of Queen Victoria,* 2d series (New York: Longmans, Greene, 1926), vol. 2, pp. 312–13.

35. See the discussion in Langer, *European Alliances and Alignments,* pp. 40–42; and Pflanze, *Bismarck and the Development of Germany,* vol. 2, pp. 264–65. The kaiser was uneasy with the bellicose tone of the speech, although in the end he followed Bismarck's language to the letter. See Friedrich Curtius, ed., *The Memoirs of Prince Chlodwig of Hohenlohe-Schillingsfürst* (New York: Macmillan, 1906), vol. 2, pp. 128–29.

36. My translation. Bismarck to Hohenlohe, ambassador at Paris, 26 February 1875, in Johannes Lepsius et al., eds., *Die grosse Politik der europäischen Kabinett: 1871–1914* (hereafter GP) (Berlin: Deutsche Verlagsgesellschaft für Politik und Geschichte, 1924), vol. 1, no. 155.

37. Pflanze, *Bismarck and the Development of Germany,* vol. 2, p. 266.

38. Colonel Krause, Section Chief, to Chief of the General Staff, Field Marshal von Moltke, 18 March 1875, GP, vol. 1, no. 157.

39. My translation. State Secretary Bülow to Münster, ambassador at London, 11 April 1875, GP, vol. 1, no. 158. The conclusion of the general staff is a classic example of worst case analysis and the assessment of intent from capability. The addition of the fourth battalions was apparently designed for no purpose other than the provision of billets for a number of French officers who had been promoted during the war. See Albert, Duc de Broglie, *La Mission de M. de Gontaut Biron* (Paris, 1896). Cited in Joseph V. Fuller, "The War Scare of 1875," *American Historical Review* 24 (January 1919), pp. 199–200.

40. Son of Friedrich Wilhelm IV's minister.

41. The Radowitz mission was deemed necessary as the ambassador, Prince Reuss, was absent from Petersburg because of prolonged illness and the chargé d'affaires

was not considered skillful enough to accomplish the task. See Carroll, *Germany and the Great Powers*, p. 109; Taffs, "The War Scare of 1875," p. 337. The best-informed work on the Radowitz mission remains Hajo Holborn, *Bismarcks Europäische Politik zu Beginn der siebziger Jahre und die Mission Radowitz* (Berlin: Deutsche Verlagsgesellschaft für Politik und Geschichte, 1925).

42. The rumor regarding a German offer of support for Russian interests in the Balkans in exchange for a pledge of neutrality was apparently begun by a person or persons in the Russian chancellery, perhaps by Gorchakov himself. See, Langer, *European Alliances and Alignments*, p. 42; Lowe, "A Famous War Scare," pp. 101–2; and Pflanze, *Bismarck and the Development of Germany*, vol. 2, p. 265. For an example of early scholarship that gives credence to the rumor, see Hans Herzfeld, *Die deutsch-französische Kriegsgefahr von 1875: Forschungen und Darstellungen aus dem Reichsarchiv*, vol. 3 (Berlin, 1922). For a refutation see Holborn, *Mission Radowitz*, pp. 53–90.

43. Langer, *European Alliances and Alignments*, p. 42. See also Holborn, *Mission Radowitz*, pp. 69–71.

44. Created in the foreign office press bureau, the authorship of these and similar articles is generally attributed Bismarck himself although he denied it at the time and afterward. See Carroll, *Germany and the Great Powers*, pp. 113–15; Pflanze, *Bismarck and the Development of Germany*, vol. 2, p. 267, n. 68; and Freiherr Lucius von Ballhausen, *Bismarck-Erinnerungen des Staatsministers Freiherrn von Ballhausen* (Stuttgart and Berlin, 1921), pp. 71–72.

45. Craig, *Germany: 1866–1945*, p. 109; Eyck, *Bismarck and the German Empire*, pp. 217–18; Langer, *European Alliances and Alignments*, p. 45–46; and Pflanze, *Bismarck and the Development of Germany*, vol. 2, p. 268.

46. Gontaut-Biron to Decazes, 21 April 1875, Ministère des Affaires Etrangères, *Documents diplomatiques français* (hereafter DDF), first series, vol. 1, no. 395. Radowitz's version of the discussion is to be found in a memorandum dated 12 May 1875, GP, vol. 1, no. 177.

47. Taffs, *Lord Odo Russell*, p. 86.

48. Ibid., pp. 89–90.

49. My translation. Decazes to Gontaut-Biron, 6 May 1875, DDF, first series, vol. 1, no. 402.

50. Quoted in Kennan, *The Decline of Bismarck's European Order*, pp. 18–19.

51. Buckle, *Letters of Queen Victoria*, 2d series, vol. 2, pp. 391–96; Eyck, *Bismarck and the German Empire*, p. 219; Pflanze, *Bismarck and the Development of Germany*, vol. 2, pp. 269–70; and Taffs, *Lord Odo Russell*, p. 96.

52. Taffs, *Lord Odo Russell*, p. 97. Bülow's contemporary account is very nearly the same. See memorandum by Bülow, Foreign Secretary, 9 May 1875, in E.T.S. Dugdale, ed., *German Diplomatic Documents: 1871–1914* (hereafter GDD) (New York: Barnes & Noble, 1969), vol. 1, pp. 5–6.

53. In doing so, I will utilize statements of the principal actors at the time of the

meetings. Although documentary evidence from the immediate period is probably less consciously biased in self-serving ways (than, for instance, memoirs), it is nonetheless likely to contain some biases. Thus, the same event is likely to be reported in very different light by different participants. The task for the analyst is to try to interpret the documentary records in terms of the most likely biases of those who wrote them. For an example of the phenomenon of biased interpretation of events from postwar American history and a discussion of the methodological implications of such biases, see Fred I. Greenstein and Richard Immerman, "What Did Eisenhower Tell Kennedy about Indochina? The Politics of Misperception," *Journal of American History* 79, no. 2 (September 1991): 568–87.

54. A facsimile of the original telegram may be found in A.Z. Manfred, *Obrazovanie russko-frantsuzkogo soyuza* (Moscow: Nauka, 1975), p. 98.

55. Fuller was the most determined proponent of the thesis that Bismarck was prepared to attack France if it did not slow the pace of rearmament. See Fuller, "The War Scare of 1875." For the counterargument, see Herzfeld, *Die deutsch-französische Kriegsgefahr von 1875,* especially p. 57.

56. The same conclusion is reached by Mitchell, *Bismarck and the French Nation,* p. 86.

57. Bismarck to Edwin von Manteuffel, commander of the German occupation troops in France, 2 June 1873, GP, vol. 1, p. 189.

58. Colonel Krause, Section Chief, to Chief of the General Staff, Field Marshal von Moltke, 18 March 1875, GP, vol. 1, no. 157. See also State Secretary Bülow to Count Münster, ambassador at London, 11 April 1875, GP, vol. 1, no. 158.

59. See Bismarck to Reuss, ambassador at Petersburg, 28 February 1874, GP, no. 151; and Odo Russell to Lord Granville, 22 December 1873, in Taffs, *Lord Odo Russell,* pp. 65–66.

60. In February the British ambassador at Berlin wired London: "The danger which Prince Bismarck dreads most at present is an understanding between Russia, France and Austria which would isolate Germany and unite her ultramontane enemies" (Taffs, *Lord Odo Russell,* p. 75). See also *Memoirs of Hohenlohe-Schillingsfürst,* vol. 2, p. 142.

61. At one point during the crisis Hohenlohe thought it doubtful war could be avoided. See *Memoirs of Hohenlohe-Schillingsfürst,* vol. 2, p. 142.

62. See Craig, *Germany: 1866–1945,* p. 107; Kennan, *The Decline of Bismarck's European Order,* p. 11; and Taylor, *The Struggle for Mastery in Europe,* p. 225.

63. The Earl of Derby to Queen Victoria, 5 May 1875, *Letters of Queen Victoria,* 2d series, vol. 2, p. 390. Although he admitted the extraordinary pace of French recovery, Derby did not regard it as a threat to Germany.

64. Quoted in Taffs, *Lord Odo Russell,* p. 76.

65. Bülow to Hohenlohe, GP, pp. 267–69.

66. Bismarck's motives were not lost on Russell, who astutely reported them to his government: "Prince Bismarck has nothing to gain from a second and aggressive

war on France, which would certainly not have the support of public opinion, because it could bring no further advantages to Germany. France is therefore safe if she will abstain first, from serious preparations for a war of revenge, and second, from seeking anti-German alliances" (Russell to Lord Derby, 28 March 1875, in Taffs, *Lord Odo Russell*, p. 80).

67. See, for example, William H. Dawson, *The German Empire, 1867–1914* (Hamden, Conn.: Archon, 1966), vol. 1, p. 363. See also Ritter, *The Sword and the Scepter*, vol. 1, pp. 255–57.

68. "Possession of Strassbourg and Metz is a national necessity for Germany, not a question of pride" (my translation; State Secretary of the Foreign Ministry von Bülow to von Hohenlohe, ambassador at Paris, 28 December 1875, GP, vol. 1, no. 195).

69. Bismarck to von Reuss, ambassador at St. Petersburg, 28 February 1874, GP, vol. 1, no. 151.

70. My translation. Bismarck to Münster, ambassador at London, 12 May 1875, GP, vol. 1, no. 176.

71. See Carroll, *Germany and the Great Powers*, p. 119; and Fuller, "The War Scare of 1875," p. 198.

72. For example, Carroll, *Germany and the Great Powers*, pp. 120–23; Dawson, *The German Empire, 1867–1914*, vol. 2, pp. 101–2; Eyck, *Bismarck and the German Empire*, p. 220; and Imanuel Geiss, *German Foreign Policy, 1871–1914* (London: Rutledge & Kegan Paul, Ltd., 1976), p. 28. The chief architects of this confusion appear to have been Decazes and Gorchakov, each of whom stood to gain politically from such an interpretation. According to one account, Gorchakov was driven by vanity and envy of Bismarck, whom he regarded as a onetime protégé (Lowe, "A Famous War Scare," p. 110). Decazes's motive may have been less personal. To the extent that Germany was regarded as the major threat to European peace, French rearmament and efforts to secure allies would not give rise to alarm among the other powers. Thus, in the aftermath of the crisis, neither corrected rumors that the tsar had deterred a German attack with a strong demarche, and Decazes contributed to their widespread circulation. For a similar line of reasoning, see Kennan, *The Decline of Bismarck's European Order*, pp. 21–22.

73. One author presents quotes from discussions between the two emperors. The tsar is said to have spoken frankly: "I will not allow France to be attacked. Germany could not move unless *we* remained neutral, and I do not mean to stand aloof if an emergency should arise" (E. M. Almedigen, *The Emperor Alexander II* [London, Bodley Head, 1962], p. 270, emphasis in the original). Almedigen cites S.S. Tatichev, *Imperator Alexandr II, Ego Zhizn' I Tsarstvovanie*, vol. 2 (St. Petersburg: Izdaniye A.S. Suvorina, 1903), as his source. Upon examination of the Russian text, however, I can find no such quotation or anything resembling it. I thank Alexander Motyl for assistance translating the Russian text.

74. My translation. Quoted (in German) in Reinhard Wittram, "*Bismarck und*

Gorĉakov im Mai 1875," *Nachrichten der Akademie der Wissenschaften in Göttingen*, Philologische-Historische Klasse (1955), p. 224.

75. Gorchakov to Oubril, 18 April 1875, in "*Franko-germanskii Krizis 1875g*," *Krasnyi Arkhiv: Istoricheskkii Zhurnal*, vol. 6, no. 91 (1938), p. 120. I thank Sergei Tikhonov for translating this document.

76. Oubril to Gorchakov, 2 May 1875, in "*Franko-germanskii Krizis 1875g*," p. 127. In this document Oubril also argues that the real threat to European peace comes not from Germany, but from France. He notes the ongoing efforts at military reorganization in France and the widespread desire for revanche. He concludes that Russia should not trust France. I thank Sergei Tikhonov for translating this document.

77. It is worth noting that direct documentary evidence to support the standard interpretation—that Russia and Britain adopted a hard line in Berlin—is nearly nonexistent.

78. My translation. Le Flô to Decazes, 6 May 1875, DDF, first series, vol. 1, no. 404.

79. Quoted in Lowe, "A Famous War Scare," p. 104.

80. Quoted in Fuller, "The War Scare of 1875," p. 215.

81. Bismarck wrote: "If he [Gorchakov] was anxious to be applauded in Paris . . . I was quite ready to assist him and have a five franc piece struck in Berlin, with the inscription: '*Gorchakov, protège la France!*' We might also have rigged up a theater at the German Embassy, where he could appear before a French audience with the same legend, in the character of a guardian angel dressed in white with wings to the accompaniment of Bengal fire" (my translation; Otto von Bismarck, *Gedanken und Errinerungen* [Stuttgart: J. G. Cotta'sche, 1922], vol. 2, pp. 200–201). For Fuller's refutation of Bismarck's account see "The War Scare of 1875," p. 196.

Bismarck's anger toward Gorchakov was not a result of what was said in their meetings on May 10. Rather, it developed in the aftermath, wherein Gorchakov and Decazes proclaimed triumph at the expense of Bismarck's reputation as the master diplomatist. Before taking leave of Berlin, Gorchakov sent two confidential telegrams for the tsar, each of which was leaked to the press in garbled form so as to cast Bismarck in poor light. The first was the aforementioned circular to Russian diplomatic missions. The second was to the tsar's sister, the Queen of Württemberg, and read "J'emporte de Berlin assurances formelles de la paix" (I bring from Berlin formal assurances of peace). It was leaked to the press and reproduced as "L'emporté de Berlin donne des assurances formelles de la paix" (The frenzied one in Berlin gives formal assurances of peace). See Kennan, *The Decline of Bismarck's European Order*, pp. 20–21.

82. Gontaut-Biron to Decazes, 11 May 1875, DDF, first series, vol. 1, no. 416. See also Kennan, *The Decline of Bismarck's European Order*, p. 20; and Langer, *European Alliances and Allignments*, p. 50.

83. René Albrecht-Carrié, *A Diplomatic History of Europe since the Congress of Vienna* (New York: Harper & Row, 1958), p. 166; and Taylor, *The Struggle for Mastery in Europe*, p. 227.

84. Kaiser Wilhelm I to Bülow, State Secretary of the Foreign Ministry, 11 May 1875, GP, no. 175.

85. Memorandum by Bülow, State Secretary of the Foreign Ministry, 9 May 1875, GDD, vol. 1, pp. 5–6.

86. My translation. Bismarck to Münster, 12 May 1875, GP, no. 176. A similar message was relayed to London via the British ambassador, Lord Russell. See Russell to Derby, 10 May 1875, in Taffs, *Lord Odo Russell*, p. 97.

87. Bismarck to Münster, 12 May 1875, GDD, p. 6.

88. Kennan makes the same point in *The Decline of Bismarck's European Order*, p. 12.

89. Press accounts quoted in Carroll, *Germany and the Great Powers*, p. 122.

90. Assurances serve to buttress a target's baseline of expectations, reducing uncertainty about the future.

91. See Bismarck to Münster, 14 May 1875, GDD, vol. 1, pp. 8–10.

92. Fuller, "The War Scare of 1875," pp. 225–26.

93. It was, perhaps, an understanding on the part of the German leadership that Britain and Russia had reason to fear a strong France that lent credibility to their assurances. See, for example, Münster to Bismarck, 28 July 1875, GDD, vol. 1, p. 298.

6 ◆ From Europe to Africa

1. For the history of German colonialism see William O. Aydelotte, *Bismarck and British Colonial Policy: The Problem of South West Africa, 1883–1885* (Philadelphia: University of Pennsylvania Press, 1937); Paul M. Kennedy, *The Rise of the Anglo-German Antagonism 1860–1914* (London: Allen & Unwin, 1980), ch. 10; John A. Moses and Paul M. Kennedy, eds., *Germany in the Pacific and Far East, 1870–1914* (St. Lucia: University of Queensland Press, 1977); Otto Pflanze, *Bismarck and the Development of Germany* (Princeton: Princeton University Press, 1990), vol. 3, ch. 5; Mary E. Townsend, *The Rise and Fall of Germany's Colonial Empire, 1884–1918*, 2d ed. (New York: Fertig, 1966); Woodruff P. Smith, *The German Colonial Empire* (Chapel Hill: University of North Carolina Press, 1978); William L. Langer, *The Diplomacy of Imperialism, 1890–1902* (New York: Knopf, 1951); A.J.P. Taylor, *German's First Bid for Colonies, 1884–1885: A Move in Bismarck's European Policy* (London: Macmillan, 1938); Maximilian von Hagen, *Bismarcks Kolonialpolitik* (Stuttgart: Deutsche Verlags-Anstalt, 1923); Hans-Ulrich Wehler, *Bismarck und der Imperialismus* (Cologne: Kiepenheuer u. Witsch, 1969).

2. Quoted in Pflanze, *Bismarck and the Development of Germany*, vol. 3, p. 114.

3. Odo Russell to Lord Granville, 11 February 1873, quoted in Aydelotte, *Bismarck and British Colonial Policy,* p. 19.

4. Friedrich Curtius, ed., *The Memoirs of Prince Chlodwig of Hohenlohe-Schillingsfürst* (New York: Macmillan, 1906), vol. 2, p. 267.

5. Whereas this discussion examines Bismarck's political motives in the adoption of a colonial policy, a full explanation for nineteenth-century imperialism requires an appreciation of the changing means of colonial conquest and imperial administration. See Daniel R. Headrick, *The Tools of Empire: Technology and the European Imperialism in the Nineteenth Century* (Oxford: Oxford University Press, 1981).

6. For the most extreme version of this argument, see Townsend, *The Rise and Fall of Germany's Colonial Empire,* pp. 68–69 and 84–91. Although her analysis of Bismarck's motives for initiating a colonial policy in the mid-1880s differs from that presented here, Townsend conceptualizes motivation in a way that is quite consistent with this study. For example, two subsections of chapter 3 are titled "A Favorable International Situation Presents Itself" and "The Opportunist Grasps the Opportunity."

7. Most prominently William O. Aydelotte, "Wollte Bismarck Kolonien?" in Werner Conze, ed., *Deutschland und Europa: Festschrift für Hans Rothfels* (Düsseldorf: Droste Verlag, 1951).

8. Taylor, *Germany's First Bid for Colonies,* p. 6. In *The Struggle for Mastery in Europe* Taylor picks up the theme: "Bismarck wanted a grievance, not colonies" (p. 295).

9. Henry Ashby Turner, "Bismarck's Imperialist Venture: Anti-British in Origin?" in Prosser Gifford and William R. Louis, eds., *Britain and Germany in Africa: Imperial Rivalry and Colonial Rule* (New Haven, Conn.: Yale University Press, 1967), pp. 47–82.

10. For a discussion of Bismarck's European policies and the goal of isolating France, see William L. Langer, *European Alliances and Alignments, 1871–1890* (New York: Knopf, 1939), p. 452. Bismarck's efforts to avoid antagonizing the British in the early period of German colonial acquisition are discussed briefly below and are detailed in Aydelotte, *Bismarck and British Colonial Policy.*

11. For Marxist interpretations, which will not be dealt with here, see G.W.F. Hallgarten, *Imperialismus vor 1914: Die soziologischen Grundlagen der Aussenpolitik europäischen Grossmächte vor dem ersten Weltkrieg,* 2 vols. (Munich: Beck, 1963); and Fritz Müller, *Deutschland-Zanzibar-Ostafrika* (Berlin: Rütten & Loening, 1959).

12. For a discussion of the move to mercantilism and its many implications for Germany, see Helmut Böhme, *Deutschlands Weg zur Grossmacht: Studien zum Verhältnis von Wirtschaft und Staat während der Reichgrundungszeit 1848–1881* (Cologne: Kiepenheuer u. Witsch, 1966), pp. 474–604.

13. Pflanze, *Bismarck and the Development of Germany*, vol. 3, pp. 118 and 121; and Wehler, *Bismarck und der Imperialismus*, pp. 158–68 and 474–85.

14. Aydelotte, *Bismarck and British Colonial Policy*, p. 18.

15. Imanuel Geiss, *German Foreign Policy, 1871–1914* (London: Rutlege & Kegan Paul, 1976), p. 44.

16. My translation. Interview with the African explorer Eugene Wolf, 5 December 1888, in Herman von Petersdorff et al., eds., *Bismarck: Die gesammelten Werke*, 15 vols. (Berlin, 1923–33) (hereafter GW), vol. 8, no. 456, p. 646.

17. Turner, "Bismarck's Imperialist Venture," especially pp. 50–51. See also William Harbutt Dawson, *The German Empire, 1867–1914, and the Unity Movement*, 2 vols. (Hamden, Conn.: Archon Books, 1966), vol. 2, p. 178.

18. Gordon A. Craig, *Germany: 1866–1945* (New York: Oxford University Press, 1978), p. 119.

19. Bismarck to Münster, 12 August 1884, in T.S. Dugdale, ed., *German Diplomatic Documents, 1871–1914*, 4 vols. (hereafter GDD), vol. 1, p. 182.

20. Dawson, *The German Empire, 1867–1914*, vol. 2, p. 201.

21. See, for example, Bismarck's Reichstag speech of 16 March 1885, *Politischen Reden*, vol. 11, pp. 141–42.

22. Quoted in *The Annual Register: A Review of Public Events at Home and Abroad, 1890* (London: Longmans, Green, 1890), p. 317.

23. See G.N. Sanderson, "The Anglo-German Agreement of 1890 and the Upper Nile," *English Historical Review* 78 (January 1963): 49–72; D.R. Gillard, "Salisbury's Heligoland Offer: The Case against the 'Witu Thesis,'" *English Historical Review* 80 (July 1965): 538–52; Langer, *Diplomacy of Imperialism*, ch. 4; Robert O. Collins, "Origins of the Nile Struggle: Anglo-German Negotiations and the MacKinnon Agreement of 1890," and W.R. Louis, "Great Britain and German Expansion in Africa, 1884–1919," both in Gifford and Louis, eds., *Britain and Germany in Africa*.

24. Sanderson, "The Anglo-German Agreement of 1890," p. 52.

25. Quoted in Kennedy, *The Rise of the Anglo-German Antagonism*, p. 204.

26. Sanderson, "The Anglo-German Agreement of 1890," p. 53. See also Salisbury to Queen Victoria, 24 February 1890, *Letters of Queen Victoria*, 3d series, vol. 1, pp. 573–74.

27. For the text of these notes, see Johannes Lepsius et al., eds., *Die grosse Politik der europäischen Kabinett: 1871–1914* (hereafter GP) (Berlin: Deutsche Verlagsgesellschaft für Politik und Geschichte, 1924), vol. 4, pp. 143–73.

28. Cabinet memorandum, 2 June 1890, in Lady Gwendolen Cecil, *Life of Robert Marquis of Salisbury* (London: Hodder and Stoughtyon, 1971), vol. 4, pp. 283–84.

29. See Cecil, *Life of Robert Marquis of Salisbury*, vol. 4, pp. 277–80; Langer, *Diplomacy of Imperialism*, pp. 115–17; Sanderson, "The Anglo-German Agreement of 1890," pp. 53–54; and Kennedy, *The Rise of the Anglo-German Antagonism*, p. 207.

30. Collins, "Origins of the Nile Struggle," p. 134.

31. Quoted in Sanderson, "The Anglo-German Agreement of 1890," p. 71.

32. By 1890 the economic arguments for colonial acquisition could no longer be sustained. Most in the German leadership came to realize that colonies were net consumers of resources. The costs of administration and protection outstripped the benefits in terms of raw materials and consumer markets in all but a very few overseas possessions. For example, in 1891 the colonies provided 123,605 marks in tax revenues to the Reich, whereas they required expenditures of 13,518,717 for administration and defense (Pflanze, *Bismarck and the Development of Germany,* vol. 3, pp. 133–42).

33. Bismarck to Münster, 25 January 1885, GDD, vol. 1, pp. 188–89.

34. The chancellor's son was State Secretary in the foreign ministry and was often sent by his father to Britain as a special emissary on colonial matters.

35. Count Herbert Bismarck to Hatzfeldt, 18 December 1889, GDD, vol. 2, p. 27.

36. Hatzfeldt to Caprivi, 30 April 1890, GDD, vol. 2, pp. 30–32.

37. See Hatzfeldt to Bismarck, 22 December 1889, GDD, vol. 2, pp. 29–30; and Hatzfeldt to Caprivi, 30 April 1890, GDD, vol. 2, pp. 30–32.

38. See Langer, *Diplomacy of Imperialism,* pp. 118–19; and Sanderson, "The Anglo-German Agreement of 1890," pp 56–58. Salisbury's initial offer of Heligoland included a provision to secure the All-Red Route, but this provision was rejected by the Germans. See Marschall to Hatzfeldt, 17 May 1890, GDD, vol. 2, p. 35.

39. There had been discussions between Count Münster and Lord Granville regarding the status of Heligoland in 1884. Bismarck showed some interest in securing the North Sea island as part of a settlement of disputes over Angra Pequena, but his interest was short-lived, and the issue was dropped. See Bismarck to Münster, 5 May, 1884, GDD, vol. 1, pp. 170–71; Münster to Bismarck, 8 May 1884, GDD, vol. 1, pp. 172–73; Bismarck to Münster, 25 May 1884, GDD, vol. 1, pp. 173–74; and Bismarck to Münster, 1 June 1884, GDD, vol. 1, pp. 175–76.

40. Hatzfeldt to Caprivi, 30 April 1890, GDD, vol. 2, pp. 30–31.

41. Marschall to Hatzfeldt, 25 May 1890, GDD, vol. 2, pp. 36–37.

42. Ibid., pp 37–38.

43. Sanderson, "The Anglo-German Agreement of 1890," p. 62.

44. In February 1890 Salisbury wrote to Odo Russell's successor at Berlin, Sir Edward Malet, that "the friction between Germans and Englishmen in Africa whenever they come into contact is increasing" (Cecil, *Life of Robert Marquis of Salisbury,* vol. 4, p. 279). See also Townsend, *The Rise and Fall of Germany's Colonial Empire,* pp. 114–15. The German foreign office likewise recognized the dangers inherent in the ongoing expeditions into the African hinterland. See Marschall to Hatzfeldt, 23 May 1890, GDD, vol. 2, p. 36.

45. Sanderson, "The Anglo-German Agreement of 1890," pp. 49–51. See also Hatzfeldt, ambassador at London, to Caprivi, 30 April 1890, GDD, vol. 2, pp. 30–

31. The Sultan of Zanzibar was widely, and quite correctly, regarded as a British client. See, for example, the Sultan of Zanzibar to Queen Victoria, 2 September 1889, *Letters of Queen Victoria,* 3d series, vol. 1, 529.

46. Salisbury's offer is detailed in Hatzfeldt to Baron von Marschall, 14 May, 1890, GDD, vol. 2, pp. 32–34. For analyses of Salisbury's decision to seek a comprehensive settlement through the Heligoland offer, see Cecil, *Life of Robert Marquis of Salisbury,* vol. 4, pp. 284–94; Sanderson, "The Anglo-German Agreement of 1890," pp. 62–63; and Collins, "Origins of the Nile Struggle," pp. 145–141.

47. Karl Peters is quoted in J. Alden Nichols, *Germany after Bismarck: The Caprivi Era, 1890–1894* (Cambridge: Harvard University Press, 1958), p. 102.

48. Of course, these facts were not lost on the British cabinet. See Salisbury to Queen Victoria, 12 June 1890, *Letters of Queen Victoria,* 3d series, vol. 1, pp. 614–15. See also Hatzfeldt's report of the difficulties Salisbury encountered in the cabinet over the cession of Heligoland in Hatzfeldt to Caprivi, 11 June 1890, GDD, vol. 2, pp. 42–43; and Sanderson, "The Anglo-German Agreement of 1890," p. 68.

49. Marschall to Hatzfeldt, 29 May 1890, GDD, vol. 2, p. 37.

50. Quoted in Townsend, *The Rise and Fall of Germany's Colonial Empire,* p. 162.

51. Marschall to Hatzfeldt, 29 May 1890, GDD, vol. 2, p. 38.

52. For example, the *Deutsche Kolonialzeitung* complained that "the acquisition of Heligoland blinds everyone to the losses sustained. With a pen's stroke, England has acquired a dominating position in East Africa. . . . Also we have lost the coast" (quoted in Townsend, *The Rise and Fall of Germany's Colonial Empire,* pp. 162–63).

53. See the analysis of public reaction to the treaty in E. Malcolm Carroll, *Germany and the Great Powers, 1866–1914* (Hamden, Conn.: Archon Books, 1966), pp. 294–95; and Kennedy, *The Rise of the Anglo-German Antagonism,* p. 208.

54. See Carroll, *Germany and the Great Powers,* p. 295.

55. *The Times,* 1 July 1891, quoted in Jean Stengers, "British and German Imperial Rivalry: A Conclusion," in Gifford and Louis, *Britain and Germany in Africa,* pp. 343–43.

56. See Salisbury to Queen Victoria, 10 June 1890, *Letters of Queen Victoria,* 3d series, vol. 1, pp. 613–14.

57. Kennedy, *The Rise of the Anglo-German Antagonism,* pp. 209–10; and Nichols, *Germany after Bismarck,* pp. 59 and 102.

58. Salisbury to Queen Victoria, 10 June 1890, in Cecil, *Life of Robert Marquis of Salisbury,* vol. 4, p. 298.

59. See Stengers, "British and German Imperial Rivalry" pp. 342–45; Kennedy, *The Rise of the Anglo-German Antagonism,* pp. 211–14; and Langer, *Diplomacy of Imperialism,* p. 7. Relations began to break down when the Germans protested elements of the Anglo-Congolese Treaty of May 1894, which according to Craig "were questionable from the standpoint of both legality and elementary honesty

and were patently designed to evade the provisions of the Anglo-German Agreement of 1890" (*Germany: 1866–1945*, p. 243). The Germans did their part to strain relations by filing a claim for sole possession of the Samoan Islands, then under joint control of Great Britain, Germany, and the United States under terms of a treaty of 1889 (see Paul M. Kennedy, "Germany and the Samoan Tridominium, 1889–98," in John A. Moses and Paul M. Kennedy, eds., *Germany in the Pacific and Far East* [St. Lucia: University of Queensland Press, 1977], pp. 89–114).

60. For example, Paul Huth and Bruce Russett, "What Makes Deterrence Work? Cases from 1900–1980," *World Politics* 36 (July 1984): 496–526; Huth and Russett, "Testing Deterrence Theory: Rigor Makes a Difference," *World Politics* 42 (July 1990): 466–502; Richard Ned Lebow and Janice Gross Stein, "Deterrence: The Elusive Dependent Variable," *World Politics* 42 (April 1990): 336–70.

61. Jonathan Mercer, *Reputation and International Politics* (Ithaca, N.Y.: Cornell University Press, 1996), chs. 3 and 5.

62. Glen H. Snyder and Paul Diesing, *Conflict among Nations: Bargaining, Decision Making and System Structure in International Crises* (Princeton: Princeton University Press, 1977), pp. 108–11, 262–68.

63. See Lebow and Stein, "Deterrence: The Elusive Dependent Variable," p. 353.

64. Huth and Russett, "What Makes Deterrence Work?" p. 506.

65. Huth and Russett, "Testing Deterrence Theory," p. 500. In the original data set Huth and Russett code the outcome of the entire case as a deterrence success, whereas in the revised data set the outcome of the first period is coded as a failure, the second, a success. Huth attributes the recoding to a fuller appreciation of the intentions and policies of Germany as well as a more comprehensive reading of multiple historical sources (private correspondence with Huth, 12 July 1994).

66. Lebow and Stein, "Deterrence: The Elusive Dependent Variable," p. 338.

67. Eugene N. Anderson, *The First Moroccan Crisis: 1904–1906* (Hamden, Conn.: Archon Books, 1966), p. 9.

68. For the history of Madrid Conference and the events that precipitated it, see Earl Fee Cruickshank, *Morocco at the Parting of the Ways* (Philadelphia: University of Pennsylvania Press, 1935).

69. In addition to recognizing French rights in Morocco, the Italian foreign minister promised that, when renewed, the Triple Alliance would contain "nothing hostile" to France. See Anderson, *The First Moroccan Crisis*, pp. 25–26. See also Kennedy, *The Rise of the Anglo-German Antagonism*, p. 269.

70. Dwight E. Lee, *Europe's Crucial Years: The Diplomatic Background of World War I, 1902–1914* (Hanover, N.H.: Clark University Press, 1974), pp. 49–80; Anderson, *The First Moroccan Crisis*, pp. 81–109.

71. Lee, *Europe's Crucial Years*, pp. 75–78; Anderson, *The First Moroccan Crisis*, pp. 118–25.

72. On the policy of *pénétration pacifique*, see Raymond Poidevin, *Les Relations economiques et financières entre la France et l'Allemagne de 1898 à 1914*

(Paris: Librairie Armand Colin, 1969), pp. 276–85; and Anderson, *The First Moroccan Crisis*, pp. 128–34.

73. Samuel R. Williamson Jr., *The Politics of Grand Strategy: Britain and France Prepare for War, 1904–1914* (London: Ashfield Press, 1990), p. 30.

74. Trade figures for the period may be found in Poidevin, *Les Relations economiques et financières*, pp. 159–61, 402–6, and in Anderson, *The First Moroccan Crisis*, p. 2.

75. Lee, *Europe's Crucial Years*, p. 79.

76. See Delcassé to Bihourd, 18 April 1904, no. 152 in Ministère des Affaires Etrangères, *Documents diplomatiques: Affaires du Maroc, 1901–1905* (Paris: 1905). Hereafter this *Livre jaune* is cited as L.j. 1901–5.

77. Anderson, *The First Moroccan Crisis*, pp. 183–85.

78. Raymond J. Sontag, "German Foreign Policy, 1904–1906," *American Historical Review* 33 (January 1928), p. 289; and Kennedy, *The Rise of the Anglo-German Antagonism*, p. 276. See also von Bülow to the kaiser, 4 April 1905, GDD, vol. 3, p. 224.

79. Bülow to the kaiser, 20 March 1905, GDD, vol. 3, p. 223.

80. Cited in Lee, *Europe's Crucial Years*, pp. 114–15. See also Anderson, *The First Moroccan Crisis*, p. 194. The kaiser's remarks went somewhat further than either von Bülow or the influential foreign office official Friedrich von Holstein had envisaged when they encouraged him to visit Tangier. See the instructions issued the kaiser on March 26 in Anderson, pp. 190–91.

81. Lee, *Europe's Crucial Years*, p. 115; and Anderson, *The First Moroccan Crisis*, p. 199.

82. Quoted in Anderson, *The First Moroccan Crisis*, p. 202.

83. See Bülow to the kaiser, 4 April 1905, GDD, vol. 3, pp. 224–25.

84. Radolin to Bülow, 30 March 1904, in GP, vol. 17, no. 5210.

85. Anderson, *The First Moroccan Crisis*, p. 208; Lee, *Europe's Crucial Years*, p. 117.

86. See the dispatch from Bülow to the kaiser, 4 April 1905, GP, vol. 20, no. 6599; and the memorandum of the same date by Holstein, GP, vol. 20, no. 6601.

87. See, for example, Kennedy, *The Rise of the Anglo-German Antagonism*, p. 415 ff.

88. Anderson, *The First Moroccan Crisis*, pp. 208–11; Lee, *Europe's Crucial Years*, 117–18; and Williamson, *The Politics of Grand Strategy*, p. 34.

89. Williamson, *The Politics of Grand Strategy*, p. 33.

90. Although Rouvier strongly disagreed with Delcassé's Moroccan policy, the foreign minister was apparently needed in the work of mediating between Russia and Japan in the East (Anderson, *The First Moroccan Crisis*, pp. 220–21).

91. See, for example, Radolin to Bülow, 30 April 1905, GDD, vol. 3, p. 226. See also Bülow, at Karlsruhe, to the German Foreign Office, 5 May 1905, GDD, vol. 3, pp. 227–28.

92. Quoted in Anderson, *The First Moroccan Crisis*, p. 225.

93. Quoted in Carroll, *Germany and the Great Powers*, p. 529.

94. Metternich to the Foreign Ministry, 27 and 28 June 1905, GP, vol. 20 (2), nos. 6859 and 6860.

95. A copy of the accord may be found in GP, vol. 20, no. 6832.

96. In December 1905 a Liberal government had come to power in London. See Holstein to Bülow, 14 January 1906, in Norman Rich and M.H. Fisher, eds., *The Holstein Papers: Correspondence, 1897–1909* (Cambridge: Cambridge University Press, 1963), vol. 4, no. 923; Holstein to Sternburg, 14 January 1906, *Holstein Papers*, vol. 4, no. 925; Holstein to Joseph Maria von Radowitz, 16 January 1906, *Holstein Papers*, vol. 4, no. 926. See also Anderson, *The First Moroccan Crisis*, pp. 315–19.

97. D.W. Sweet, "Great Britain and Germany, 1905–1911," in F.H. Hinsley, ed., *British Foreign Policy under Sir Edward Grey* (Cambridge: Cambridge University Press, 1977), p. 217.

98. Lee, *Europe's Crucial Years*, p. 139; Anderson, *The First Moroccan Crisis*, pp. 348–96.

99. For example, Immanuel Geiss argues that "it was a resounding defeat for Germany, which attained none of its aims, short-term or long-term, because it had overreached itself" (*German Foreign Policy, 1871–1914* [London: Rutledge & Kegan Paul, 1976], p. 105). For similar arguments see Norman Rich, *Friedrich von Holstein: Politics and Diplomacy in the Era of Bismarck and Wilhelm II* (Cambridge: Cambridge University Press, 1965), vol. 2, p. 742. See also Sontag, "German Foreign Policy, 1904–1906," p. 298.

100. After presenting the arguments that might suggest Holstein intended to provoke another war with France, Rich reaches this same conclusion. See Rich, *Friedrich von Holstein*, vol. 2, pp. 696–99 and 745.

101. Memorandum by Baron von Holstein, 3 June 1904, GDD, vol. 3, pp. 220–21.

102. Bülow to the kaiser, 26 March 1905, GP, vol. 20, no. 6576. Cited in Anderson, *The First Moroccan Crisis*, p. 187.

103. My translation. Bülow to Sternburg, ambassador at Washington, 3 April 1905, GP, vol. 19, no. 6302.

104. Holstein to Bülow, 5 April 1905, *Holstein Papers*, vol. 4, no. 882.

105. See Anderson, *The First Moroccan Crisis*, pp. 141 and 217. The ultra-nationalist Pan-German lobby, however, remained committed colonialists. See Carroll, *Germany and the Great Powers*, pp. 495–98.

106. My translation. Bülow to Tattenbach, German Envoy at Fez, 30 April 1905, GP, vol. 20, no. 6643. German objectives remained constant. See "Enclosure I: Instructions for the German Delegates to the Moroccan Conference," 3 January 1906, GP, vol. 20, no. 6922. The instructions begin "During the Spring of 1904, His

Majesty the Kaiser and King declared at Vigo to his Majesty the King of Spain that above all, he had no territorial, only commercial, interests in Morocco."

107. For example, S.L. Mayer writes: "It would not be sufficient to suppose that Germany merely sought to deflect France from her 'penétration pacifique' of Morocco, which had been going on for some time previously. It has generally been assumed that the German Foreign Office hoped to humiliate France diplomatically in a contrived show of force that could have resulted in the rupture of the Entente Cordiale" ("Anglo-German Rivalry at the Algeciras Conference," in Gifford and Louis, eds., *Britain and Germany in Africa*, p. 216).

108. For a similar conclusion see Williamson, *The Politics of Grand Strategy*, p. 32. But see Acton to Grey, 31 December 1905, cited in Anderson, *The First Moroccan Crisis*, p. 328.

109. My translation. Memorandum by Hammann, 7 April 1905, GP, vol. 20, no. 6609.

110. See Bülow to Kaiser Wilhelm II, 4 April 1905, GP, vol. 20, no. 6599; memorandum by Holstein, 4 April 1905, GP, vol. 20, no. 6601; and Holstein to Radolin, 11 April 1905, *Holstein Papers*, vol. 4, no. 883.

111. See Christopher M. Andrew, *Théophile Delcassé and the Making of the Entente Cordiale: A Reappraisal of French Foreign Policy* (London: Melbourne, 1968).

112. See Williamson, *The Politics of Grand Strategy*, pp. 33–38; Kennedy, *The Rise of the Anglo-German Antagonism*, pp. 277–83; and Mayer, "Anglo-German Rivalry at the Algeciras Conference," p. 219.

113. Williamson, *The Politics of Grand Strategy*, p. 34; and Kennedy, *The Rise of the Anglo-German Antagonism*, p. 277.

114. On the continuity of British policy from Lansdowne to Grey, see Kennedy, *The Rise of the Anglo-German Antagonism*, pp. 281–84.

115. General von Schlieffen, Chief of the General Staff, to Bülow, 20 April 1904, GP, vol. 19 (1), no. 6032; Schlieffen to Bülow, 10 June 1905, GP, vol. 19 (2), no. 6195.

116. Lieutenant-General von Moltke to Bülow, 23 January 1906, GDD, vol. 3, pp. 238–39.

117. Bülow to Sternburg, 27 April 1905, GP, vol. 20, no. 6634; and Holstein to von Radolin, 1 May 1905, *Holstein Papers*, no. 886. See also Rich, *Friedrich von Holstein*, vol. 2, pp. 696–97; and Kennedy, *The Rise of the Anglo-German Antagonism*, p. 279. The danger of war was not insignificant, and arguments in support of preventive war were found not only in Berlin. For much as the German General Staff spoke of a window of opportunity that favored Germany, the British Admiralty considered 1905 a "golden opportunity for fighting the Germans in alliance with the French" (quoted in Kennedy, *The Rise of the Anglo-German Antagonism*, p. 279).

118. This characterization was used by both Holstein and Bülow. See Holstein

to Radolin, 1 May 1905, *Holstein Papers,* vol. 4, no. 886; and Berhard von Bülow, *Reden* (Leipzig: Johannes Penzler, 1903), vol. 2, p. 303.

119. My translation. Holstein memorandum, 5 June 1904, GP, vol. 20 (1), no. 6461.

120. Quoted in Kennedy, *The Rise of the Anglo-German Antagonism,* p. 277. See also Anderson, *The First Moroccan Crisis,* pp. 198, 207.

121. See Radolin to Foreign Office, 14 April 1905, GP, vol. 20, no. 6621; memorandum by Mühlberg, 19 April 1905, GP, vol. 20, no. 6623; Bülow to Tattenbach, 18 April 1905, GP, vol. 20, no. 6624. See also Anderson, *The First Moroccan Crisis,* pp. 197–99.

122. Anderson, *The First Moroccan Crisis,* pp. 213–14.

123. See, for example, Richthofen to Radowitz, 24 September 1903, GP, vol. 17, no. 5200; Bihourd to Delcassé, 21 April 1904, L.j. 1901–5, no. 153; and memorandum by Lord Sanderson, 25 February 1907, in G.P. Gooch and H. Temperley, eds., *British Documents on the Origins of the War* (London: Her Majesty's Stationery Office, 1926–1938) (hereafter BD), vol. 3, p. 421.

124. My translation. Bülow to Flotow, 6 June 1905, GP, vol. 20 (2), no. 6683.

125. See Bülow to Tattenbach, 30 April 1905, GP, vol. 20, no. 6643; see also Holstein to Radolin, 14 June 1905, *Holstein Papers,* vol. 4, no. 891.

126. Delcassé's dismissal was seen by the German leadership as a reflection of his unpopularity at home and the political skill of Rouvier who outmaneuvered him (Flotow to Bülow, 7 June 1905, GDD, vol. 3, pp. 228–29).

127. Bülow to Flotow, 6 June 1905, GP, vol. 20 (2), no. 6683. Holstein's instructions to the German ambassador at Paris were the same: "You can tell Rouvier and his confidants in all sincerity that we would very much like to get out of the impossible situation in which Delcassé has placed us and arrive at a better relationship with France, but Rouvier must show us a decent way out. We cannot violate the Sultan" (Holstein to Radolin, 14 June 1905, *Holstein Papers,* vol. 4, no. 891).

128. Quoted in Anderson, *The First Moroccan Crisis,* pp. 241–42.

129. Interview with M. Tardieu of *Le Temps,* 3 October 1905, quoted in Anderson, *The First Moroccan Crisis,* p. 275.

130. Ibid., p. 276.

131. Ibid., p. 277.

132. Holstein to Maximilian von Brandt, 14 November 1905, *Holstein Papers,* vol. 4, no. 915.

133. See Flotow to Holstein, 8 December 1905, *Holstein Papers,* vol. 4, no. 916. See also Mayer, "Anglo-German Rivalry at the Algeciras Conference," pp. 220–21; Anderson, *The First Moroccan Crisis,* pp. 311–12.

134. See Deputy Secretary of State von Mühlberg to Flotow, 29 November, 1905, GP, vol. 21, no. 6904; see also memorandum by Mühlberg, 30 November 1905, GP, vol. 21, no. 6906.

135. Flotow argued that it was the work of an overzealous member of the for-

eign service. See Flotow to Holstein, 8 December 1905, *Holstein Papers,* vol. 4, no. 916. It is now widely accepted that Rouvier himself was behind the offer. See Mayer, "Anglo-German Rivalry at the Algeciras Conference," p. 221; and Anderson, *The First Moroccan Crisis,* p. 312.

136. Mayer, "Anglo-German Rivalry at the Algeciras Conference," p. 222.

137. Bülow to Sternburg, 19 March 1906, GDD, vol. 3, p. 247.

138. See, for example, Bülow to Holstein, 14 March 1906, *Holstein Papers,* vol. 4, no. 941; same to the same, 17 March 1906, *Holstein Papers,* vol. 4, no. 942; and memorandum by Holstein, 29 March 1906, *Holstein Papers,* no. 948.

139. Bülow to Holstein, 25 March 1906, *Holstein Papers,* vol. 4, no. 946.

140. See *Holstein Papers,* vol. 4, pp. 405–6.

141. See Ima Christina Barlow, *The Agadir Crisis* (Hamden, Conn.: Archon Books, 1971), pp. 68–84; and Lee, *Europe's Crucial Years,* pp. 239–41. The accords may be found in GP, vol. 24, nos. 8490–92.

142. Townsend, *The Rise and Fall of Germany's Colonial Empire,* p. 322.

143. See Barlow, *The Agadir Crisis,* pp. 86–87; Lee, *Europe's Crucial Years,* pp. 241–42; G. Lowes Dickenson, *The International Anarchy, 1904–1914* (London: Allen & Unwin, 1926), p. 200; and Williamson, *The Politics of Grand Strategy,* p. 143.

144. See Barlow, *The Agadir Crisis,* pp. 167–95; Lee, *Europe's Crucial Years,* pp. 243–46.

145. See Seckendorff to Bethmann-Hollweg, 10 April 1911, GP, vol. 29, no. 10530; and Seckendorff to the Foreign Office, 16 April 1911, GP, vol. 29, no. 10531.

146. Kiderlen to Cambon, 7 April 1911, GP, vol. 29, no. 10527.

147. Quoted in Barlow, *The Agadir Crisis,* p. 181; and Lee, *Europe's Crucial Years,* p. 248.

148. See memorandum by Kiderlen, 28 April 1911, GDD, vol. 4, pp. 1–2.

149. See Barlow, *The Agadir Crisis,* pp. 179, 184–85, 190–94, 202–05; Lee, *Europe's Crucial Years,* pp. 249–50; and Williamson, *The Politics of Grand Strategy,* p. 142.

150. For British policy in this period, see M.L. Dockrill, "British Policy during the Agadir Crisis of 1911," in Hinsley, ed., *British Foreign Policy under Sir Edward Grey,* pp. 271–87; see also Kennedy, *The Rise of the Anglo-German Antagonism,* pp. 446–50.

151. Quoted in Barlow, *The Agadir Crisis,* p. 211.

152. Ibid., pp. 212–13.

153. See instructions from Kiderlen to Metternich, ambassador at London, 30 June 1911, GDD, vol. 4, pp. 6–7. See also "Aide-Mémoire Communicated by Count Metternich," 1 July 1911, BD, vol. 7, no. 338. The justification was based on a fiction. Agadir was a closed port; there were no German nationals living there or engaged in any economic activity. The choice of Agadir may have reflected the fact

that there would be no chance that the German seamen might come into contact with French or Spanish police forces.

154. Lee, *Europe's Crucial Years,* p. 253.

155. Metternich to Foreign Office, 4 July 1911, GDD, vol. 4, p. 8.

156. Williamson, *The Politics of Grand Strategy,* p. 146. Despite their long-held opposition to a German port in Morocco, the British government had apparently decided that a nonfortified port was acceptable, provided it was not located on Morocco's Mediterranean coast.

157. These talks are detailed in Barlow, *The Agadir Crisis,* pp. 253–65.

158. Ibid., p. 264.

159. See Bethmann-Hollweg to the kaiser, 15 July 1911, GDD, vol. 4, p. 11; Bethmann-Hollweg to the kaiser, 20 July 1911, GP, vol. 29, no. 10613; and Bethmann-Hollweg to the Foreign Office, 21 July 1911, GP, vol. 29, no. 10614. The kaiser remained a voice of caution throughout the crisis. See Townsend, *The Rise and Fall of Germany's Colonial Empire,* pp. 323–25.

160. Historians debate whether the real target of the warning was Germany or France. A.J.P. Taylor put forward the proposition that it was targeted at France, "a warning that Britain could not be left out of any new partition of Morocco" (Taylor, *The Struggle for Mastery in Europe, 1848–1918,* p. 471). For the debate see Richard A. Cosgrove, "A Note on Lloyd George's Speech at the Mansion House 21 July 1911," *Historical Journal* 12 (December 1969): 698–701; Keith Wilson, "The Agadir Crisis, The Mansion House Speech, and the Double Edgedness of Agreements," *Historical Journal* 15 (September 1972): 513–32; and Timothy Boyle, "New Light on Lloyd George's Mansion House Speech," *Historical Journal* 23 (June 1980): 431–33.

161. Speech quoted in Barlow, *The Agadir Crisis,* p. 298. See also "Extract from Speech of Mr. Lloyd George on July 21, 1911, at the Mansion House," BD, vol. 7, no. 412.

162. Barlow, *The Agadir Crisis,* p. 307. See also the discussion of its effects in Michael Fry, *Lloyd George and Foreign Policy* (Montreal: McGill-Queen's University Press, 1977), pp. 141–42.

163. Barlow, *The Agadir Crisis,* p. 305.

164. *Journal des Débats,* 22 July 1911, cited in Barlow, *The Agadir Crisis,* p. 305.

165. See Lee, *Europe's Crucial Years,* p. 259. See also Metternich to Bethmann-Hollweg, 22 July 1911, GP, vol. 29, no. 10621.

166. Kiderlen to Metternich, 24 July 1911, GP, vol. 29, no. 10623; and Metternich to the Foreign Office, 25 July 1911, GDD, vol. 4, pp. 15–16.

167. As quoted in Lee, *Europe's Crucial Years,* p. 260. For Metternich's instructions see Kiderlen to Metternich, 24 July 1911, GP, vol. 29, no. 10623; see also Kiderlen to Metternich, 25 July, 1911, GP, vol. 29, no. 10625.

168. Winston S. Churchill, *The World Crisis: An Abridgement of the Classic 4-Volume History of World War I* (New York: Scribner's Sons, 1931), p. 32.

169. Barlow, *The Agadir Crisis*, p. 313. French concerns over a German invasion were evident as early as May. See the memorandum by Bethmann-Hollweg, 23 May 1911, GDD, vol. 4, p. 5.

170. See Schön to the Foreign Office, 31 July 1911, GP, vol. 29, no. 10681.

171. See, for example, Gerhard Ritter, *The Sword and the Scepter: The Problem of Militarism in Germany*, 4 vols. (Coral Gables, Fla.: University of Miami Press, 1969), vol. 2, p. 172.

172. The words were those of Alexander von Benckendorff, Russian ambassador at London. See Benckendorff to Neratov, 1 August 1911, in G.A. Schreiner, ed., *Entente Diplomacy and the World* (New York: Knickerbocker Press, 1921), no. 689.

173. The entire speech can be found in *Parliamentary Debates*, 5th series, vol. 27, pp. 1827–28.

174. Barlow, *The Agadir Crisis*, p. 315

175. See Schön to the Foreign Office, 26 July 1911, GP, vol. 29, no. 10675; and the same to the same, 27 July 1911, GP, vol. 29, no. 10678.

176. Barlow provides the most comprehensive treatment. See *The Agadir Crisis*, pp. 325–75.

177. Schön to the Foreign Office, 5 August 1911, GP, vol. 29, no. 10686.

178. Kiderlen to Schön, 5 August 1911, GP, vol. 29, no. 10687.

179. Ibid., no. 10688.

180. See Wilhelm II to Kiderlen, 9 August 1911, GP, vol. 29, no. 10696.

181. My translation. Jenisch to the Foreign Ministry, 9 August 1911, GP, vol. 29, no. 10698.

182. See Kiderlen to Jenisch, 8 August 1911, GP, vol. 29, no. 10691; and Admiralty to Wilhelm II, 8 August 1911, GP, vol. 29, no. 10692.

183. Barlow, *The Agadir Crisis*, p. 342. See also Jenisch to the Foreign Office, 9 August 1911, GP, vol. 29, no. 10698.

184. Williamson, *The Politics of Grand Strategy*, p. 162; Lee, *Europe's Crucial Years*, p. 264–65. The idea of a transfer of Paris's preemption rights to the Belgian Congo had been raised by Rouvier in December 1905. See the discussion of the First Moroccan Crisis above.

185. Lee, *Europe's Crucial Years*, p. 265.

186. Memorandum by Kiderlen, 3 May 1911, GDD, vol. 4, pp. 2–4.

187. See Baron von Jenish, in the kaiser's suite at Achilleion in Corfu, to Kiderlen, 30 April 1911. GDD, vol. 4, p. 2; and memorandum by Bethmann-Hollweg, 23 May 1911, GDD, vol. 4, p. 5.

188. The Russian foreign minister reached this conclusion at the time. See Neratoff to Benckendorff, 2 July 1911, *Entente Diplomacy*, no. 680.

189. In fact, when Mulay Hafid offered Germany a coaling station on Morocco's Atlantic Coast, the German leadership turned him down, concluding that a coaling station would be "against the integrity of Morocco guaranteed by the Algeciras Act" and "against [Germany's] Moroccan Accord with France" (Schön's note for

Bethmann-Hollweg, 14 December 1909, GP, vol. 29, no. 10489). See the discussion in Barlow, *The Agadir Crisis,* pp. 86–87.

190. Schön to Bethmann-Hollweg, 7 May 1911, GDD, vol. 4, p. 4.

191. Zimmerman note, 12 June 1911, GP, vol. 29, no. 10572.

192. Kiderlen memorandum, 3 May 1911.

193. Ibid.

194. Memorandum by Bethmann-Hollweg, 23 May, 1911, GDD, vol. 4, p. 5. King George later admitted to the Austrian ambassador: "I will not deny that he perhaps could have said something of a ship, although I do not remember it. If he did, I thought of Mogador; in any case he did not mention Agadir" (Mensdorff to the Austrian Foreign Office, 29 September 1911, as cited in Barlow, *The Agadir Crisis,* p. 226).

195. Bethmann-Hollweg to Metternich, 4 July 1911, GDD, vol. 4, pp. 7–8.

196. Kiderlen to Metternich, 30 June 1911, GDD, vol. 4, p. 7; and Kiderlen to Bethmann-Hollweg, 20 July 1911, GDD, vol. 4, p. 12.

197. Huth and Russett, "Testing Deterrence Theory," especially "Appendix: Summaries of 58 Cases of Extended Deterrence" (unpublished), pp. 22–24.

198. Kiderlen to Metternich, 24 July 1911, GDD, vol. 4, no. 14.

199. Quoted in Fritz Fischer, *War of Illusions: Germany's Policies from 1911 to 1914* (New York: W.W. Norton, 1975), p. 82.

200. Metternich to the Foreign Office, 25 July 1911, GP, vol. 29, no. 10625.

201. *Parliamentary Debates,* 5th series, vol. 27, pp. 1827–28.

202. See Metternich to the Foreign Office, 27 July 1911, GP, vol. 29, no. 10635. See also Kiderlen to Treutler, 28 July 1911, GP, vol. 29, no. 10679.

203. Quoted in Carroll, *Germany and the Great Powers,* pp. 672–73.

204. My translation. Kiderlen to Schön, 5 August 1911, GP, vol. 29, no. 10688.

205. My translation. Wilhelm II to Kiderlen, 9 August 1911, GP, vol. 29, no. 10696.

206. Quoted in Konrad H. Jarausch, *The Enigmatic Chancellor: Bethmann-Hollweg and the Hubris of Imperial Germany* (New Haven, Conn.: Yale University Press, 1973), p. 124.

207. Barlow, *The Agadir Crisis,* p. 381.

208. Kiderlen memorandum, 3 May 1911.

209. For a sampling of such charges, see Carroll, *The Agadir Crisis,* pp. 697–98.

210. See, for example, Bertie to Grey, 18 July 1911, BD, vol. 7, no. 392, and the marginalia of Eyre Crowe of the same date.

211. Volker R. Berghan, *Germany and the Approach of War,* 2d ed. (New York: St. Martin's Press, 1992), p. 108.

212. Jarausch, *The Enigmatic Chancellor,* pp. 123–24.

213. Barlow, *The Agadir Crisis,* p. 380.

214. Curiously, the same belief obtained in France, where the majority of public

opinion believed France had suffered a major diplomatic defeat. See Barlow, *The Agadir Crisis*, pp. 283–384; and Carroll, *Germany and the Great Powers*, pp. 697–98.

7 ◆ The July Crisis

1. See Raymond Sontag, *European Diplomatic History, 1871–1932* (New York: Appleton-Century-Crofts, 1933), pp. 59–95.

2. Bernhard von Bülow, *Memoirs of Prince von Bülow*, 4 vols. (Boston: Little, Brown, 1931), vol. 3, p. 166.

3. This is the thesis of Fritz Fischer and his student Imanuel Geiss. See Fischer, *Griff Nach der Weltmacht* (Düsseldorf: Droste, 1961), translated as *Germany's Aims in the First World War* (New York: W.W. Norton, 1967); and *War of Illusions: German Policies from 1911 to 1914* (New York: W.W. Norton, 1975); Geiss, *Das Deutsche Reich und die Vorgeschichte des Ersten Welt Kriegs* (Munich: Hanser, 1978); *July 1914: The Outbreak of the First World War: Selected Documents* (New York: Scribner's Sons, 1967); and *Das Deutsche Reich und der Erste Weltkrieg* (Munich: Hanser, 1978).

4. For versions of this thesis see Michael Howard, "Lest We Forget," *Encounter* (January 1964), p. 65; Luigi Albertini, *The Origins of the War of 1914*, ed. and trans. Isabella Massey, 3 vols. (London: Oxford University Press, 1952–57), vol. 2, pp. 479–83, 579; and L.C.F. Turner, *Origins of the First World War* (New York: W.W. Norton, 1970), pp. 1, 99. For discussions of the failure of political leadership in Germany, see Gerhard Ritter, *The Sword and the Scepter: The Problem of Militarism in Germany*, 4 vols. (Coral Gables, Fla.: University of Miami Press, 1969); Karl Heinz Janssen, *Der Kanzler und der General: Die Führungskriese um Bethmann-Hollweg und Falkenhayn, 1914–1916* (Göttingen, Musterschmidt Verlag, 1967); and Admiral Georg von Müller, *The Kaiser and His Court* (London: MacDonald, 1961).

5. For variants of this argument see Albertini, *The Origins of the War of 1914*, vol. 2, pp. 514–15; Jack S. Levy, "Preferences, Constraints, and Choices in July 1914," *International Security* (winter 1990/91): 151–86; Scott D. Sagan, "1914 Revisited: Allies, Offense, and Instability," *International Security* (fall 1986): 151–76; Bernadotte Schmitt, *The Origins of the War, 1914*, 2 vols. (New York: Howard Fertig, 1966), vol. 2, p. 409; and Zara Steiner, *Britain and the Origins of the First World War* (London: Macmillan, 1977), p. 227.

6. See Robert Jervis, *Perception and Misperception in International Politics* (Princeton: Princeton University Press, 1976), pp. 58–107, especially 94–95; Aaron Wildavsky, "Practical Consequences of the Theoretic Study of Defense Policy," in Wildavsky, *The Revolt of the Masses and Other Essays on Politics and Public Policy* (New York: Basic Books, 1971), p. 65. The widespread belief among European decision makers in the dominance of offensive military strategies produced a par-

ticularly virulent manifestation of spiral dynamics: the system of interlocking mobilization schedules. Once one state mobilized, countermobilizations began in the others. The reciprocal and mutually reinforcing nature of military preparations severely constrained the capacity of the political leaders to de-escalate the crisis and avert war. See Stephen Van Evera, "The Cult of the Offensive and the Origins of the First World War," *International Security* (summer 1984): 58–107; and Jack Snyder, "Civil-Military Relations and the Cult of the Offensive, 1914 and 1984," *International Security* (summer 1984): 108–46. But see the rebuttal offered by Marc Trachtenberg, "The Meaning of Mobilization in 1914," *International Security* (winter 1990/91), pp. 120–50.

7. Paul W. Schroeder, "World War I as Galloping Gertie: A Reply to Joachim Remak," *Journal of Modern History* 44 (September 1972), p. 320.

8. For an excellent review of the literature on German war aims, see Wolfgang J. Mommsen, "The Debate on German War Aims," *Journal of Contemporary History* 1 (July 1966): 47–72. Among those who argue that Germany policy was essentially defensive, the result of encirclement and threats to Germany's continental position, are Ritter, *The Sword and the Scepter*, especially the introduction to volume 3 of the German edition: *Staatskunst und Kriegshandwerk: Das Problem des "Militarismus" in Deutschland. Vol. 3: Die Tragödie der Staatskunst: Bethmann-Hollweg als Kriegskanzler* (Munich: Oldenbourg, 1964–68); Egmont Zechlin, "Deutschland zwischen Kabinetts- und Wirtschaftskrieg," *Historische Zeitschrift* 199 (1964): 347–458; and David Calleo, *The German Problem Reconsidered: Germany and the World Order, 1870 to the Present* (Cambridge: Cambridge University Press, 1978).

9. See Van Evera, "The Cult of the Offensive," pp. 79–85; Konrad Jarausch, *The Enigmatic Chancellor: Bethmann-Hollweg and the Hubris of Imperial Germany* (New Haven, Conn.: Yale University Press, 1973), pp. 157–59; and Zechlin, "Deutschland zwischen Kabinetts- und Wirtschaftskrieg."

10. Jarausch, *The Enigmatic Chancellor,* pp. 155–59; Albertini, *The Origins of the War of 1914,* vol. 2, pp. 258–64, 453–60; Tschirschky to Bethmann-Hollweg, 14 July 1914, no. 22 in Geiss, *July 1914,* pp. 114–15; Berchtold to Szögyény, 15 July 1914, no. 23 in *July 1914,* pp. 116–17; and Szögyény to Berchtold, 25 July 1914, no. 71 in *July 1914,* p. 200.

11. See Albertini, *The Origins of the War of 1914,* vol. 2, pp. 504, 522–25.

12. Trachtenberg, "The Meaning of Mobilization in 1914," p. 136.

13. See Albertini, *The Origins of the War of 1914,* vol. 2, pp. 514–20, vol. 3, pp. 3–4. Fischer likewise maintains that Bethmann-Hollweg expected British neutrality. See *Germany's Aims in the First World War,* pp. 78–80, and *War of Illusions,* pp. 495–96.

14. Albertini himself offers this interpretation of Bethmann's expectations, then abandons it. See *Origins of the War of 1914,* vol. 2, pp. 424–29. See also Bassermann's letter to Schiffer of 5 June: "Bethmann said to me with fatalistic resignation: 'If there is war with France, England will march against us to the last man'" (quoted in

Mommsen, "The Debate on German War Aims," pp. 59–60); and Lerchenfeld to Hertling, 4 June 1914, *Bayerische Dokumente zum Kriegsausbruch und zum Versailler Schuldspruch* (Munich, Oldenbourg, 1922); Lichnowsky to Jagow, 24 July 1914, no. 57 in *July 1914*, pp. 183–84; and the same to the same, 25 July 194, no. 73 in *July 1914*, pp. 205–6.

15. Albertini, *The Origins of the War of 1914*, vol. 2, pp. 453–60.

16. For a similar conclusion see Konrad H. Jarausch, "The Illusion of Limited War: Chancellor Bethmann-Hollweg's Calculated Risk, July 1914," *Central European History* (March 1969): 60–62.

17. The text of the ultimatum is reprinted in *July 1914*, pp. 143–46.

18. Bethmann-Hollweg to the ambassadors at St. Petersburg, Paris, and London, 21 July 1914, no. 39 in *July 1914*, pp. 149–50.

19. Quoted in Albertini, *The Origins of the War of 1914*, vol. 2, pp. 442–43.

20. Bethmann-Hollweg to Lichnowsky, 28 July 1914, no. 101 in *July 1914*, pp. 243–44.

21. To his ambassador at Paris, Bethmann wrote: "We cannot mediate in the conflict between Austria and Serbia, but probably [we will do so] between Austria and Russia" (Bethmann-Hollweg to Schön, 26 July 1914, cited in Jarausch, "The Illusion of Limited War," p. 64). See also Bethmann-Hollweg to Tschirschky, 28 July 1914, no. 115 in *July 1914*, p. 259. The chancellor hoped that agreement could be reached on the basis of an Austrian occupation of Belgrade as a material guarantee for Serbian compliance with the ultimatum. The kaiser had proposed the idea of a "Halt in Belgrade" earlier that day. See Wilhelm II to Jagow, 28 July 1914, no. 112 in *July 1914*, p. 256.

22. Quoted in Albertini, *The Origins of the War of 1914*, vol. 2, p. 428.

23. Trachtenberg, "The Meaning of Mobilization in 1914," pp. 132–33.

24. Again Trachtenberg provides the evidence; see "The Meaning of Mobilization in 1914," p. 138. For more on deliberations over the *Kriegsgefahrzustand*, see Albertini, *The Origins of the War of 1914*, vol. 2, pp. 491, 599, and vol. 3, p. 15.

25. Trachtenberg, "The Meaning of Mobilization in 1914," p. 136.

26. Quoted in Albertini, *Origins of the War of 1914*, vol. 2, p. 523.

27. See Schroeder, "World War I as Galloping Gertie," pp. 338–39.

28. Count Czernin to the Foreign Minister, Count Berchtold, 22 June 1914. Quoted in ibid., p. 337.

29. Memorandum by Conrad, 22 June 1914. Quoted in Albertini, *The Origins of the War of 1914*, vol. 1, p. 539.

30. James Joll, *The Origins of the First World War*, 2d ed. (London: Longman, 1992), p. 111; Ritter, *The Sword and the Scepter*, vol. 2, p. 228; and Samuel R. Williamson Jr., *Austria-Hungary and the Origins of the First World War* (London: Macmillan, 1991), p. 194.

31. Albertini reaches a similar conclusion; see *The Origins of the War of 1914*, vol. 2, pp. 658–59.

32. William C. Fuller Jr., *Strategy and Power in Russia, 1600–1914* (New York: Free Press, 1992), p. 448. See also D.C.B. Lieven, *Russia and the Origins of the First World War* (London: Macmillan, 1983), pp. 140–50.

33. Albertini, *The Origins of the War of 1914,* vol. 2, pp. 524, 527, 655–58, 667–71, and 679–86.

34. Van Evera, "The Cult of the Offensive," especially pp. 71–75.

35. Thomas C. Schelling, *Arms and Influence* (New Haven, Conn.: Yale University Press, 1966), p. 4.

8 ♦ *Conclusions*

1. Gerald F. Seib, "Rewarding Virtue Is a Good Policy in Curbing Nukes," *Wall Street Journal,* 8 December 1993, p. A16; and William Safire, "Reactor Roulette," *New York Times,* 2 June 1994, p. A23. When North Korea agreed to abandon nuclear power facilities that had as their by-product weapons-grade plutonium and pledged to halt their nuclear weapons program in exchange for $4 billion in oil and the construction of an advanced-technology light-water reactor, Safire was indignant: "The threat of war by North Korea forced Bill Clinton to fold his hand. But war was a false alternative" ("Clinton's Concessions," *New York Times,* 24 October 1994, p. A17.)

2. Elaine Sciolino, "Top U.S. Officials Divided in Debate on Invading Haiti," *New York Times,* 4 August 1994, pp. A1, A10.

3. See Joseph Fitchett, "Use of Force in Kosovo Splits NATO," *International Herald Tribune,* 8 February 1999, p. 7; Thomas L. Friedman,"Redo Dayton on Bosnia, and Do a Deal on Kosovo," *International Herald Tribune,* 8 February 1999, p. 8; and Charles Trueheart, "Albright Brings Serbs and Rebels Together," *International Herald Tribune,* 15 February 1999, pp. 1, 4.

4. For a discussion of the methodological problems confronting the scholar in this regard, see Robert Jervis, *Perception and Misperception in International Politics* (Princeton: Princeton University Press, 1976), ch. 2. For some historical examples of statesmen's efforts to discern their adversary's motives, see Melvyn P. Leffler, *A Preponderance of Power: National Security, the Truman Administration, and the Cold War* (Stanford, Calif.: Stanford University Press, 1992), ch. 1; and Barbara Rearden Farnham, *Roosevelt and the Munich Crisis: A Study of Political Decision-Making* (Princeton: Princeton University Press, 1997), especially chs. 3 and 4.

5. See Kenneth N. Waltz, *Theory of International Politics* (Reading, Mass.: Addison-Wesley, 1979), especially pp. 102–28. For Waltz fear is a rational reaction to the condition of anarchy, but such fears are probably reinforced by psychological processes that may deviate from a strict definition of rationality. See Jervis, *Perception and Misperception in International Politics,* pp. 117–202, 372–78.

6. See, for example, Arnold Wolfers, *Discord and Collaboration: Essays on In-*

ternational Politics (Baltimore: Johns Hopkins University Press, 1962), pp. 98–102. On the inconsistency between the assumptions of most deterrence theorists and those of structural realism, see Charles L. Glaser, "Political Consequences of Military Strategy: Expanding and Refining the Spiral and Deterrence Models," *World Politics* 44 (July 1992): 506–8.

7. Jack L. Snyder, *Myths of Empire* (Ithaca, N.Y.: Cornell University Press, 1991).

8. Jervis, *Perception and Misperception in International Politics,* pp. 117–202. Sometimes ambiguity is the intended result of a state's foreign policy. The strategic value of ambiguity is discussed in Robert Jervis, *The Logic of Images in International Relations* (Princeton: Princeton University Press, 1970), pp. 113–38.

9. See, for example, Allan Bullock, *Hitler: A Study in Tyranny* (New York: Harper, 1962), pp. 490–559; and Gerhard L. Weinberg, *The Foreign Policy of Hitler's Germany,* 2 vols. (Chicago: University of Chicago Press, 1970–1980), vol. 2: *Starting World War II, 1937–1939.* Telford Taylor argues that the bulk of the British cabinet understood this at the time and supported the Munich accords not because they believed Hitler could be appeased, but because they hoped the accords might delay the onset of war, thus providing the allies with more time to rearm; see *Munich: The Price of Peace* (New York: Vintage, 1979), pp. 978–1004.

10. For the impact of the "lessons" of the 1930s on postwar American foreign policy, see Ernest R. May, *"Lessons" of the Past: The Use and Misuse of History in American Foreign Policy* (New York: Oxford University Press, 1973), especially pp. 52–86; Yuen Foong Khong, *Analogies at War: Korea, Munich, Dien Bien Phu, and the Vietnam Decisions of 1965* (Princeton: Princeton University Press, 1992), especially pp. 175–205; and Harry S. Truman, *Memoirs,* 2 vols. (New York: Doubleday, 1955–56), vol. 2, pp. 332–33.

11. This may result from the process whereby analogies become salient. Foreign policy analogies are often generated by salient national episodes and shared by members of the generation that experienced them. When policy makers are of the same generation, implicit assumptions based on the "lessons" of shared experience are probably frequent. See Michael Roskin, "From Pearl Harbor to Vietnam: Shifting Generational Paradigms," *Political Science Quarterly* 89 (fall 1974): 563–88; Robert Jervis, *Perception and Misperception in International Politics,* pp. 353–257; and R. Ned Lebow, "Generational Learning and Conflict Management," *International Journal* 40 (autumn 1985): 555–85.

12. Jervis, *Perception and Misperception in International Politics,* p. 112. The shortcoming may be subject to remedy. Psychologists find that people who are explicitly encouraged to think of reasons their assessments might be wrong are less likely to persist with initially incorrect assessments and more likely to adjust their views to discrepant information. See Susan Fiske and Shelley Taylor, *Social Cognition,* 2d ed. (Reading, Mass.: Addison-Wesley, 1991); and Philip Tetlock and J. Kim, "Accountability and Overconfidence in Personality Prediction Task," *Journal of Personality and Social Psychology* 52 (1987): 700–709.

13. The concept of the "security dilemma" was introduced to international relations theory by John Herz, who recognized that many of the means by which a state tries to increase its security have the effect of decreasing the security of other states. This produces countermeasures that negate any gains that might have accrued to the first state. See John H. Herz, *Political Realism and Political Idealism* (Chicago: University of Chicago Press, 1951); see also Robert Jervis, "Cooperation under the Security Dilemma," *World Politics* 30 (January 1978): 167–214.

14. Jervis, *Perception and Misperception in International Politics*, p. 109.

15. Richard Ned Lebow and Janice Gross Stein, *When Does Deterrence Succeed and How Do We Know?* (Ottawa: Canadian Institute for International Peace and Security, 1990), p. 72.

16. Susan Peterson examines the sequencing of threats and promises in light of states' domestic structures. See *Crisis Bargaining and the State: The Domestic Politics of International Conflict* (Ann Arbor: University of Michigan Press, 1996).

17. For an example of analysis from an international law perspective, see Louis Henkin, *How Nations Behave: Law and Foreign Policy*, 2d ed. (New York: Columbia University Press, 1979), especially pp. 54–56, 76–87. For a more recent treatment rooted in the regime approach, see Friedrich V. Kratochwil, *Rules, Norms, and Decisions: On the Conditions of Practical and Legal Reasoning in International Relations and Domestic Affairs* (Cambridge: Cambridge University Press, 1989), pp. 47–57.

18. Robert Jervis, "Security Regimes," in Stephen Krasner, ed., *International Regimes* (Ithaca, N.Y.: Cornell University Press, 1983), p. 359.

19. Trade figure computed for 1898 from data in B.R. Mitchell, *International Historical Statistics, Europe: 1750–1988* (New York: Stockdon Press, 1993), p. 555; and Raymond Poidevin, *Les Relations Economiques et Financières entre la France et L'Allemagne de 1898 à 1914* (Paris: Librairie Armand Colin, 1969), p. 160. Aggregate German external trade amounted to 8,833,000,000 marks in current value, whereas for the same year the total value of Moroccan trade was 7,268,000 marks.

20. Kratochwil, *Rules, Norms, and Decisions*, pp. 130–54.

21. That Germany's self-image as a great power appears to have been in part a function of rights accorded Germany in the Treaty of Madrid suggests that the Moroccan crises may provide data for the testing of constructivist notions on identity formation in international politics. For example, Alexander Wendt argues that "the process of creating institutions is one of internalizing new understandings of self and other, of acquiring new role identities, not just of creating external constraints on the behavior of exogenously constituted actors" (Wendt, "Anarchy Is What States Make of It: The Social Construction of Power Politics," *International Organization* 46 [spring 1992]: 417).

22. Thomas C. Schelling, *Arms and Influence* (New Haven, Conn.: Yale University Press, 1966), ch. 3; Alexander George and Richard Smoke, *Deterrence in American Foreign Policy* (New York: Columbia University Press, 1974), pp. 527–30.

23. Schelling, *The Strategy of Conflict* (Cambridge: Harvard University Press, 1960), ch. 8.

24. Robert Jervis presents the case for crises between nuclear powers who possess secure second-strike capability. See *The Meaning of the Nuclear Revolution: Statecraft and the Prospect of Armageddon* (Ithaca, N.Y.: Cornell University Press, 1989), especially pp. 81–85.

25. For example, it is unlikely that a U.S. threat to destroy North Korea in the event of North Korea's building an atomic weapon would deter a nuclear arms program. The threat lacks credibility—not because the United States lacks technical capability, but rather as the threat flies in the face of any sense of proportionality.

26. Winston S. Churchill, *The World Crisis: An Abridgement of the Classic 4-Volume History of World War I* (New York: Scribner's Sons, 1931), p. 33.

27. Ibid., p. 45.

28. Ibid., p. 33. Churchill is not alone in arguing that the Mansion House speech led the German leadership to recalculate the utility of an assertive policy that risked war with France. For similar accounts see Gordon A. Craig, *Germany: 1866–1945* (New York: Oxford University Press, 1978), p. 328; G.P. Gooch, *History of Modern Europe, 1878–1919* (New York: Henry Holt, 1922), p. 479; Fritz Fischer, *War of Illusions: German Policies from 1911–1914* (New York: W.W. Norton, 1975), p. 79; and Paul Huth and Bruce Russett, "Appendix: Summaries of 58 Cases of Extended Deterrence" (unpublished manuscript), pp. 22–24. Barlow accords the British threat a more limited role. In her conclusion she lists Lloyd George's speech as "one of the forces that influenced [Kiderlen] to modify his demands" and hypothesizes that without it France would have had to offer Germany more. See Ima Christine Barlow, *The Agadir Crisis* (Hamden, Conn.: Archon Books, 1971) p. 399.

29. Schelling, *Arms and Influence*, p. 74.

30. Jervis makes the same point. See Jervis, *The Illogic of American Nuclear Strategy* (Ithaca, N.Y.: Cornell University Press, 1984), pp. 84–85. See also Fred C. Iklé, *Every War Must End* (New York: Columbia University Press, 1971), pp. 84–105. Even when one side capitulates, influence is not always unidirectional. One study found that defeated states often secure assurances from the victor before they surrender. See Paul Kecskemeti, *Strategic Surrender: The Politics of Victory and Defeat* (Stanford, Calif.: Stanford University Press, 1958).

31. Zbigniew Brzezinski, *Power and Principle* (New York: Farrar, Straus & Giroux, 1983), p. 429.

32. See Jonathan Mercer, *Reputation and International Politics* (Ithaca, N.Y.: Cornell University Press, 1995).

33. Jervis, *The Logic of Images in International Relations*, and "Domino Beliefs and Strategic Behavior," in Robert Jervis and Jack Snyder, eds., *Dominoes and Bandwagons: Strategic Beliefs and Great Power Competition in the Eurasian Rimland* (New York: Oxford University Press, 1991), pp. 20–50.

34. Queen Victoria to Salisbury, 9 June 1890, in George E. Buckle, ed., *Letters of Queen Victoria*, 3d series (New York: Longmans, Green, 1926), vol. 1, p. 612.

35. Salisbury to Queen Victoria, 12 June 1890, *Letters of Queen Victoria*, 3d series, vol. 1, pp. 614–15.

36. These costs would have to be judged against the costs of standing firm in the immediate crisis and risking war as well as the long-run costs associated with standing firm in all contingencies. For an analysis of precedents in international relations, see Elizabeth Kier and Jonathan Mercer, "Setting Precedents in Anarchy: Military Intervention and Weapons of Mass Destruction," *International Security* 20 (spring 1996): 77–106.

37. See Paul Huth and Bruce Russett, "What Makes Deterrence Work?" *World Politics* 36 (July 1984), p. 498.

38. Lebow and Stein, *When Does Deterrence Succeed*, p. 50.

39. See Patrick M. Morgan, *Deterrence: A Conceptual Analysis* (Beverly Hills, Calif.: Sage, 1983); Lebow and Stein, *When Does Deterrence Succeed*, p. 9; and more recently James D. Fearon, "Selection Effects in Deterrence," in Kenneth Oye, ed., *Deterrence Debates* (Ann Arbor: University of Michigan Press, forthcoming).

40. See James D. Fearon, "Signaling Versus the Balance of Power and Interests: An Empirical Test of a Crisis Bargaining Model," *Journal of Conflict Resolution* 38 (June 1994): 236–69.

41. The same appears to have been true in U.S. policy-making circles. See Steven Kull, *Minds at War: Nuclear Reality and the Inner Conflict of Defense Policymakers* (New York: Basic Books, 1988), ch. 4.

42. For a discussion of the three "waves" of deterrence theory, see Robert Jervis, "Deterrence Theory Revisited," *World Politics* 31 (January 1979): 289–324.

43. See Fearon, "Signaling Versus the Balance of Power and Interest."

44. Marschall to Hatzfeldt, 25 May 1890, in E.T.S. Dugdale, ed. and trans., *German Diplomatic Documents*, 4 vols. (New York: Barnes & Noble, 1969), vol. 2, pp. 30–31.

INDEX